MW00412929

# Digital Deals

# Digital Deals

## Strategies for Selecting and Structuring Partnerships

George T. Geis
George S. Geis

McGraw-Hill

New York   Chicago   San Francisco   Lisbon   London
Madrid   Mexico City   Milan   New Delhi   San Juan
Seoul   Singapore   Sydney   Toronto

**Library of Congress Cataloging-in-Publication Data**

Geis, George T.
    Digital Deals: strategies for selecting and structuring partnerships/
George T. Geis, George S. Geis.
        p.      cm.
    Includes bibliographical references and index.
    ISBN 0-07-137497-3
    1. Strategic alliances (Business).   2. Partnership.   3. Joint ventures.
  4. Consolidation and merger of corporations.   I. Geis, George S.
II. Title.
  HD69.S8G45    2001
  658'044—dc21                                              2001030277

*McGraw-Hill*

A Division of The McGraw-Hill Companies

Copyright © 2001 by George T. Geis and George S. Geis. All rights reserved. Printed
in the United States of America. Except as permitted under the United States Copyright Act of 1976, no part of this publication may be reproduced or distributed in any
form or by any means, or stored in a data base or retrieval system, without the prior
written permission of the publisher.

1 2 3 4 5 6 7 8 9 0   DOC/DOC   0 9 8 7 6 5 4 3 2 1

ISBN 0-07-137497-3

This publication is designed to provide accurate and authoritative information in
regard to the subject matter covered. It is sold with the understanding that the
publisher is not engaged in rendering legal, accounting, or other professional
service. If legal advice or other expert assistance is required, the services of a
competent professional person should be sought.
                *—From a declaration of principles jointly adopted by a committee of*
                *the American Bar Association and a committee of publishers.*

Printed and bound by R. R. Donnelley & Sons Company.

This book is printed on recycled, acid-free paper
containing a minimum of 50% recycled, de-inked fiber.

To our wives Penny and Laurel—the best nondigital
partnerships we ever structured

# Contents

# Foreword

Time is, without a doubt, the most perishable asset on the planet. Where and with whom we spend our time now defines our social and workplace identities. The efficacy associated with our use of time charts our career trajectory. Spending time "strategically" on "strategic issues" is what executives are supposed to do. In almost two decades serving as a trusted advisor to executives, I have never heard an executive say, "We have no time for strategy." Having huddled around my fair share of top-of-the-house campfires, I find that as the libations taken at CXO watering holes loosen tongues and the executive elders start to tell stories, the most memorable narrative that emerges revolves around a review of past decisions. I have heard, stated quietly and in confidence, "We focused on the wrong things. We made the wrong decision." The payback on time spent strategically was, in many instances, negative.

Is time spent strategically a bad thing? Is strategy dead? Was time spent on strategy wasted? Does strategic planning have a place in our time-crazed, execution-obsessed New Economy? In 1983, the uber-executive of our age—General Electric Chairman Jack Welch—dismantled the company's once heralded planning department. We have empirical evidence that those spending the most on traditional forms of resource-centric "strategy consulting" (the cerebrally challenged SWOT—Strengths, Weaknesses, Opportunities, and Threats dance) performed the poorest in the marketplace. The biggest strategic planner of them all, the Soviet Union, appears to have just about finished its premillennial journey from totalitarianism to disintegration. Strategy is not dead, but it has certainly fallen out of favor. There are few companies that do not have strategic plans. Yet few devote the resources to them that they used to. Most disturbing is that efforts to fix the problem often had the effect of making things worse—or at least making them bad in a different way.

Crusades and reforms that were intended to reinvent, relaunch, and reposition the practice strategy have failed.

Lewis Mumford divided history into epochs characterized by their power sources. Traditional strategy tended to emphasize a focused single line of attack, executed by a single economic enterprise—a clear statement of where, how, and when to compete. Noticeably lacking was the question of "with whom?" The new power source in the New Economy is the ability to assemble the most resource-rich, market-savvy, technology-gifted, fleet-of-foot, known-and-trusted-by-the-consumer armada of partners possible. The way you do that is the subject of *Digital Deals*.

No book can promise infallibility. No book can guarantee that good decisions will be made. This book will help you spend the time you can allocate to strategic thinking more efficaciously. As such, this is not a coffee-table book. This is not a Great-Title-No-Content book. This is not a Good-article-unbelievable-they-stretched-it-into-a-book-book. This most definitely is not an I'll-buy-it-but-I-won't-read-it book. *Digital Deals* is the new, new thing in strategic thinking.

Using the framework in *Digital Deals* to analyze the ur-protagonists of our evolving New Economy (Cisco, Intel, Microsoft, AOL, AT&T, Amazon), I experienced something akin to the joy that Galileo must have felt when he used the telescope to study the heavens or that Robert Hooke felt when he used the microscope to study bacteria. The tools contained in these pages will let you see new things. It will simplify what heretofore has been an incoherent jumble of pieces. This book has helped me understand the players, the deals, and the deal rationales of the market I work in—digital security and privacy.

As I read the book, I continued to ask myself whether the two Georges were adding words to the existing vocabulary of strategic planning or creating a new grammar into which the old words might be conjugated. There is no doubt that the process of market modeling described within these pages fundamentally changes the types of conversations we will be having as we try to plan our respective futures.

*Thornton May*
*Corporate Futurist & Chief Awareness Officer*
*Guardent, Inc.*
*www.guardent.com*

# Acknowledgments

This book would not have been possible without the generous help of many individuals and organizations. In particular, we would like to thank the following students and faculty associated with UCLA's Anderson School of Management: Martina Aufiero, Jeff Cole, Keala Dickhens, Shari Gunn, Jack McDonough, Kevin Watson, and many others. We are also grateful to friends and colleagues at McKinsey & Company for their support and assistance, including Derek Alderton, Byron Auguste, Viva Bartkus, Joe Berchtold, Shona Brown, David Ernst, John Hagel, Jeff Long, and the other members and leaders of the Los Angeles office.

We owe a gracious note of thanks to our friends and family who took the time to read this manuscript or endured our long absences from hospitable conversation. Special thanks go to Debbie Foster, Terri Geis, and Olaf Westheider for their conceptual insight. Thanks also to the dozens of people who shaped the book by sharing their companies' successes and frustrations at selecting, structuring, and implementing digital deals.

Finally, we sincerely appreciate the support of McGraw-Hill, with abundant thanks going to our editor, Michelle Williams, for her kinetic energy and insight throughout the entire process.

Of course, any errors or shortcomings in this manuscript are the authors' sole responsibility.

# Preface

About five years ago, we launched a research effort that began by analyzing investments and alliances of two towers of technology: Intel and Microsoft. With whom and in what markets were these companies partnering? How were they structuring deals? And perhaps most importantly, what strategic benefits did the companies hope to get out of these deals?

In the late 1990s, the "deal flow" for Intel and Microsoft accelerated. By the end of the century, Microsoft had assembled a portfolio of deals worth nearly $20 billion. It had purchased almost 50 companies, made scores of minority investments, and structured some 25 joint ventures. Intel had built a portfolio that was unprecedented in business history, which consisted of over 400 minority equity investments valued at around $10 billion. Flush with success, Intel decided to punctuate its investment efforts in early 2000 by establishing a new division dubbed "Intel Capital."

Although 2000 brought dot-com shakeout and "value compression," doing digital deals, had become a fixture in global strategy. The twenty-first century began with maxims linking return to risk. Nevertheless, for Intel and Microsoft (and other corporate leaders analyzed in this book), an intensified level of investments and alliances was not just some passing late twentieth-century trend. In fact, tumultuous markets made it even more important for all companies to establish thoughtful methods for selecting and structuring partnerships.

As we continued to study the deals of these two companies, it became clear that the real value did not lie in studying each deal in isolation, but in understanding patterns. Their webs of investments and partnerships were growing so complex that we needed a way to step back from individual deals to comprehend broader patterns and strategic implications.

By then, our database of deals had grown to many thousands of companies and relationships. Drawing on this information, we began to experiment with meaningful ways to organize the players and deals into markets and submarkets. We developed software to visually analyze the relationships over time to see how a beachhead position might evolve into a strong market presence. We cut the data by product, geography, value activity, customer segment, deal structure, and time. We began to discern distinct patterns—there was a method behind much of what Microsoft and Intel were doing.

We decided to expand our research efforts to explore other "lighthouse companies" that could offer insight into how companies were succeeding (and failing) in using digital deals for competitive positioning. We used our same methodology to research Cisco, AOL Time Warner, AT&T, News Corp., Amazon.com, and others. In some cases, these companies were doing deals for the same reasons as Intel and Microsoft. But we also uncovered additional deal rationales, expanding our universe of deal strategies.

As we continued our research and conducted seminars on this topic, we found that corporate executives seemed hungry for a systematic way to make sense of complex markets and to manage their own deal strategies. Their worlds had become more complicated, more partnership oriented, and invariably presented many more possibilities. We were struck by the fact that many managers were suffering from real pain—they knew that they needed to act, but they were unsure of how to systematically think about the increasing intricacy of their markets.

We now wanted to move from the retrospective to the prospective. Instead of researching what Microsoft, Intel, AOL, and Cisco *had done*, could we develop a methodology that would guide executives as they thought through what their deal strategy *should be*? Over time—and after testing and interacting with a number of companies across different industries—we developed such an approach.

\*\*\*

We believe that the market modeling methodology we present can be used by large and small companies across a wide range of industries.

This book addresses three main topics:

1. *How can firms systematically understand the profound changes occurring within their markets?* To successfully compete in the new economy, executives need to get their hands around a much broader range of competitors and players. What "armadas of partnerships" are forming? How can firms make sense of industry moves to determine what's happening, what is really happening, and what's likely to happen?

2. *What types of deals should firms pursue and why?* As companies analyze other industry players, they must understand why deals are taking place. This book presents a framework for uncovering deal rationales. What do competitors hope to accomplish in executing specific deals? And, most importantly, how should firms design their own deal strategy? What rationales should drive their arrays of partnerships and investments?

3. *What steps should firms take to execute their deals successfully?* Here we move from analysis to action. Having developed a deal strategy, firms need to select specific partners and structure deals. How should they design the structure of a deal? Should they attempt to buy a company, make a minority investment, establish a joint venture, form an alliance, or do something else? Does a given deal rationale suggest one deal structure over another? What lessons can firms learn from the home runs and strikeouts of lighthouse companies that have had many "at-bats" relating to a particular deal form?

\*\*\*

Part 1 of this book explores how forces of the "new economy" have moved partnerships and other deals to the center stage of corporate strategy. We then lay out and illustrate an eight-step methodology (market modeling) for systematically analyzing and executing deal strategies.

In Part 2, we examine five deal structures: mergers and acquisitions, joint ventures, minority investments, advertising and commerce alliances, and spin-offs and tracking stocks. Drawing on examples and insight derived from our deal database and case studies, we illustrate how firms—both large and small—have used these deal structures to support specific deal rationales. We seek to inform new deal strategies by exploring how and why lighthouse firms have structured their investments and partnerships.

In Part 3, we pull together the connections between deal rationale and deal structure. We also make specific suggestions about building a dedicated system for selecting and executing digital deals. Taken together, the book provides a guide for firms embarking on a strategy that requires superior competitive positioning and partnership planning.

# Crafting a Systematic Deal Strategy

What is new about the "new economy"? Although the concept has attracted both hyperbole and cynicism, fundamental business norms are, in fact, changing as several forces combine to create opportunity and reduce the costs of transacting business. While there are many implications of the new economy, this book addresses just one: the increased importance of corporate investments and partnerships.

Over the past few years, both the pace and value of business deals have grown rapidly. However, many executives charged with planning and executing business development activity feel increasingly challenged as they realize that old ways of corporate strategy are no longer adequate. Unfortunately, most companies currently lack basic processes for capturing the information that they need to craft an informed deal strategy. The next few chapters explore the new significance of partnerships and present a systematic framework for selecting the right digital deals.

1

# The Era of Digital Deals

For thousands of years Lake Ontario teemed with fish. Diverse species—trout, salmon, catfish, and perch—each gathered in a different part of the water. The fish divided up the lake and lived in a predictable, balanced ecology.

In 1819 the Erie Canal opened to bring barge traffic into Lake Ontario from the Hudson River. Along with boats and freight, the canal brought new "competitors" into the lake, including a parasitic fish from the North Atlantic Ocean known as the sea lamprey. The lamprey swam into Lake Ontario via the canal and sucked body fluids out of unsuspecting trout, whose small scales were easily removed by the lamprey's teeth-covered tongue. Over the next few years, attacking lampreys decimated the trout.

Some time later, a fish called the alewife followed the sea lamprey through the Erie Canal into Lake Ontario. It was a gray, sickly fish, about the length of a finger. Trout love to eat alewives and surely would have devoured them, but few trout had survived the lampreys' attack. In a twist of fate, salmon gobbled up the alewives instead. This proved deadly, as the alewife carries an enzyme that destroys vitamin $B_1$ concentrations in salmon. Female salmon fed extensively on the alewife and grew vitamin $B_1$ deficient. As a result, their babies invariably died after only a few

3

weeks. Ultimately, "poison" alewives would kill every single salmon in Lake Ontario.[1]

## COMPLEXITY OF COMPETITION

Forces of the new economy are fundamentally changing the way businesses compete. Just as the Erie Canal exposed Lake Ontario to previously unseen species, new technologies and macroeconomic forces are subjecting traditionally isolated markets to new competitors. According to venture capitalist and writer Bill Gurley, "The least obvious, but most interesting, way the Internet is changing competition is through the blurring of boundaries that have historically existed between markets. Imagine if you will, a large body of land covered by independent lakes. Think of these lakes as markets, and the species that inhabit each lake as competitors. . . . Now imagine what would happen if a canal were established between each and every lake, thereby enabling the fish to swim freely. . . . Your competition is no longer limited to your lake, and you may find yourself face to face with a species you have never seen before."[2] The structural protection that traditional market borders used to provide is no more.

This newly intensified competition can take on several forms. Like the sea lamprey, some attackers are directly threatening traditional incumbents. For example, AT&T, one of the most powerful icons of American business in the twentieth century, has struggled as smaller competitors take advantage of new technologies to attack its core long-distance and wireless services markets.[3] In other cases, industries are changing more subtly. Just as the sea lamprey established the preconditions for the alewife to destroy Lake Ontario salmon, serial competitive battles are leading to surprising outcomes. Amazon.com enters and transforms the book market, an event that influences players and dynamics in markets from toys to groceries. Both primary and secondary effects must be considered. The complexity of competition is enhanced by periodic dot-com implosions coupled with an ongoing march of wireless, broadband, and digital video.

This book is grounded in two fundamental premises:

◆ In the new economy, competitive positioning has become significantly more complex, raising the need for refined methodologies to analyze market dynamics.

◆ Superior business models increasingly require a network of deals, alliances, and other partnerships for every market or submarket in which a firm competes. Given these complexities, executives need new information systems to help select and implement deals.

## NEW IMPORTANCE OF PARTNERSHIPS

The number of deals is mushrooming. Partnership and investment activity have become an enduring dimension of corporate strategy that occurs during ebbs and flows of the business cycle. Virtually no one goes to market alone anymore—it's too costly, too risky, and too slow.

Nineteen of the world's 20 largest mergers of the twentieth century were announced in the two-year period starting in 1998. During the same time frame, it became commonplace for companies to build corporate venture groups to make Internet-related minority investments in other firms. Internet commerce and business development partnerships occupy an increasing amount of executive attention. According to Robert Spekman and Lynn Isabella at the University of Virginia's Darden School, "The rate of alliance formation has exploded—the number of alliances formed each year is estimated to run into the tens of thousands."[4] Startups seeking venture capital funding now require a good idea, a great management team, and a set of marquee partnerships.

By the year 2000, Intel had made over 400 minority equity investments. (During 2000, Intel continued at a torrid investment pace and ended the year as the most active venture capital investor, having made over 200 deals.) Microsoft had pulled together more than 25 joint ventures and amassed a corporate investment portfolio valued around $20 billion. Cisco had completed over 50 acquisitions. AOL had strung together thousands of business commerce deals with a backlog (contracted, but not-yet-booked, revenue) of at least $3 billion.[5] Equity-for-advertising deals, clicks-to-bricks partnerships, cobranding initiatives, and a host of other alliances were all part of a digital-deal landscape.

Companies other than technology and/or Internet organizations were actively engaged in corporate ventures and alliances. In fact, companies in every industry were involved in the deal flow. Corporate venture capital had reached new heights. In 1998 U.S. companies set up venture arms that invested $1.5 billion, around 8 percent of total venture money. The next year, they more than quadrupled their level of investment, channeling nearly $7 billion (16 percent of total venture capital investments) into young firms, according to the National Venture Capital Association. Over 200 firms made corporate venture investments in 1999.

The deal frenzy brought together all combinations of partners. Old-world companies were forming alliances with Internet dot-coms. Start-ups struck deals among themselves. Incumbent companies were spinning off Internet units. From alliances completed over lunch to acquisitions requiring months of regulatory approval, cross-company dealing was at an all-time high.

However, the dot-com burnout of 2000 proved that deal volume alone was no guarantee of success. Business development screens were needed as it became increasingly hazardous to deal with just any dot-com (or incumbent) company.

Today, firms must select deals that create real value. Frequent press releases will not substitute for a well-crafted deal strategy. Business has entered a new era where, more than ever, success requires considered cooperation.[6]

Exactly what is a digital deal? Simply stated, it involves two or more companies joining forces to compete, using bits more than atoms. Nicholas Negroponte, founder of MIT's Media Lab, explored this distinction in his 1995 book *Being Digital*: "The best way to appreciate the merits and consequences of being digital is to reflect on the difference between bits and atoms. Most information is delivered to us in the form of atoms: newspapers, magazines, and books . . . physical materials in real packages . . . . The information superhighway is about the global movements of weightless bits at the speed at light . . . . It [a bit] is a state of being: on or off, true or false, black or white."[7] In a digital deal, firms team up to compete primarily using bits. In a conventional deal, they remain predominantly in the realm of atoms.

Whether or not a deal is digital depends on the partners' intent. Why have the companies formed the deal? What do they hope to accomplish? How will the deal change the way they compete? This distinction is not always transparent. For example, consider a merger between two mining companies designed to cut the cost of processing minerals—hard to find a deal based more in the world of atoms. But now suppose that the primary motivation for entering the deal is to establish the critical mass needed to join an Internet supply hub for the minerals. Definitely a digital deal.

The rise of the digital economy—accelerated by powerful processors and fatter communication pipes—is transforming the world from one made up of atoms to one made up of atoms and bits. These changes add a new dimension to corporate strategy, forcing most companies to focus on a new array of partnership opportunities. Digital deals take on many different forms. They can involve marketing, operations, finance, or organizational design. They utilize structures that include alliances, minority investments, joint ventures, acquisitions, and even spin-offs. (This book broadly uses the term *partnerships* to refer to all of these deal structures.) Winning firms need to understand why digital deals have become more important and how they can structure partnerships to take advantage of the new business climate. The age of digital deals has dawned.

## FORCES OF THE NEW ECONOMY

The forces of the new economy are pushing companies to form digital deals at a torrid pace. The value chains of every industry are being reinvented, and in almost all cases digital deals play an integral part in the value reshuffling. In *Race for the World*, managers are advised to "think of an industry as a picture puzzle with each piece representing a part of the chain of suppliers, manufacturers, and service providers that currently make up its structure. On the back of each piece is a number representing its value. Now take the puzzle apart and change the shape of the pieces—cut them in half, attach them to others, discard a few, and create new ones. Then assign new values to each piece, but use a much broader and higher range of numbers. Winning . . . will be about shaping and owning the right pieces at the right time and putting them together in new ways."[8] In our view, digital deals are the primary method of reshaping and reassembling the pieces of a market puzzle.

To understand why deals are so important, let's step back to explore briefly how three powerful forces—technology, free flowing capital markets, and deregulation—are transforming the environment in which firms operate.

## Technology and the digital triangle

The relentless pace of technological progress—and the resulting business opportunities and pressures—have been well documented over the past few years. By any unit of measurement, advances in technology are awesome. The number of semiconductors currently pulsing has already passed 6 billion, which means there are more chips than humans on Earth. *Race for the World* explains how the cost of raw computing power has fallen precipitously: The cost of processing a million instructions per second (MIPS) was nearly $600 in 1980. In 1995 one MIPS cost $1.30, and by 2005, a MIPS is estimated to cost one-tenth of a penny. The book also explores the drop in communications costs: "In 1930, a three-minute call between New York and London cost $300 in 1996 dollars; today it costs only $1.26."[9] Arguably, recent advances in voice over Internet Protocol (IP) technology (which supports long-distance voice communication using Internet technology) will drive these costs down even further.

These rapid advances in computer processing and communications technology are creating new dimensions in business opportunity and complexity. One way to depict this complexity is via a digital triangle (see Figure 1-1), which plots the new economy along three key dimensions: (1) products and services, (2) technology, and (3) distribution and communications. Historically, most companies have succeeded by concentrating on the top corner of the triangle—focusing on producing a better car, movie, newspaper, or airline flight. But today, every company needs to incorporate the other two corners of the triangle—technology and communications—into its competitive positioning and partnership strategy.

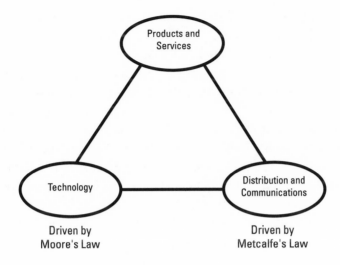

**FIGURE 1-1**
*The digital triangle.*

First, consider the lower left corner of the triangle—technology. The classic way of underlining advances in technology is via Moore's law. Named after Gordon Moore, cofounder of Intel, Moore's law is now discussed as often in business schools as in engineering departments. It states that for the same cost, computer processing power doubles every 18 months. For the past 30 years, electrical engineers have been able to shrink down the circuits on semiconductors creating smaller chips or doubling processing power without increasing size. Larry Downes and Chunka Mui summarize the implications of Moore's Law in *Unleashing the Killer App*: "Everything having to do with digital technology gets relentlessly smaller, faster, and cheaper . . . . [Previously uneconomical applications] suddenly have the wherewithal to enter the market, taking advantage of low cost computer power, memory, and storage to perform complex tasks."[10]

Technological progress will roll on. Craig Barrett, Intel's CEO, believes that Moore's law will continue for 15 more years. A chip with the power of the Pentium will shrink from measuring about 2 inches square to fit on the head of a pin. Ultimately, conventional chip technology will begin to run into limits—the line widths etched in a chip can only be shrunk to about 0.1 microns (less than one-thousandth the width of a human hair). Furthermore, below measurements of 0.02 microns, the quantum limit is reached, where conventional laws of physics break down and electrons behave unpredictably. However, scientists continue to experiment with new materials and quantum technologies that may enable Moore's law to continue even beyond Barrett's current estimate.[11]

Moving to the  bottom right corner of the digital triangle, the power of ubiquitous communications can be seen in Metcalfe's law, named after Robert Metcalfe, founder of 3Com. He asserts that the overall value of a network increases exponentially with every additional user. When someone else buys a fax, phone, or MP3 player, everyone else in the group benefits. Carl Shapiro and Hal Varian calculate the impact of Metcalfe's law in *Information Rules*: "If the value of a network to a single user is $1 for each other user on the network, then a network of size 10 has a total value of roughly $100. In contrast a network of size 100 has a total value of roughly $10,000. Multiplying the number of users by ten increases the value by a factor of one hundred."[12] As communication bandwidth becomes faster and cheaper, users continue to join groups, exponentially increasing benefits for everyone.

Likewise, advances in communications are continuing at a rapid pace. Fiber capacity expands relentlessly, and quantum leaps in optical technology will allow firms to transmit massive volumes of information at the speed of light. Broadband technologies in the home, such as DSL and cable, are beginning to reach critical mass. Virtual Private Networks (VPNs) allow companies to communicate securely and seamlessly using the infrastructure of the Internet. The rise of wireless communications is making it easier than ever to communicate remotely.

As computer processing and communication technologies continue to improve, companies must devise and revise strategies that consider and incorporate all relevant parts of the digital triangle. A few companies, such as AOL, attempt to position themselves in the middle of the triangle by developing core capabilities involving all three corners—products, technology, and distribution and communications. Others, such as Sun Microsystems, pride themselves on building and defending a core bastion in the technology corner. Even these companies, however, must develop a coherent partnership strategy with respect to communications and vertical product markets.

Large and small companies in diverse markets frequently need to work with partners in other corners of the digital triangle to build effective new economy business models. For example, in 1999, financial giant Merrill Lynch—having long scoffed at the need to embrace the Internet technology corner of the digital triangle—awoke to dramatically reposition itself in the retail investing market by offering online trading for $29 per transaction. Under threat from competitors such as Charles Schwab, Merrill assembled an armada of partners to execute its new efforts, including Standard & Poors, Intuit, Cisco, Exodus, and others. Similarly, Boeing announced in 2000 that it was launching a new service called Connexion, designed to offer air travelers high-speed data communication via a space-based network. The world's premier aircraft manufacturer, having decided to move toward the communications corner of the digital triangle, embarked on an extensive partnership strategy that involved CNN, CNBC, Mitsubishi, and others. Digital disruption knows no market boundaries and has no limits on company size.

The need for positioning and digital partnering in existing and new submarkets seems endless. And as illustrated throughout this book, a company must think through competitive positioning and partnering submarket by submarket, taking into account the digital triangle.

## Free flowing capital markets

A second major force has driven the new economy: free-flowing global financial markets. During the 1990s the world became awash with capital waiting to be invested in compelling opportunities. It has been estimated that the world's stock of liquid financial assets was $80 trillion in 2000, more than seven times the amount of capital available 20 years earlier.[13]

During the past few years, this glut of capital reached an apex. In 1999, venture capital firms invested $36.5 billion in 1500 companies, nearly tripling the $14.3 billion invested in 1998. In the first three months of 2000, venture capitalists poured $23 billion into start-ups. The National Venture Capital Association and the Venture Economics group of Thomson Financial Securities Data reported that 50 percent of the 544 initial public offerings (IPOs) in 1999 were venture-backed, up from 20 percent in 1998. Furthermore, 271 venture-backed companies went public in 1999 with the total valuation of these companies on the IPO date reaching $136.2 billion.[14] Dozens—if not hundreds—of companies ranging from Intel to Starbucks set up corporate venture capital groups to fund promising opportunities.

By the middle of 2000, the spigots of capital flow seemed to be shut off for some submarkets. Many dot-coms could not raise the capital needed to continue operations and were forced to shut down. Other start-ups slashed their burn rates to preserve existing capital. In particular, venture capitalists shunned investments in saturated sectors such as new media content or B2C ecommerce. One sensed, however, that this was more of a pause than an absolute stoppage of capital flow for these sectors.

Massive stockpiles of capital can now be moved around the globe at the speed of bits. Historically, capital markets, governed by the post–World War II Bretton Woods system, operated only in limited geographic regions. However, during the 1970s, the existing financial system broke down and the foreign exchange markets rapidly integrated into a single, global market. This integration continued during the 1980s and 1990s as the debt and equity markets converged. As a result, capital can now move very quickly to reward the strong and punish the weak. As the 1998 economic crises in Asia demonstrated, erosion of confidence can quickly decimate assets as the premium for risk rises. Likewise, during 2000, the U.S. equity market demonstrated that free-flowing capital could result in highly volatile stock prices.

Capital markets will continue to integrate. Equity markets are consolidating as bourses in Europe join with the U.S. Nasdaq market. Additional countries in Europe are likely to adopt the Euro as their sole currency (although some nations continue to resist change). Soon waves of money will seamlessly flow from debt to equity to foreign exchange markets around the world. This mass of mobile capital has profound implications for the new economy.

## Deregulation

As global financial markets gained power, most governments have realized that free market economies are the fastest way to create wealth.

When countries open up their borders, they gain access to new investment, learn new business skills, and enjoy new bases of customers. As their economic productivity multiplies, these countries enjoy a higher standard of living. To this effect, trade barriers are falling, opening up opportunities in every corner of the world. The General Agreement on Tariffs and Trade (GATT), the North American Free Trade Agreement (NAFTA), and an expanding World Trade Organization (WTO) are only a few examples.

Within the United States, the ebb and flow of regulation has largely ebbed. Many regulatory bodies are proving cooperative to business. For example, the Securities and Exchange Commission (SEC) now works with lawyers to get IPO registrations completed in record time. What used to take six to nine months can often be done in three. The SEC is also working with different groups to simplify and streamline the entire securities registration process.

Antitrust enforcement has been lenient in general, with the exception of a few high-profile cases. The U.S. Department of Justice and the Federal Trade Commission (FTC) are approving most mergers, even as industries grow more and more concentrated. Clearly there are major exceptions—Microsoft has learned the hard way that Washington, D.C., matters in the corporate boardroom. An attempt by MCI WorldCom to acquire Sprint met FTC resistance in 2000, and the America Online/Time Warner merger received intense scrutiny in the United States, as well as in Europe. However, to a large extent, U.S. regulators have limited antitrust intrusions, wary of interfering with the economy. According to one Federal Communications Commission (FCC) commissioner, Gloria Tristani, the focus of the commission has shifted. With a mandate to protect the public policy, the FCC has, by and large, reinterpreted "public policy" to mean the country's economic well-being and has approved mergers that it might have questioned in an earlier era.[15] Furthermore, under the Bush administration, the FCC has signaled that it will reduce its market intervention.

To be sure, the death of government regulation is nowhere near a reality. There have been periodic backlashes, as some cry out for additional protections to cope with the complexities brought on by the new economy. In 2000, for example, the FTC was investigating whether actions taken by Amazon.com, DoubleClick, and Yahoo! violated privacy laws, and was exploring whether an auto parts exchange run by Ford, GM, DaimlerChrysler, and other automobile companies would violate antitrust laws. Underlying political currents will continue to support some level of regulation. Complicating matters, the global reach of corporations often subjects them to multiple jurisdictions. A firm may clear a U.S. antitrust hurdle only to find its deal blocked by the European Union in Brussels. But, in general, deregulation is uniting the world, leading to new business opportunities and increasing the complexities of competition.

# IMPLICATIONS OF NEW ECONOMY FORCES

Web gurus and economists debate the impact of these forces on fundamental economic tenets. Kevin Kelly insists that the new economy has changed everything—toss out old textbooks and invert supply and demand curves. Carl Shapiro and Hal Varian counter that little has changed—plain old economic rules still govern market behavior. Academics and executives are struggling to interpret and profit from the new economy.[16]

In our view, new technology, ubiquitous capital markets, and global deregulation lead to three important implications: lower transaction costs (the costs of coordinating and conducting business), an explosion of business opportunity, and (central to our efforts) a more prominent role for digital deals.

## Lower transaction costs

Ronald Coase has become an unexpected apostle of the new economy. Coase, a University of Chicago Nobel laureate, explored why people organize into firms to conduct business.[17] According to Coase, it all boils down to transaction costs, the efforts required to search out a buyer, advertise products, conduct negotiations, draw up the contract, and so on. Groups of people organize into firms to save transaction costs whenever the cost of coordinating within a firm is less than that of conducting business in the open market. Coase felt that firms would reach an upper size limit, when it became so difficult to coordinate within the firm (think bureaucracy) that there would be no advantage over an open market transaction.

Larry Downes and Chunka Mui illustrate transaction costs and the nature of the firm: "Let's say you work for an averaged-sized firm and you've run out of paper clips. Almost assuredly, you will get your paper clips not by going out on the open market but by going down the hall to the supplies department of your office, which has purchased and maintains an inventory of paper clips in your building . . . . The reason? Even if you could get paper clips on your own for the same price, you would still have to *get them* . . . . Better to . . . buy in bulk and avoid all that trouble."[18] That "trouble" reflects transaction costs.

The forces of the new economy are acting in concert to reduce transaction costs. Advances in technology and communications networks have increased the efficiency of data gathering, written and oral communication, and group problem-solving interaction. Deregulation, open market borders, and free flowing capital markets compound these efficiencies. More can be done in less time as new economy marketplaces cut transaction costs not just incrementally, but exponentially.

## Opportunity explosion

Around 550 million years ago, the Earth exploded with life. By the early Cambrian Period, the atmosphere finally developed enough oxygen to support large, complex animals. Over the next 20 million years, an extraordinary number of distinct species evolved. In fact, almost all of our modern animal groups first appear in this relatively short period of time. One critical event, increasing levels of oxygen in the atmosphere, sparked enormous change. Jeff Bezos of Amazon.com compares the new economy to the Cambrian explosion of life. New species of corporate life forms are rapidly evolving to display unique, even outlandish, business models previously unseen in the corporate boardroom.[19]

Lower transaction costs act like Cambrian oxygen, spawning dozens of new business models as industry value chains are reshuffled and new corporate strategies are tested. Business opportunity abounds. The exact nature of that opportunity—how firms should strategically take advantage of lower transaction costs—is less clear. Consider three plausible strategies: specialization, massification, and vertical integration.

SPECIALIZATION

One reasonable conclusion is that firms will increasingly need to specialize as transaction costs shrink. They should shed unrelated business processes, focus on particular core strengths, and team up with other specialized firms to complete larger projects or ventures. As it becomes easier to coordinate with outside parties, the value of doing everything under one corporate umbrella shrinks. It's much easier to establish and monitor agreements with third parties.

The value of specialization is not new. Think back to Henry Ford, who used assembly lines to divide up labor and improve efficiency not only through mass production but also through specialization. Each worker focused on steering wheels, hubcaps, or brake pedals instead of building the entire car. The difference now is that instead of people specializing within a firm, companies arguably will specialize within an industry or even across industries.

Consider changes in the movie-making business. Fifty years ago Hollywood was dominated by seven major studios that made every aspect of a movie in-house. MGM, for example, assembled a permanent team of writers, artists, editors, lighting technicians, and props makers. But the rise of foreign films and television forced Hollywood to restructure. Over the next few decades, the big studios fragmented into a number of smaller, specialized companies. This atomization of Hollywood into mostly small, uniquely skilled companies has transformed the way movies are made. Movie producers no longer deploy a rigidly structured workforce completely under internal control. Instead, successful producers must now cultivate relationships and alliances that allow them to craft a coalition of small firms that work together to make a movie. The competitive edge belongs to those who can navigate Hollywood's network of flexible small businesses to assemble the best talent quickly.[20]

MASSIFICATION

A second plausible strategy is to pursue scale. In addition to promoting specialization, lower transaction costs can also trigger massification in which large firms efficiently knit together vast empires. In *The Social Life of Information*, John Seely Brown and Paul Duguid reject the argument that firms are growing more specialized by pointing to empirical evidence, including a spate of high-profile mergers. "Ninety years after the era of trust busting, oil, banking, and tobacco are all consolidating again."[21]

Some firms are successfully pursuing a strategy of size. Cisco gobbles up new companies every year, feeding its marketing muscle with new network infrastructure technologies. Archrivals Lucent and Nortel have attempted a similar strategy. AOL is amassing music, news, and other content and deploying new technology and business models to leverage these assets. Charles Schwab gains an upscale market presence by purchasing U.S. Trust, an asset manager for wealthy clients. Giants in the financial, industrial, and media sectors continue to merge, using scale to lower costs, increase leverage over suppliers and customers, and take advantage of the transaction costs dynamics of the new economy.

## VERTICAL INTEGRATION

A third set of firms may choose to follow a vertical integration strategy, assembling all steps in an industry value chain under one roof. Classically, vertical integration has been defined as combining distinct economic processes within a single firm.[22]

In the new economy, the notion of vertical integration is undergoing a subtle extension that is explored in this book. By establishing digital deals with players in other key activities, companies can often create a business model that effectively integrates a market offering, even if all such activities are not housed under one "roof." Firms must consider a strategy that links together—via partnerships or outright ownership— all the key pieces of a particular value chain.

This vertical integration strategy allows a firm to iron out inefficiencies in the value chain by controlling information at each link of the chain. For example, by gathering constant information on gas consumption in consumers' cars, the local gas station, regional storage tankers, extraction sites, and so on, an integrated energy firm could monitor and optimize the movement of gas to boost profitability. The key to this newer form of vertical integration is gathering, controlling, and synthesizing new types of information to develop a holistic market picture.

One common thread runs through all three of these new economy strategies—specialization, massification, and vertical integration. Each requires a successful deal strategy to thrive. Specialist firms must develop a series of partnerships to accomplish larger, more complex projects. Firms in pursuit of scale are likely to focus on mergers and acquisitions to supplement organic growth. And companies that choose to position themselves across all activities of an industry value chain will often require a network of alliances and partnerships to do so. Regardless of the particular strategy that a firm chooses to pursue, it will need to skillfully select and structure digital deals.

## TRADITIONAL APPROACH TO DEALS INADEQUATE

Partnerships have always been important to corporate strategy. John D. Rockefeller positioned Standard Oil through a network of deals. Henry Ford and Alfred P. Sloan built automobile empires through an elaborate series of acquisitions and partnerships. What's different, if anything, about digital deal making? This book offers two suggestions: (1) competitive and partnership arenas have grown more complicated, and (2) the reasons why deals are being done—deal rationales—have (at least in part) changed.

In the early 1900s Henry Ford had a good sense for the limited set of players in the automobile industry. He could assess the impact of a deal intuitively by thinking through how major competitors, suppliers, or customers were likely to react. Today these types of calculations are difficult to make and require much more sophisticated analysis. Even the basic idea of competition has changed. Firms face an increasingly subtle world of "co-opetition," where they must both cooperate and compete with one company at the same time. As Adam Brandenburger and Barry Nalebuff state: "There's a fundamental duality here: whereas creating value is an inherently cooperative process, capturing value is inherently competitive. . . . Co-opetition means cooperating to create a bigger business 'pie,' while competing to divide it up."[23] There is also a new imperative for speed; companies have to be ready to assess partners and make decisions virtually overnight. As competition grows more complex in the digital economy, firms that lack basic processes for systematically gathering and understanding the information that they need to make deal decisions are increasingly disadvantaged.

Second, the reasons for forming deals are changing in the new economy. Not everything is revolutionary; some deals seek to accomplish age-old objectives. But many of today's partnership rationales are very different than before—often in subtle ways. Firms need new methods to uncover their competitors' motives for partnerships, and to clarify and select their own digital deal rationales.

For example, one of the main reasons for partnering with other companies has historically been to improve sales of an existing product through geographic expansion. In these types of alliances, success came from transferring competencies across borders by retaining key managers from acquired companies and by employing strategies designed to transfer the best practices of each partner.[24]

In today's economy, international deals remain highly relevant. However, many more deals are about securing a new technology or effectively combining digital activities of a value chain. As the reasons for deals change and expand, firms need to adopt new ways of analyzing, executing, and managing a broader range of partnership and investment possibilities.

# DEVELOPING A SYSTEMATIC DEAL STRATEGY

Chapters 2 through 5 present a new way of thinking about deal strategy. They explore methods for understanding market changes and intelligently selecting deals and partners. Later this book examines how to select between different deal structures and discusses key steps that managers can take to execute deals successfully.

To guide this effort, we developed a systematic framework to help executives craft a strategy for effective positioning and partnering in the digital economy. This approach is called *market modeling*. This eight-step process, which is described in detail over the next few chapters, summarizes the essence of digital deal making (see Figure 1-2).

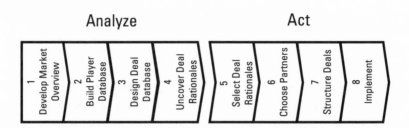

**FIGURE 1-2**
*Market modeling framework.*

1. Develop a market overview that depicts the value activities of the market.

2. Build a database of players relevant to the market being analyzed.

3. Design and build a deal database for the market.

4. Uncover deal rationales using direct deal analysis or by analyzing constellations of deals.

5. Within the context of a company's core strengths, select deal rationales that will contribute to a superior business model.

6. Choose target partners.

7. Structure the partnership or investment.

8. Implement the deal successfully.

Steps 1 to 4 involve analyzing the market, its players, and its deals. Steps 5 to 8 move from analysis to action on digital deals. Steps 1 and 2 are discussed in the next chapter.

## SUMMARY

What's new about the "new economy"? Three forces—technology, capital markets, and global deregulation—are combining to reduce the costs of transacting business. Lower transaction costs act as Cambrian oxygen, spawning new business models as industry value chains are reshuffled and new corporate strategies ensue. This turmoil has increased the pace and importance of deals. Not surprisingly, it has also led to confusion and pain as managers realize that old ways of corporate strategy are no longer adequate. Structuring the right deals is more important than ever, but unfortunately, most companies lack basic processes for capturing the information that they need to craft an informed deal strategy. This must change. The next four chapters present a systematic framework that firms can use to understand how markets are evolving and select the right digital deals to execute.

# CHAPTER 2

# Market Overview and Player Database

In a classic essay that remains provocative, Nobel award–winning economist Herb Simon illustrates how both scientists and executives must gather a large number of "chunks of knowledge" to make world-class contributions. "In neither science nor business does the professional look for a fair bet. Rather the creative professional has superior knowledge that comes from persistence in acquiring more chunks than others."[1]

Market modeling involves chunk building—developing meaningful pieces of information about markets, companies, and relationships. A robust market model does not happen all at once, but requires persistent effort. An organization must put in place a system that enables the continual building of market-specific knowledge. Over time, as more and more information chunks are accumulated, the market modeling resource grows increasingly valuable in supporting competitive positioning and partnership planning for executives.

Most areas within a company use automated systems to capture and analyze information. Accountants use financial information systems. Analysts build spreadsheet models. The Human Resources department has personnel systems. Operations planners deploy enterprise resource planning (ERP) software. Sales managers have sales force automation (SFA) technology and customer relationship management (CRM) systems.

So what do corporate strategists and business development professionals have?

There is a dire need for organizations to build systems that support competitive analysis and partnership planning. In 1998 Peter Drucker lamented that information technology had barely impacted how top management develops business strategy. He predicted that during the next 10 to 15 years, systematic collection of outside information would become the next frontier for information technology.[2]

To successfully design and implement strategy, informational emphasis has to move from internal operations to the external worlds of markets, competitors, and partners. The complexity and rate of change present unique challenges for corporate strategists. In the face of these challenges, successful corporate development demands the systematic gathering of real-time outside information. Digital deal analysis and execution must not be discrete, unitary actions, but rather a continuous process involving information about multiple markets and dozens if not hundreds of partnerships or investments.

This chapter begins to develop the market modeling framework introduced in Chapter 1. This framework is an eight-step process designed to help executives analyze and execute digital deals in the new economy (see Figure 1-2). In particular, this chapter focuses on the first two steps: developing a market overview that depicts value activities and building a database of relevant players.

In addition, brilliant corporate positioning and partnership planning depend on an organization's developing and utilizing these market knowledge chunks. Chapter 12 discusses how to tune both the analytical and deal-making resources of a company toward this effort.

Let's begin by examining the music industry—a rapidly changing market at the vanguard of the digital economy—as a context for illustrating the first two steps of market modeling.

## MORPHING MUSIC

The music industry provides a prime example of a "market space" where intense deal making permeates all aspects of the business. There is growing consensus that the way music will be manufactured, distributed, and sold in 2010 will scarcely resemble the current process. Facing new technology, new standards, and other catalysts of change, every old and new music company is wrestling with positioning and partnering decisions (see Table 2-1). Music is an ideal market to illustrate digital deal making.

**Table 2-1 Trends in the Music Industry**

| Trend | Examples |
| --- | --- |
| **Consolidation** | Big Five record labels |
| **New technology** | Digitized music; new hardware devices |
| **New standards** | Competition for codecs and digital rights management |
| **New channels** | Online retail; Internet downloads; Internet radio |
| **New business models** | Download sites; streaming sites; direct-to-consumer subscription |
| **New legal questions** | Online intellectual property; security and digital rights management |

Music also provides a leading indicator as to how other markets—such as video entertainment, publishing, education and training, and even investment banking—will evolve in the new economy. The music industry has been compared to "a canary in the digital coal mine," sniffing out colorless, odorless, and tasteless methane gas, thereby offering early warning to explosive dangers for other markets.[3]

## Industry background and consolidation

The music industry was created in 1877 when Thomas Edison invented his talking machine. Through the next 70 years it continued as an oligopoly with four or fewer companies controlling the majority of sales.[4] However, by the early 1960s, as Rock and Roll increased the demand for music, dozens of new companies sprang up. Before long, over 40 record labels had one or more *Billboard*-charted albums.

During the next 20 years the major record companies reclaimed the industry via acquisition. Large labels bought out smaller ones, preserving the distinct names but consolidating production, distribution, and control behind the scenes. The year 2000 found the world recording industry dominated by the Big Five: Warner, EMI, Sony, Universal, and BMG. (In 2000, Warner and EMI attempted to merge and consolidate the industry from the Big Five to a Bigger Four, but European Union regulatory authorities blocked the effort.) Other labels found it tough to compete because the Big Five jealously guarded the distribution of music—independent labels could not sell into many retail stores. Only the Big Five could assemble an international distribution system that got albums to consumers on a massive scale.

## DIGITAL ECONOMY BEGETS DEALS

By 2000, the digital economy had transformed the music industry. The rise of new technology, standards, business models, and legal questions led to unprecedented changes and an outbreak of innovative partnerships.

### New technology and standards

Analog music had long ago been digitized, a process in which sound wave positions are converted to a series of 1's and 0's. Digitized music could then be pressed into compact discs to store and play songs. But digital music had historically demanded large amounts of memory, explaining why a traditional CD could only hold about an hour of music. And for most listeners, digitized songs were too large to download from the Internet.

The music market quickly became more dynamic as barriers to digital distribution began to crumble. Bandwidth continued to increase, making it faster to stream or download digital music files. (Streaming involves "broadcasting" music over the Internet, whereas downloaded music is stored on a listener's hard drive or other storage device.) Another breakthrough came as audio researchers developed ways to digitize music in a variety of more compact formats called codecs (compression/decompression algorithms). Each codec technology could create song files, with extremely good sound quality, using less than one-tenth the size of normal CDs.[5] This compressed music could now be downloaded (or streamed) over the Internet in a reasonable period of time and played on the sound systems of computers or other digital devices.

Engineers at MPEG, Microsoft, AT&T, RealAudio, and other companies created distinct codecs, each with relative advantages and disadvantages. These codecs competed to become the universal standard, and backers all vied to become the media format preferred by artists and listeners. The pace of deals and partnerships centered on digital music format accelerated.

## New channels and business models

The Big Five didn't fully realize how much their world would change when online retailers like Amazon.com and CDNow first started selling traditional CDs over the Internet. This move threatened a competitive advantage of the Big Five: access to scarce distribution and shelf space at the local retail stores. With unconstrained shelf space, CDNow offered 10 times the selection of a brick-and-mortar store. Although online sales of CDs began to climb, the Big Five didn't view this hybrid model (order online, fulfill offline) as a major industry transformation. It was just another channel to them.

Not much later, however, as the MP3 codec gained momentum with artists, the media, and Internet listeners, the Big Five began to sweat. Encouraged by an almost fanatical group of fans, download or streaming sites such as MP3.com sprang up to offer a wide variety of songs to eager listeners who had downloaded free player software from AOL or RealNetworks. A multiplicity of download sites, software player technology, and hardware devices for listening added to the deal-making frenzy.

As the industry continued to morph, new business models arose to exploit the change. MP3.com (in an early incarnation) pioneered a garage band upload model, where aspiring musicians could upload their songs to MP3.com to be sampled and sold to the public. Artists could customize their own CDs by choosing the songs, artwork, and price via online configurators. Artists also enjoyed unprecedented information: how many people were listening to each song, where their fans lived, and how downloads grew in California after a concert. (MP3.com later launched a service called MyMP3.com delivering music from licensors that included large record companies.)

Companies would also use streaming technology to deliver music over the Internet. To listen to streamed music, users did not need to download an entire song, making the music faster to play and freeing up hard drive storage space. Internet radio business models started to provide listeners with a "better radio." For example, Yahoo! Radio developed a database of hundreds of thousands of digitized songs, which could be played on specialized channels. Another California-based company, Launch Media, allowed users to create a customized radio station. They started by listing favorite traditional radio stations. Then, as songs were streamed, listeners could rate how much they liked the song or artist, even demanding that lousy songs never be played again. As users listened to their personal stations longer, Launch got smarter about what type of music they liked to hear, as well as what types of ads to display.

AOL was also moving aggressively into the music space by acquiring and building brands around companies that included Spinner, an Internet music broadcast service. Then in 2000, AOL showed just how serious it was about digital music by acquiring Time Warner, parent of the Warner Music Group. With the announcement of the AOL deal, other music industry giants were moved from confusion to panic. The deal was finalized in 2001.

Companies (including the Big Five record companies) started exploring models to sell per-use or subscription rights to streaming music over the Internet. Instead of buying the right to store the song on their hard drive and play it endlessly, users would just buy a per-use license to stream the song whenever they wanted to listen to it. Imagine having access to every song ever recorded; a listener picks exactly what he or she wants to hear and pays pennies each time he or she listens. Or imagine paying a flat $15 per month for a subscription to favorite music, old and new. What would be next—Amazon.com making payments to a music publisher for a listener to hear favorite songs while he or she shops on its site?

## New legal questions

By now the record labels were panicked, facing growing threats to their market control and margins. In particular, new legal questions emerged that potentially restricted their ability to control distribution and protect intellectual property rights.

MP3 proliferation was causing a major headache. It became very easy to put MP3 files on the Internet for others to download for free. In addition, listeners could quickly convert a Garth Brooks single or CD into MP3 format and email it to their friends. The situation was inflamed when Diamond Multimedia Systems came out with a Rio MP3 player, which could store files into memory for portable listening. Soon "MP3" was appearing in more Yahoo! searches than "sex."

Then Napster emerged on the scene, providing a software application that allowed listeners to share music files among PCs, rather than between a Web server and a PC. College students (and soon many others) were telling Napster where music files were located on their hard drives, and Napster would tell the world. This made it easier than ever for listeners to find and download free music files.

Security and digital rights management became crucial issues, as the Big Five feared losing millions to illegal copying. The Recording Industry Association of America (RIAA) established the Secure Digital Music Initiative (SDMI) to create secure standards for Internet music delivery. Some 110 companies—including the Big Five record labels and the "4C team" of IBM, Intel, Matsushita, and Toshiba—joined the SDMI to defend against easy piracy offered by MP3. Both MP3.com and Napster were sued by the RIAA for "blatant infringement" of copyright laws.[6]

To solve the problem, the SDMI looked to deploy watermarking technology, where digital songs would be encoded with an inaudible stamp that could be traced throughout all music formats, no matter how a song was compressed. This watermark would identify the owner of the song, and perhaps whether it was an illegal copy. Dozens of watermarking companies sprang up to develop this security feature, and the war for standards began anew. Other companies worked to develop cryptography for secure music transfer, and firms like Reciprocal were created to provide the auditing and royalty management clearinghouse services that secure music distribution required.

As legal concerns continued to grow, a flurry of new players entered (and often exited) the market and old players repositioned themselves. The Big Five, dazed by the rapid change, moved forward with other deals. They joined with IBM on a widely publicized (and criticized) Madison project, which piloted a solution for "pirate-proof" delivery of music over the Web. Over 1000 high-speed Internet users in San Diego tested IBM's system for downloading secure music from the libraries of the Big Five. Some of the Big Five partnered with non-SDMI watermarking firms, attempting to develop their own solutions. BMG even signed a deal with the devil, agreeing to loan Napster $50 million and drop its lawsuit if the company "went legit." Deal-making activity accelerated as all players staked out positions relating to secure music delivery.

Whether or not they would thrive, services such as MP3.com and Napster had clearly demonstrated that enormous demand existed for digital music—at least when price equaled zero. One point on a demand curve had been clearly established. What now needed to be determined were the demand curves and elasticities that related to pay services.

A tornado of confusion was wreaking havoc on the music market. On the one hand was enormous opportunity—the industry had been characterized as a "$100 billion market trapped in a $40 billion body." Eventually, the new economy could unleash this ensnared value. On the other hand was the horrendous threat in which music morphed into a $0 billion market ravaged by free distribution. The digital economy was spawning hundreds of new companies making thousands of deals with and apart from the major record companies. Exactly how power and profits would shake out was yet to be determined.

How could one understand such a complicated business situation? Using the music industry in 2000, let's illustrate the first two steps of market modeling.

# STEP 1: MARKET OVERVIEW

*Develop a market overview that depicts the value activities of the market.*

During more conventional periods, companies operated within a stable value chain[7] that tracked the physical flow of products or services through a given market. For example, in the music industry, album sales traditionally followed a rather predictable value chain (see Figure 2-1), reflecting a standard series of activities. The process started with an artist placing responsibility for his or her business arrangements in the hands of a management company or agent. The artist then signed with a label and made recordings with the creative and technical support of producers and engineers. Physical representations of the music (mainly CDs) were then manufactured, marketed (largely via radio stations and other advertising), and distributed through established channels. The CDs eventually reached retail stores where they were merchandised and purchased by consumers.

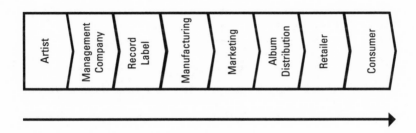

**FIGURE 2-1**
*Traditional music industry value chain.*

The first step of market modeling involves developing a market overview that depicts the value activities of a market. In the digital economy, many markets are finding their linear value chains replaced by a market web consisting of traditional, hybrid, and digital activities. Linear value chain analysis is no longer sufficient to support competitive positioning and partnership decisions, in part because multiple market activities—traditional, hybrid, and digital—are occurring simultaneously.

Let's illustrate this step for the music industry. Figure 2-2 presents a high-level overview of the traditional, hybrid, and digital value activities in the music space. Traditional activities are rooted in the pre-Internet world. Hybrid activities utilize digital ordering, but still rely on physical manufacturing and shipping. With digital value activities, virtually the entire process moves from atoms to bits.

The hybrid value activities of searching, sampling, and ordering music occur online (at a Web venue such as Amazon.com or CDNow), while fulfillment still occurs through physical distribution channels. Product delivery typically flows through a new media distributor, possibly through a retailer's distribution center, and then to a consumer's house via a package delivery service (such as UPS).

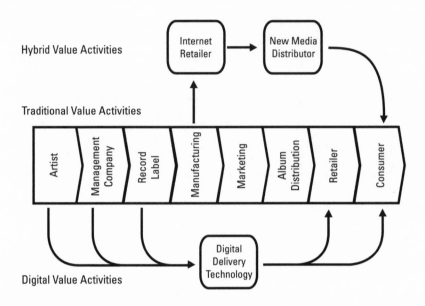

**FIGURE 2-2**
*Traditional, hybrid, and digital value activities in music.*

The real revolution comes as the market moves exclusively to digital value activities disintermediating traditional manufacturing plants, distributors, and retailers. Once music is placed in a digital format and stored on a server, it can be distributed directly to the public via the Internet. The server can be owned and operated by an artist, a management company, a music portal, an established label, another consumer, or other genres of players in the digital music space. The entire industry is transformed as consumers receive music directly from any player on the traditional value chain. Although digital value activities in other markets may not be as pervasive, hybrid and digital value activities are becoming more significant in every industry. All firms need to consider how the flow of their goods and services will change in the new economy.

## Value activity areas

What is a value activity, anyway? And why is it so important to identify? *Value activities* are areas of a market (traditional, hybrid, and digital) where value capture can occur—in other words, where someone will pay more than it costs to provide the good or service. Identifying these activities helps a manager recognize potential regions inside and outside of a company's core competency where it wants to expand or supplement capabilities. The clarification of value activities drives partnership and investment decisions.

In building a market overview, begin from a top-down perspective and identify value activity areas for the market. As an executive continues to model the market, these activity areas are typically refined through bottom-up insights derived from how new and traditional market players are working to capture value. As mentioned earlier, market modeling is not a one-time effort, but involves an iterative, chunk-building process. Systematic development of player and deal databases will trigger new understanding of existing and emerging value activities. Given dynamic market conditions—including entry of new players with novel positioning—digital value activities are certain to change over time.

Figure 2-3 shows how the value activities for the music industry might be portrayed as of mid-2000, with special emphasis on digital value activities or subsectors. Here's a brief description of these digital value activities.[8]

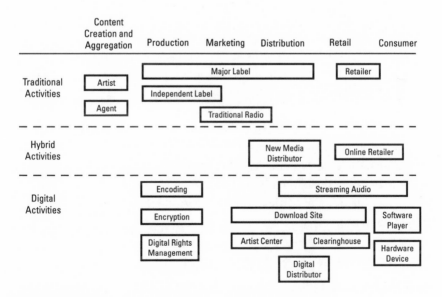

**FIGURE 2-3**
*Value activities in the music market* (© 2000).

◆ Encoding involves placing music in a compressed digital format.

◆ Encryption protects a digital music track, often by placing a "watermark" or alteration in the digital file to indicate genuineness.

◆ Digital Rights Management (DRM) technology places copying, distribution, and listening rights into the music file.

◆ Download sites make music files available for retail customers.

◆ Artist centers promote individual artist's music and collateral products and services (including concerts).

◆ Clearinghouses enforce copying and distribution rights and can also monitor and distribute music royalties.

◆ Digital distributors host libraries of music and distribute digital music to retailers.

◆ Streaming audio broadcasts music over the Internet, using "stations" organized by genre or subscription services where consumers can customize the music they hear.

◆ Software players play downloaded or streamed digital music.

◆ Hardware devices for playing music include personal computers as well as an increasing array of portable players and home entertainment centers.

Once again, keep in mind that the value activities in this market are dynamic. Both incumbent and insurgent companies generate novel products and services. In addition, new enabling technologies (for example, peer-to-peer distribution networks like Napster) can quickly give rise to innovative value activities. To effectively support corporate positioning and development, a market model must accommodate such rapidly changing activities. The music industry clearly makes this case.

Having now developed a market overview that identifies at least an initial pass at value activities for the music space, let's turn to building a player database.

## STEP 2: PLAYER DATABASE

*Build a database of players relevant to the market being analyzed.*

The second step in market modeling is to systematically build a database of players relevant to the market being analyzed. This player database will consist of companies that are directly operating in the market or have established alliances with companies operating in the market. In addition, include players likely to enter the market, given the opportunity or a competitor threat.

A player database for a market can ultimately consist of hundreds or even thousands of companies. But don't be daunted by the potential size of the effort. When establishing the database, the initial set will be much smaller and typically include prominent players already on the radar screen. As the market modeling evolves, systematically add companies to the player database in an iterative process of chunk building. The effort will pay dividends, as a well-designed and up-to-date player database enables an executive to cut through confusion and respond quickly and confidently to partnership opportunity.[9]

Include both descriptive and structural information about companies in a player database. Descriptive information includes items such as a company profile or contact essentials. Structural information involves characterizing the company by key market variables that will directly support competitive analysis and partnership decisions. This section emphasizes structural information.

The market overview and related value activities developed in Step 1 provide an initial framework for classifying companies. For example, Figure 2-4 depicts a small sample list of players for the music industry as of mid-2000. Notice that each company's market value activities are indicated in the database. For example, Sony is shown as owning record labels, developing encoding technology, and providing hardware in this market. In order to support robust partnership analysis, it is important to properly characterize each player's value activities.

In building a database, limit the number of players included for some value activities. For example, all Big Five record companies would undoubtedly be included in a music database. However, select only a subset of artists or independent labels, given the thousands of possible players in each of these areas. The specific strategic context will determine which entities are essential to include in the database. Building a company database is a selective process.

| Company | Artist | Record Label | Traditional Retailer | Encoding | DRM* | Digital Distributor | Streaming Audio | Download Site | Software Player | Hardware Player |
|---|---|---|---|---|---|---|---|---|---|---|
| Britney Spears | ✓ | | | | | | | | | |
| Tom Petty | ✓ | | | | | | | | | |
| BMG | | ✓ | | | | | | | | |
| EMI | | ✓ | | | | | | | | |
| Sony | | ✓ | ✓ | | | | | | | ✓ |
| Warner Music | | ✓ | | | | | | | | |
| Universal Music | | ✓ | | | | | | | | |
| Edel | | ✓ | | | | | | | | |
| Microsoft | | | | ✓ | ✓ | | | | ✓ | |
| AOL/Winamp | | | | | | ✓ | ✓ | ✓ | | |
| Sam Goody | | | ✓ | | | | | | | |
| Best Buy | | | ✓ | | | | | | | |
| AT&T (A2B) | | | | ✓ | | | | | | |
| Intertrust | | | | | ✓ | | | | | |
| Preview | | | | | ✓ | | | | | |
| Liquid Audio | | | | ✓ | ✓ | ✓ | ✓ | | ✓ | |
| Real Networks | | ✓ | | | | | ✓ | ✓ | | |
| Napster | | | | | | ✓ | | ✓ | | |
| Amazon.com | | | | | | | | ✓ | | |
| CDNow | | | | | | | | ✓ | | |
| MP3.com | | | | | | | | ✓ | | |
| Listen.com | | | | | | | | ✓ | | |
| Diamond | | | | | | | | | | ✓ |
| Sanyo | | | | | | | | | | ✓ |

\* Digital Rights Management

**FIGURE 2-4**
*Assigning music players to value activities.*

Furthermore, in moving on to the next step of market modeling—building a deal database—additional companies will be "pulled" into the player database by virtue of their digital deals. For example, a company such as Intel may not initially appear in a music player database, but certainly will be included once Intel's range of investments in this space is uncovered. Building a company database is an iterative process.

Finally, anticipate companies likely to enter a market. This is easy to determine when a company preannounces intentions. For example, in 2000 Microsoft stated it would enter the gaming console market with a platform dubbed the XBox—albeit not for at least another year. In other cases, although it may be less certain that a company intends to move into a market, it should still be included in a player database so that its moves can be watched.

In summary, a company enters a player database as a direct market player, an indirect participant by virtue of a digital deal, or as a possible new entrant. Value activities are regularly added to or removed from market players. Over time, a player database becomes an increasingly valuable asset for both competitive analysis and partnership planning.

## Database dimensions and granularity

What core structural dimensions should be included in a player database? Meaningful market modeling requires a database that can be searched or filtered to answer specific strategic questions. A manager must be able to identify a set of companies that is neither too broad nor too restrictive for each digital deal being considered. Using too broad a universe is like painting a portrait with a four-inch brush—necessary details can't be discerned. Using too restrictive a universe is like painting the portrait with a palette lacking a primary color—vital elements are missing. A player database must be set to a level of granularity that supports meaningful market analysis and deal selection.

Here are three dimensions for classifying companies that will help to achieve the appropriate level of precision in a player database.

### BY VALUE ACTIVITIES

Earlier, this chapter explored how to develop a market overview and identify specific traditional, hybrid, and digital value activities. As illustrated in Figure 2-4, managers should then assign the appropriate set of value activities to each company. A company can take part in multiple value activities (partially or fully vertically integrated) or specialize in one value activity. In the illustration, Sony and Microsoft participate in several value activities in the music market, whereas Intertrust focuses on digital rights management technology. Capturing precise value activities that each player embodies is crucial for analyzing partnership possibilities.

## BY GEOGRAPHIC FOCUS

As Internet penetration accelerates throughout the world, geography has become an important dimension by which to classify companies in a player database. The digital economy has rapidly expanded global reach for many organizations. Consequently, it is often important to identify and categorize players in each regional market of interest.

For example, when Cisco wanted to analyze the drivers of broadband adoption worldwide, the company began by targeting key countries to study. Next, it analyzed players involved in value activities for markets important in stimulating broadband technology in each of these countries. The analysis was conducted market-by-market, country-by-country, and suggested partnerships for Cisco's consideration.

Suppose a manager is investigating the market for sports content on the Web. Players such as ESPN and SportsLine would, of course, be included. For specific deal analysis, however, players with a given geographic focus may need to be isolated. The manager may want to analyze potential partners involved in specific geographic markets, such as "sports content (Europe)" or "sports content (Germany)." To do so, relevant geographic information about companies must be captured in a database.

## BY CUSTOMER SEGMENT

Customer segmentation is a third important dimension in searching or filtering a player database. Players can be classified by the particular customers that they target—including race, gender, age, price sensitivity, product preferences, vertical markets, size of company, and so on. Analyzing players by the segments they are pursuing often leads to partnership insights.[10]

Microsoft, for example, in 1999 launched its bCentral Web service for the small business sector. As a result, the company initiated a series of investments and alliances with a range of application and service companies targeting this customer segment. In building bCentral, Microsoft was acutely interested in identifying and then carefully selecting partners to provide a portfolio of offerings to small business.

## MULTIPLE DIMENSIONS

At times, an executive will be interested in identifying players that meet more than one database dimension. A player database should enable each market to be analyzed by one or more dimensions (value activity, geography, customer segment, and so forth) at the desired level of granularity. For example, assume an enterprise security services firm is seeking partnerships with technology companies. It may want to identify companies that have developed intrusion detection technology (search by value activity). It may also want to find companies targeting the financial services vertical (search by customer segmentation). Finally, it may want to identify partners by the type of financial institution and region they serve, such as consumer banks in the Southeast (search by specific customer segment and by region). Anticipated queries should guide the database design.

# SUMMARIZING STEPS 1 AND 2

Let's summarize what's been said so far about market modeling. Steps 1 and 2 involve collecting outside information that will later be used in deal analysis and execution. In Step 1, develop a market overview that depicts traditional, hybrid, and digital value activities. In Step 2, systematically develop a player database by identifying companies directly competing, doing deals, or likely to enter the market. Gather descriptive and structural information about each player within the context of specific strategic goals. In particular, characterize each company by its value activities, geographic focus, or customer segmentation at an appropriate level of granularity.

A market overview and player database is a dynamic system. In the new economy, the value activities of a market are subject to rapid change. Companies enter and leave markets, and modify the value activities, geographies, and customer segments they are targeting. Movement in a market modeling system is unending, but so is the partnership payoff from being able to effectively track it.

The next chapter shifts from markets and players to deals and deal rationales. It discusses how to classify deals and uncover why firms are executing specific partnerships. By analyzing the deal rationales of other companies (including competitors), an executive will be in a better position to fine-tune strategy and select partnerships. A deal database, when combined with a market overview and player database, will provide the foundation for developing a digital deal strategy.

# INTRODUCING EDEL

Having dissected the new economy's transformation of the music industry, let's now take a closer look at one player in this space—Edel Music. We will use Edel here and in the next two chapters as a case study to illustrate key concepts of crafting a deal strategy.

Edel is one of the largest independent music companies in Europe. Founded in 1986, Edel has evolved from a film score mail-order catalog in Germany to a full-scale music company involved in value activities from artist management to music distribution.

Edel has endeavored to introduce young, no-name artists and generate superior financial returns from low initial costs. The company has used independence as a competitive advantage, capitalizing on flexibility in its creative offerings and business partnerships. In 2000, Edel set the aggressive goal of increasing its global share of the music market from 1 to 4 percent over the next few years.

## Edel's history

As a mail-order catalog, Edel was essentially a marketing company run out of founder Michael Haentjes' home in Hamburg. Over time, the company licensed content and moved into manufacturing. By the mid-1990s, Edel had developed its own Artists & Repertoire (A&R) arm to attract talent. As sales increased, it looked to gain a foothold outside of the German market through European subsidiaries.

Edel has used partnerships to great effect in growing its business. As a smaller label, Edel established strategic alliances with larger record companies and distributors to gain access to markets, while using its independence to attract talent and remain flexible. Edel has deployed a range of deal structures, including a joint venture with Hollywood Records (a Disney company); a coinvestment in Viva Media with Universal, Warner Music, and EMI; a minority investment in Eagle Rock Entertainment (a U.K.-based record, video, and television producer); and multiple acquisitions.

Largely through its partnership and deal strategy, Edel Music has become one of the largest independent labels in Europe (see Table 2-2). The company is vertically integrated with operations and partnerships in publishing, A&R, production, marketing, and distribution.

**Table 2-2  Edel's Evolution**

| Year | Event |
|------|-------|
| 1986 | Founded as mail-order catalog called "Cinema Soundtrack Club" |
| 1989 | Established licensing agreements with U.S. and European companies |
| 1990 | Created own sales force |
| 1991 | Opened CD manufacturing plant to provide flexible, 48-hour turnaround time for CDs |
| 1992 | Incorporated into holding company and launched subsidiaries in Austria and Switzerland |
| 1994 | Launched own A&R activities |
| 1995 | Launched international affiliates and subsidiaries |
| 1998 | IPO on Neuer Market; entered U.S. market with artist sensation Jennifer Paige |
| 2000 | Exploring digital music strategy |

Through the 1990s, Edel's activities spread across the traditional music industry value chain. However, by 2000 Edel had developed only a nascent Internet strategy. Our interest lies in exploring how and where the company might partner in a digital music value web. We will look closer at Edel's historical deals and deal rationales in Chapter 3 and then suggest a digital deal strategy in Chapter 4.

# CHAPTER 3

# Deal Database
# and Deal Rationale

Chapter 2 focused on the first two steps of market modeling: developing a market overview that depicts value activity areas and building a player database. Market modeling involves a novel strategic initiative, leading to an information resource that is quite different from traditional, internally focused systems. This new system is tuned to external information about companies, relationships, and markets.

This chapter describes Steps 3 and 4 of a market modeling system, focusing on building a database to capture essential deal information. Which patterns of deals are likely to be successful? Which ones augur failure? To answer these questions, firms must order alliances, investments, and other deals into key descriptive and structural elements. Special emphasis is also placed on understanding why deals are occurring—the business rationales behind the deals (see Figure 1-2 for the complete eight-step market modeling framework).

The research and analysis effort described here (and in Chapter 2) builds a knowledge base to use and reuse in executing a deal strategy. Remember that, as with all knowledge resources, deal-related content is built sequentially. All chunks are not accumulated simultaneously. Deal databases and related deal rationales become increasingly useful (and valuable) over time. The information generated by developing a market overview, building a player universe, creating a deal database, and uncovering deal rationales will provide the core components for actions discussed throughout the book. These market, company, and deal components will be combined and recombined to simulate and select "optimal deal DNA" for an enterprise.

## STEP 3: BUILDING A DEAL DATABASE

*Design and build a deal database for the market.*

The third step in market modeling involves building a deal database by identifying relevant alliances, investments, and other relationships in a given market. The deal database typically begins as a direct extension of the player database. The easiest way to start is by analyzing the deals of companies that are the most important players in the market space—the equivalent to the Big Five of music for an industry. If the market is fragmented, start by identifying a short list of companies considered to be the most significant players. Research these companies, studying their significant deals and creating a database containing key information about each deal.

This section does not emphasize the technical mechanics of developing a deal database or how to source information on specific deals (corporate Web sites, periodicals, press releases, SEC filings, and analyst reports can provide a good start). But it is important to ask what types of information should be gathered and how the database should be designed to develop an information resource of increasing strategic value that can be used and reused in corporate development decisions.

Figure 3-1 identifies some of the key elements for a sample digital deal database pertaining to the music industry. Notice that the database shown in Figure 3-1 starts with significant players in the music space, such as AOL, Warner Music, and EMI. It then describes deals for each of these players, including important deals that failed to be consummated. This sample database illustrates a variety of deal structures ranging from mergers and acquisitions to spin-off activities. At a minimum, the fields for the database should include:

◆ Deal description—a high-level characterization of the deal.

◆ Date announced—when the deal was first announced; there are other milestone dates to potentially include in a database, such as the completion date for an acquisition or the date when an alliance was expanded.

◆ Type—the structure of the deal: merger and/or acquisition, joint venture, minority equity investment, alliance (commerce, marketing, technology, or other), spin-off, and so on. Each of these structures is examined in Chapter 5 and in even greater detail in Part 2 of this book.

◆ Primary company—the company or companies that initiated the deal; for example, the acquirer, investor, or lead partner of an alliance.

◆ Targets and/or Partners—the acquired company, the investee, the joint venture company, or secondary partner companies in an alliance.

◆ Deal facts—information summarizing other important details of the deal.

Other fields can be added to a deal database, including one to capture information relating to the current status of a deal. Business relationships are more like mobiles than statues—they are sure to change over time. Seeing how a partnership evolves allows an executive to better understand the context of the relationship. For example, consider the complex relationship between Microsoft and AOL involving AOL's use of Microsoft's Internet Explorer browser. The firms signed a browser agreement back in March 1996, but the nature of this partnership has changed significantly as both companies entered new business lines and AOL acquired Netscape. Our deal database currently contains eight separate "date-stamped" events that update the status of this Microsoft-AOL deal, thereby providing texture for understanding the subtlety of this relationship.

Furthermore, like the player database (see Chapter 2), be sure to capture structural information relating to the value activities, geographic focus, or customer segments that the deal involves. Later in this chap-

| Deal Description | Date Announced | Type | Primary Company | Targets and/or Partners | Deal Facts |
|---|---|---|---|---|---|
| AOL to acquire Time Warner | 01/10/2000 | Merger / acquisition | AOL | Time Warner | AOL will acquire Time Warner and plans to form AOL Time Warner in a massive combination of new and old media. Time Warner shareholders would receive 1.5 shares of AOL Time Warner for each Time Warner share. |
| Warner Music to combine with EMI; deal scrapped after EU regulatory scrutiny (10/00) | 01/24/2000 | Joint venture | Time Warner | EMI | Time Warner and EMI will merge their music interests. The combination will be achieved through joint venture in which both companies contribute their recorded music and music publishing assets. Time Warner would control the new venture through a majority of its board and plans to pay EMI's shareholders more than $1 billion as a control premium. |
| Intel invests in Supertracks | 04/03/2000 | Minority investment | Intel | Supertracks | Intel invests in Supertracks as part of an $18 million funding round. Supertracks is an enabler of digital distribution of music (DDM) over the Internet. The company provides Internet distribution services, systems and technology integration, commerce and clearinghouse solutions, and back-end operations to retailers and record labels. |

| Deal Description | Date Announced | Type | Primary Company | Targets / Partners | Deal Facts |
|---|---|---|---|---|---|
| Universal launches Farm Club | 11/09/1999 | Commerce alliance | Seagrams/ Universal Music | AOL, MTV, USA Networks | Farm Club is a digital music label that enables artists to upload music and compete for a major record contract. AOL is providing $100 million in promotional support for Farm Club and will receive offline cross-promotion and exclusive content as well as a 3 percent equity stake in Farm Club. MTV Networks and MTVi has a cross-promotional alliance with Farm Club. USA Networks will broadcast a weekly one-hour program (FarmClub.com). |
| S3 spins off graphics-chip business to concentrate on Internet music and other devices | 04/05/2000 | Spin-off | S3 | Via | S3 repositions itself as a maker of Internet music players and information appliances. S3 will spin off its graphics-chip business to a joint venture controlled by Via Technologies for $323 million in cash and stock. S3 already plays in the information appliance market through its Diamond Multimedia division, which manufactures the Rio for storing music downloaded from the Web. |

**FIGURE 3-1**
*Deal database entries for the music market.*

ter, we'll see how this structural information can be used to understand deal patterns.

One additional information field will be of particular importance in a deal database—the deal rationale. This field involves uncovering and capturing information about why each party has entered into a deal. What do they hope to accomplish or gain? What motivated each company to do the deal? Let's discuss some ways to uncover deal rationales.

## STEP 4: UNCOVERING DEAL RATIONALES

*Uncover deal rationales using direct deal analysis or by analyzing constellations of deals.*

The fourth step of the market modeling process is to determine the reasons why companies in a market are partnering or investing. This involves uncovering deal rationales to understand not just what's happening, but what's really happening. Why is a partnership or investment taking place? What specific business goals is each party striving to accomplish? Essentially, every entry in the deal database is augmented to include a strategic assessment of the deal.[1]

The ultimate objective is to organize a market's deal activity into a conceptual framework that will help in the selection of digital deals. In other words, a firm must uncover the reasons behind the deal strategy of competitors and potential partners in order to better craft its own deals. Systematically gathering this information is likely to trigger creativity and lead to new partnership insights. Deal making requires a large dose of managerial intuition and judgment, but systematic deal analysis must play an increasing role in planning entry into new markets or revitalizing positioning in old ones. Institutional knowledge management, moving far beyond what's inside an individual's head, is vital. Building a database of deal rationales can support the need to be both fast and smart in selecting partners and executing deals.[2]

There are a number of ways to organize deal rationale information. To start, firms can classify deal rationales by four basic business functions: marketing, operations, finance, or organizational design. Was the deal formed to comarket services, to streamline operational processes, to earn financial return through investment, retain employees, and so on?

Of course, the same deal often impacts more than one functional area. Nevertheless, breaking deal rationales down by the business function(s) driving the partnership is a good way to classify deals and uncover common patterns.

Figure 3-2 shows three deals relating to different markets with rationale classified by four business functions. (Each of these deals is analyzed in detail later in this chapter.) The figure captures distinct rationale for each company in the partnership. Notice that deal rationale data can be viewed as a direct extension of the deal database, providing additional information for each deal.

There are two primary benefits of analyzing and classifying deal rationales by these four functional areas. First, accessing this information by functional area will support strategic thinking in planning a deal portfolio in each of these areas—marketing, operations, finance, and organizational design.

Second, whether a company is a large incumbent, midsize challenger, or small start-up company, identifying how a deal will support either marketing, operations, finance, or organizational design underscores the need to integrate deals into core business activities. To date, many deal integration efforts have been far from effective as organizations have commonly formed partnerships without adequately thinking through how the deal will be implemented.

How are digital deal rationales uncovered? Two methods involve direct deal analysis and deal constellation analysis. Direct deal analysis involves an in-depth review of facts and statements surrounding a specific deal as well as inferences based on market experience. As illustrated above, one goal of direct deal analysis may be to classify the deal according to one or more functional areas (marketing, operations, finance, or organizational design) by explaining what the deal provides from each party's point of view.

Deal constellation analysis involves discerning higher-level patterns in the deal-making activity of an organization or market. For example, by examining the broader array of partnerships and investments that America Online (AOL) is establishing in the music industry, it becomes easier to determine what each new deal is intended to accomplish and where AOL is moving in this market. Examining patterns will help

| Deal Description | Market | Date Announced | Company | Functional Areas Impacted | | | |
| --- | --- | --- | --- | --- | --- | --- | --- |
| | | | | Marketing | Operations | Finance | Organizational Design |
| Amazon and Sotheby's launch auction site; site closed in October 2000 after Sotheby's antitrust violations | Auctioning | 11/01/1999 | Amazon | Brand building through association by selling items authenticated by Sotheby's | Quality inventory to sell from dealers committed to auction format | | Access to a new talent base, including art expertise |
| | | | Sotheby's | New distribution channel, with access to Amazon's large customer base | Access to easy-to-use, customer-centric technology | Minority equity investment of $35+ million from Amazon | |
| Bank One/First USA signs five-year exclusive deal with AOL to market Visa and MasterCard credit cards | Financial Services | 02/01/1999 | America Online | Establish a new high-water mark for its business commerce partnership portfolio | | Up-front cash, new customer bounty, percentage of outstanding credit balance; high margin recurring revenue stream | |

Functional Areas Impacted

| Deal Description | Market | Date Announced | Company | Marketing | Operations | Finance | Organizational Design |
|---|---|---|---|---|---|---|---|
| | | | Bank One | Exclusive access to AOL's brands (AOL, AOL.com, Digital Cities, and CompuServe) for online credit card marketing | | Was the price tag for Bank One/First USA for this deal too high? | |
| Intel invests in Liquid Audio | Music | 05/01/1996 | Intel | Stimulate growth in digital music market to sell higher end microprocessors | | Achieve financial returns from investment portfolio | |
| | | | Liquid Audio | | | Minority investment funding; halo effect from Intel investment | |

**FIGURE 3-2**
*Extending the deal database to include rationale by function.*

uncover the motivation behind a deal by establishing its context within a broader deal strategy. Of course, deal constellation analysis requires firms to develop or have access to a relevant deal database. It requires extra effort, but deal constellation analysis is an extremely powerful methodology.

## Direct deal analysis

Let's use the deals in Figure 3-2 to illustrate direct deal analysis and deal constellation analysis.

### OLD WINE IN NEW SKINS

One common deal theme involves partnerships between old companies and new ones, between traditional brick-and-mortar firms and dotcoms. Old economy assets can find new expression from virtual partners, and new economy assets can benefit from classic dimensions of time-honored venues. Consider this tale of two "book companies," one old and one new. (This section performs a direct deal analysis of the Sotheby's-Amazon partnership without portraying a more complete constellation of deals established by either player. Later, Chapter 11 analyzes Amazon's partnership strategy more comprehensively.)

In 1744 Sotheby's started selling books and over its 250+-year history has developed enviable expertise in valuing and auctioning art and other valuable objects. In 1995 Amazon.com started selling books and over its 5+-year history has developed well-known expertise in ecommerce. In November 1999, the two companies partnered to launch sothebys.amazon.com, an auction site that hoped to marry Sotheby's expertise in art and collectibles with Amazon's experience in Internet marketing. To cement the deal, Amazon purchased 1 million shares of Sotheby's for around $35 per share and spent another $10 million on three-year warrants for an additional million shares.

Each side brought different strengths to the table. Internet commerce involves establishing trust at a distance. Sotheby's sterling reputation—and the cadre of experts associated with the renowned auctioneer—intrigued Amazon. It expected that online auction participants, given a Sotheby's stamp of approval, would buy with confidence.

What appealed to Sotheby's about Amazon was its obsession with building ease-of-use technology for customer-centric ebusiness. Amazon used state-of-the-art technology, combined with a solid understanding of customer needs, to quickly establish itself as a leading ecommerce company. Of course, Sotheby's was also attracted to Amazon's large customer base and to Amazon's financial commitment.

The deal combined old-economy expertise with new-economy technology for customer service and support. Encompassing both digital and traditional marketing and sales activities, sothebys.amazon.com was launched as a "hybrid value activity" business with a broad product range. The venture intended to demonstrate that business-to-consumer ecommerce need not be constrained by a price ceiling. The companies hoped that auction enthusiasts would be clicking on items presented in rich digital media to bid sums greater than $100,000.

In addition to the Amazon partnership, Sotheby's developed its own auction site, Sothebys.com, to focus on high-end art. Likewise, Amazon continued to conduct auctions on Amazon.com, apart from Sotheby's. Nevertheless, the partnership attempted a blend of business-past and business-future, illustrating an "old marrying new" pattern for digital deals.

A direct analysis (see Figure 3-2) of this deal suggests several deal rationales for Amazon: (1) marketing—building its brand through association by selling items authenticated by Sotheby's; (2) operations—acquiring quality inventory to sell from dealers committed to the auction format; and (3) organizational design—accessing a new talent base, including unrivaled art experts. Deal rationale for Sotheby's included: (1) marketing—securing access to Amazon's large customer base; (2) operations—accessing easy-to-use, customer-centric technology; and (3) finance—receiving a minority equity investment of $35+ million from Amazon. Note that for both companies, the sothebys.amazon.com venture involved deal rationales associated with multiple functional areas.

Unfortunately, as originally conceived, this deal failed. Sotheby's reputation was sullied in early 2000 as the U.S. Justice Department investigated possible price fixing in the fine-art industry, and two company executives resigned. Stories about Sotheby's former CEO pleading guilty to felony charges certainly didn't add any cobranding luster to Amazon. In addition, the multiple auction sites confused customers, and sothebys.amazon.com failed to attract enough users. Finally, Wall Street continued to pressure Amazon to focus its business efforts and deliver profits sooner rather than later. In October 2000, Amazon and Sotheby's announced they were shutting down sothebys.amazon.com. Under a new agreement buyers and sellers would be sent to Sothebys.com, and Amazon would receive cash payments for referrals as well as a percentage of transaction sales.

Although the restructuring was disappointing for the partners, firms can often learn as much from failed deals as successful ones. In this case, direct deal analysis of the original deal and its postmortem help uncover valid deal rationales in both the auctioning and collectibles markets.

## LEVERAGING EYEBALLS

A second example of direct deal analysis, also summarized in Figure 3-2, involves America Online. While many companies have successfully aggregated subscribers or members and then generated advertising and commerce revenue, in 2000 AOL was head and shoulders above the rest in executing this deal strategy.

Chapter 9 analyzes AOL's "adcom" activities and deal rationales in detail. For now, look at one example. In February 1999, AOL announced an exclusive five-year deal with Bank One's credit card subsidiary, First USA, worth up to $500 million. First USA became the sole marketer of Visa and MasterCard credit cards on AOL's properties—AOL, AOL.com, Digital Cities, and CompuServe. AOL would receive an initial up-front payment and additional performance payments based on customer acquisition benchmarks.

Although AOL did not disclose the size of the up-front cash component, estimates were in the range of $60 to $90 million. AOL would also receive a bounty per customer acquired, including a flat fee as well as a percentage of the monthly credit balance. AOL could capture more than $25 per customer and could receive 50 basis points of a customer's outstanding credit balance.[3] This deal was a coup for AOL, allowing it to monetize its vast subscriber base with a high-margin, annuity revenue stream.

From the First USA–Bank One perspective, the AOL deal promised exclusive access for marketing credit cards using the brands of the most significant consumer presence on the Internet. (First USA had been a partner of AOL's since 1996, but its contract was to expire in May 1999. This new agreement suggested that AOL was overdelivering against the previous contract.) First USA saw AOL as a new marketing, distribution, and transaction vehicle that could continue to drive forward First USA's share of the credit card market. First USA's credit card operation was second in size only to Citigroup's and had been growing at more than 20 percent a year, despite a flooded credit card market. As events moved forward, however, all would not go smoothly for First USA. In December 1999, John McCoy, former CEO of Bank One, took early retirement, facing an earnings shortfall at Bank One and growing problems at First USA's credit card division.[4] Sometimes digital deals work more favorably for one side than the other—not all deal rationales are fully realized.

Not many companies command an audience as large as AOL's. Nevertheless, many firms can strike digital deals involving business commerce partnerships and sponsorships centered on leveraging their online members or subscribers. Chapter 9 presents AOL—the "king" of commerce partners—as a shining example of this type of deal. It examines typical issues involved in a business development deal and when the price can become too high. For now, looking at the AOL–First USA partnership serves as a rich illustration of advertising and commerce direct deal analysis.

Let's move on to explore how deal rationales can be uncovered using constellation analysis.

## Deal constellation analysis

Analyzing a digital deal in isolation does not always provide the context needed to understand why the deal is being done. It is often useful to combine multiple deals into a deal constellation[5]—a visual pattern of deals intended to help spot significant trends, market movements, or new value creation opportunities. These visual representations (which we call *Infographics*[6]) highlight one or more dimensions of a deal pattern in a market including:

◆ Select deals of one or more key companies

◆ Deal structures (license, alliance, joint venture, minority investment, acquisition, and so on)

◆ Value activity areas

◆ Geographic areas

◆ Deals occurring within a given time frame

For example, Figure 3-3 shows a deal constellation for Microsoft (key company) relating to broadband infrastructure (value activity) in Europe (geographic area). In this case Microsoft was investing in and partnering with these companies to stimulate bandwidth delivered via all possible means. Ultimately Microsoft sought to build demand for its set-top boxes and other technologies. A constellation can be portrayed as a simple cluster centered on a key company or can display a network of deals with no central company.

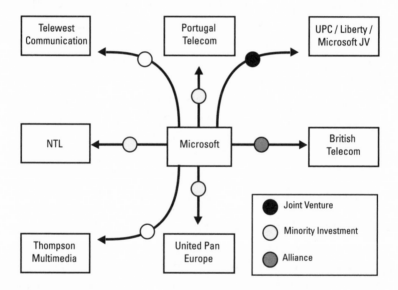

**FIGURE 3-3**
*Microsoft's broadband infrastructure deals in Europe.*

THE ECOSYSTEM

Analyzing deals in constellations makes it easier to clearly discern market patterns and possibly predict the next moves of players in the market.[7] As importantly, it promotes insight into how clusters or ecosystems of companies work together to grow markets. For a long time, private venture capitalists, as well as corporate venture groups, have established market ecosystems in attempts to foster intercompany synergies. For example, no organization has been more actively involved in corporate venture funding than Intel, and at times, Intel has deliberately worked toward establishing a market ecosystem.

Let's dig deeper into one such ecosystem. In the late 1990s, Intel made numerous investments in companies that provided content, products, services, and applications supporting the delivery of digital music and video. Intel established a Content Group to provide funding and marketing support to companies such as Liquid Audio (technology for digital music encoding and distribution—also see Figure 3-2), Broadcast.com (Internet broadcasting), Launch Media (personalized digital music), Audible (digital audio delivery of published content), and Spinner.com (Internet music broadcaster). Figure 3-4 depicts a constellation of these deals organized by primary value activity. The constellation shows that Intel's investments were designed to stimulate movement across a number of digital music value activities.

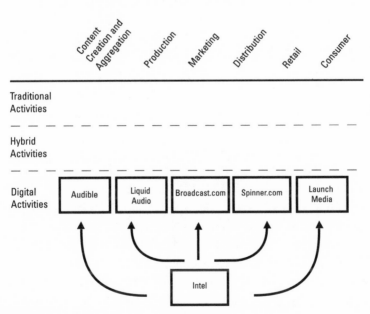

**FIGURE 3-4**
*Intel's minority investments in an audio ecosystem.*

Two of these companies (Broadcast.com and Spinner.com) were later acquired by Yahoo! and AOL—to Intel's financial benefit. Although Intel stressed that its venture investments are grounded in strategic reasons, financial return clearly plays an important role as well. Chapter 8 explores Intel's rationales for building its minority equity investment portfolio—which by the end of 2000 consisted of more than 500 companies (including many other investments in the digital audio-music ecosystem). Deal constellation analysis is crucial for understanding Intel's and other firms' market ecosystems.

EVENT ANALYSIS

Sometimes a company announces a constellation of deals all at once. This event is often a particularly useful time to supplement or refine a deal database and deal rationales. Often the announcement can impact the company's valuation or trigger a direct stock market response, especially if the constellation presents a compelling deal rationale.[8] While a market reaction is not always an accurate gauge of ultimate deal significance, movement in a company's stock price does at least indicate perceived importance of a deal. Indeed, for some organizations a portfolio of digital deals is arguably the most important off–balance sheet asset (although subsequent market events can quickly change the perceived significance of any deal). Consider an announcement by Liquid Audio, one of the Intel portfolio companies mentioned on p. 57.

Liquid Audio develops technology that allows music to be encoded and delivered electronically over the Internet. The company's format provides labels and artists with technology for secure online preview and purchase of CD-quality digital music. Liquid Audio's digital format was distinct from the popular MP3 format, but the company also supported MP3 as well as other formats. On September 3, 1999, Liquid Audio's stock was trading at $27 per share. On that day, the company announced several music content, distribution, and retail deals that suggested broadened industry adoption of its technology.

Figure 3-5 depicts how this partnership constellation positioned Liquid Audio with players in digital, hybrid, and traditional value activities of the music industry. It struck content deals with major record companies and labels (such as Warner Music), online distribution arrangements with portals (such as Yahoo!), and click-and-mortar deals with traditional retailers (such as Musicland). The range and reach of Liquid Audio's new partners signaled new business momentum. The company stated in a press release: "These new music sales and promotions demonstrate that Liquid Audio is building the label and retail relationships it needs to succeed as an Internet music distributor."[9]

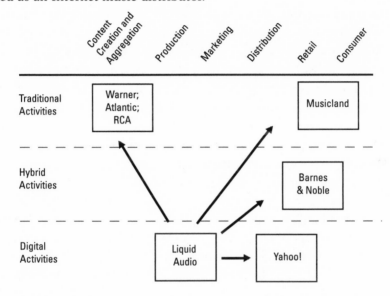

**FIGURE 3-5**
*Liquid Audio forms content, distribution, and retail digital deals.*

Over the next two trading days, Liquid Audio's stock rose nearly 25 percent. The market agreed that the company had pulled together a constellation that would create value. It interpreted the deals to mean that Liquid Audio was marshaling key partners, throughout a music value web, to make its digital format a significant distribution standard.

Liquid Audio's success was far from assured. During 2000, the company experienced significant ups and downs as competitors fought back with new business models for digital music. There was great uncertainty as to how this new form of music would be monetized. But the company's digital deal portfolio remained a major intangible asset as Liquid Audio moved to establish additional partnerships with BMG, Microsoft, Real-

Networks, and Road Runner. Its rapid deal making illustrates the need for deal constellation analysis to understand the significance of partnership portfolios in the music industry.

## BLOCKING DEALS BY COMPETITORS

Sometimes deal rationale is more about what a partnership will do to block a competitor than what the deal will do for the company. Consider the following account.

MP3.com (introduced in Chapter 2) began by distributing music from lesser-known artists who uploaded free songs to the site in exchange for exposure, digital distribution, and other promotional support. As the company evolved, it started to provide music from well-known artists over the Internet (offering consumers instant digital access to their CD collection) and was promptly sued by the music establishment. By the end of 2000, MP3.com had worked through several costly settlements and licensing agreements with major record companies and others.

MP3.com's stock price has mirrored the firm's wild ride. In July 1999, it went public, enjoying a successful offering that raised $344 million. On its first day of trading, MP3.com's stock jumped as high as $105 before settling down to close its first day near $63 per share, thereby providing MP3.com with a $3.9 billion market capitalization. November 8, 1999, found MP3.com's stock trading at $61 per share. But the next day it skidded to $54 and two weeks later had plummeted to $38. What happened? MP3.com, a pre-Napster lightning rod for the digital music revolution, had been attacked by Universal Music Group (UMG), one of the industry's Big Five. The attack from Universal centered on what was then MP3.com's core strategic thrust—the discovery and promotion of new talent.

A competing deal constellation had hammered MP3.com's stock. On November 9, UMG launched a new label, Jimmy and Doug's Farm Club, a subsidiary aimed at musicians not signed to a recording contract. The new label mimicked MP3.com by enabling unknown musicians to put their material on the Internet as a first line of marketing and promotion. Artists would also have the opportunity to compete for a major record contract. UMG had strategically aligned with an impressive array of forces to discover, develop, and market musical careers, including America Online, USA Networks, MTV Networks, and Sprite. Taking its name from a major league baseball metaphor, Farm Club and its allies would make a direct strike at the core of MP3.com.

Here's the armada of partners with which Farm Club would sail (see Figure 3-6):

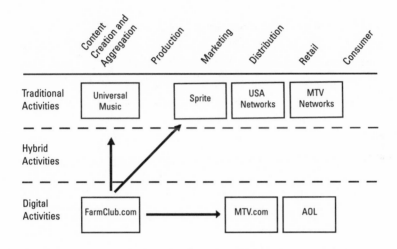

**FIGURE 3-6**
*Deal constellation for Farm Club.*

◆ Universal Music Group—UMG would help market and distribute Farm Club releases. If artists were selected for a record contract, their recordings would be marketed through both Internet and traditional record label resources.

◆ America Online—AOL would provide Farm Club with exposure on AOL and AOL.com. AOL agreed to supply $100 million in promotional support for Farm Club. In return, AOL would receive offline cross-promotion and exclusive content from UMG as well as a 3 percent stake in Farm Club.

◆ USA Networks—USA, a popular basic cable network, would broadcast a weekly one-hour program (FarmClub.com). At that time USA

Networks was partly owned by Seagram, UMG's parent.

◆ MTV Networks—MTV Networks and MTVI (a portfolio of music Web sites) established a cross-promotional alliance with Farm Club to have the artist communities sections linked to Farm Club.

◆ Sprite—Sprite (soft drink) would be the flagship sponsor of Farm Club.

As the deal constellation in Figure 3-6 shows, this partnership pulled together a wide range of players. Jimmy and Doug's partners included a soft drink (Sprite), a cable TV channel (USA Networks), an online service (AOL), as well as another major music player (MTV and its Internet affiliates). Digital deals join content, distribution, and technology companies—often right out of the starting gate.

While the formation of the Farm Club deal constellation had a chilling effect on MP3.com's value, the announcement did not impact Seagram's (UMG's parent at the time) stock price at all. In fact, questions lingered in 2000 about the long-term success of Farm Club and the company began to reposition itself in 2001. At the same time, MP3.com's CEO, Michael Robertson, showed continued resolve and insight in his efforts to pioneer digital music distribution. The case proves, however, that to fully understand a company's strategic position, the deal constellations of its competitors as well as the firm's own array of digital deals must be analyzed.

The ability to generate and analyze deal constellations is a powerful strategic tool. Digital deal ecosystems provide perspective on overall company or market movements. Identifying gaps and seizing resultant opportunities to build strong partnership armadas can create real value and drive up a firm's stock price. Understanding competitors' deal constellations clarifies their strategic moves and provides insight on how to respond.

There are many other ways to use deal constellations. Table 3-1 lists several powerful analyses. For example, a manager may wish to conduct a time series analysis, showing how a firm's partnerships have evolved over time from a beachhead position into a strong market presence. Likewise, depending on a given strategic situation, a company may find value in a gap analysis (suggesting new areas for business development or competitor weaknesses) or a conflict analysis (depicting potential clashes that could result from a new partnership).

If based on a well-designed deal database, these classes of company and market constellations become organizing mechanisms to rapidly and smartly discern deal rationales and analyze a company's positioning and partnerships.

**Table 3-1  Selected Deal Constellation Analyses**

| Analysis | Description |
| --- | --- |
| Ecosystem | Depicts synergistic collection of company partnerships or investments |
| Event | Depicts cluster of partners arising from a significant company announcement or beachhead |
| Blocking move | Illustrates group of competitor's partnerships designed to blunt another company |
| Side-by-side | Provides head-to-head comparison of partnerships for two companies in a market |
| Focal point | Shows how one company is emerging as a pivot of market attention |
| Cross-country | Compares how market players are evolving in distinct countries or regions |
| Time series | Shows a company's partnerships within a discrete time period |
| Gap | Identifies a hole in a company's partnership portfolio |
| Conflict | Depicts potential clashes that could emerge from a partnership |

# Simulating what could happen

Identifying deal rationales involves more than cataloging what has happened. It also involves modeling what could happen—keeping one's ear to the ground and anticipating movements that have not yet been formalized, including new entrepreneurial initiatives. In addition to direct deal analysis and deal constellation analysis involving known deals, simulating company and market movements relating to deals not yet announced is often important. Consider the following story.

"Hello, my name is Steve Perry, and I own the domain name steveperry.com. Can you help me with a research study?" Steve Perry is a well-known classic rock musician who enjoyed fame as the lead singer for the group Journey. However, we were not talking to this Steve Perry, but an MBA student with the same name. Just prior to calling us, the student was told by the musician's attorney that in owning steveperry.com, he was infringing on his client's trademark. The student replied that since Steve Perry was also his name and since there was no commercial activity at steveperry.com, how could he be guilty of trademark violation?

About a week later, the student got a call from Steve Perry asking him to lunch. Steve Perry had left Journey and was no longer under contract with Sony Music. He was a free agent and was interested in exploring options for using the Internet in making, marketing, and distributing music. After some discussion, our student said he would give Steve Perry the domain name steveperry.com if he and a team of other students could conduct a market research study and make recommendations to the musician about how best to use the domain. This was the research study he wanted us to sponsor.

Imagine the various possibilities. Should Perry establish a site to directly promote and sell his own new music? Or should he build a classic rock portal developing a consortium with other musicians of the same genre? Or should he think on an even grander scale and assemble a cross-genre armada of well-known "digital musicians"?

A major component of deal rationale analysis involves studying deals that have been formed by existing companies. But sophisticated strategists will move beyond what's happening to simulate what could happen. No one can foresee all possible combinations of digital deals in a market, but that should not stop an executive from simulating likely scenarios—including new movements and deals from both existing players and start-ups. Consider a market's value activities and explore how clusters of firms could assemble a new value web. Study a competitor's deal history for clues about its likely next steps. Explore how a creative start-up with connections might attack the market. Great companies will be distinguished from also-rans by superior external market knowledge and systems that can be used to model competitor moves and simulate one's own deal strategies and resultant business models.

## REVIEWING STEPS 1 THROUGH 4

Let's summarize what's been said so far about market modeling. The first four steps involve collecting outside information to analyze markets, companies, and deals.

First, develop a market overview, which identifies traditional, hybrid, and digital value activities. Subsequent steps of market modeling will refine this market overview.

Second, systematically build a player database. Start by including significant companies that are known competitors in a market. Then add other players by identifying firms that are doing deals in that market—even if the company does not operate directly in the market. Also include new companies and potential competitors in the player database. As appropriate, assign each player to important submarkets defined by value activity, geographic focus, or customer segment.

Third, build a deal database that captures basic deal facts including announcement date, deal structure (alliance, minority investment, joint venture, merger or acquisition, spin-off, and so on) and other essential deal facts. This database also includes the role of each company involved in the deal, the current status of the deal, and structural information relating to value activity, geographic focus, or customer segment.

Fourth, extend the deal database by uncovering the reasons why each deal has been done. While several case examples and tools have been presented to help, uncovering deal rationales is an art as well as a science. Start by using direct deal analysis, where deals are analyzed in isolation. What does each side really hope to gain? Sometimes it helps to break down the different "gives and gets" of the deal by business function. In other cases, researching the value activities implicated by the deal makes more sense. As a deal database becomes more fully developed, employ deal constellation analysis as a richer context for understanding deal rationales. Major events, such as company announcements of significant deals, are particularly useful times to refine the deal database and rationales. Finally, at a more sophisticated level of analysis, move beyond what's happening to simulate movement and deals that could happen.

An executive is now intelligently armed to develop deal strategy on a market-by-market basis. The next chapter focuses on how to use a market overview, player database, deal database, and deal rationales as a foundation for establishing competitive positioning and for building partnership strategy. Now the creative part begins with the four remaining steps: select deal rationales, choose target partners, structure the partnership or investment, and implement the deal successfully.

The final four steps of market modeling are more intuitive and impressionistic than the first four steps. There will be no precise calculation to determine with whom to partner, how the deal should be structured, or exactly how it should be implemented. Nevertheless, if an executive has done a good job on the first four steps of market modeling, he or she will have in place a system that can yield semi-intelligent recommendations for digital deals. The efforts will provide a vital, external information-based system for thoughtful business development.

## EDEL'S DEAL HISTORY

This chapter concludes by continuing the discussion of Edel Music in 2000, summarizing Edel's deal history (primarily in the traditional value activities of the music industry). The next chapter explores Edel's possible moves into digital deals.

As described in Chapter 2, Edel focused initially on the German market, establishing the core of its business in music distribution, marketing, and production. From there, Edel expanded its reach, using its distribution efficiency and lower distribution fees to attract new artists while working to build a modest international presence.

Recall that traditional music industry activities follow a predictable value chain (see Figure 2-1). The process begins when artists create a new song and are then "discovered" by a label's A&R group. Producers, engineers, and artists record the album. Record companies manufacture and distribute albums to retail stores, where fans buy the music.

By 2000, Edel had moved into nearly every one of these traditional value activities. It attracted content (A&R) through publishing and record label deals. Between 1997 and 1999, Edel formed partnerships with or acquired record labels to reach target demographics and expand its A&R presence in Europe and the United Kingdom. It expanded its music publishing business, acquiring Megason Publishing and investing $40 million in a joint venture with singer-songwriter Desmond Child's Deston Songs, a New York–based publishing company for writers and catalogs.

Edel was also expanding its distribution. In 1994 it formed a joint sales venture with Roadrunner Records, a Dutch company. Four years later, Edel formed a joint venture with Hollywood Records to promote, distribute, and market artist Jennifer Paige, in the United States. In 1999, Edel acquired 80 percent of RED, Sony's U.S. independent distribution company and formed a joint venture for distribution with Disney. That same year, it acquired K-Tel, a Finnish company that owned distribution facilities. Edel used licensing agreements in parts of the world where it had a limited presence, such as with SWAT Marketing in Asia and Shock Records in Australia.

Edel began to look at other media to expand its content and provide new marketing and distribution channels. In late 1998, Edel structured a licensing agreement with EM.TV Merchandising, a leading supplier of children's programming, and in early 1999, Edel created Junior.TV, a joint venture with EM.TV and the Kirchgruppe. Later that year, Edel invested in MTV rival music channel, Viva, with coinvestors that included Universal, Warner Music, and EMI. Edel also took a minority position in Eagle Rock Entertainment, a U.K.-based record, video, and television producer.

## Digital deals

By 2000, Edel realized that digital value activities of music were becoming much more important, but the company was not certain how to proceed. In February 2000, Edel announced plans to digitize a "significant amount" of titles for distribution over the Internet.

The digital transformation of the music industry was creating a complex set of value activities and interactions that Edel needed to understand. What partnerships should Edel consider? In Chapter 4, some options for Edel will be analyzed as the company repositions itself for the dramatic changes occurring in music.

# CHAPTER 4

# Selecting Deals and Partners

1999 and early 2000 brought an era of excess. Investor speculation and free-flowing capital led to inflated stock prices, which firms used to fund thousands of acquisitions, alliances, and minority investments. The IPO market was red hot with first-day stock price increases of 500 percent or more.[1] This flood of successful IPOs gave many newer companies currency to make a series of targeted deals right out of the IPO box. Unfortunately, many of these partnerships did not pass long-term muster.

To some extent, Wall Street encouraged nonsense deals by supporting revenue-based stock valuations. Historically, firms have been valued on earnings or cash flow. But revenue figures were now being used as a benchmark to set stock prices. This encouraged companies to structure a variety of creative deals just to boost revenues. Consider, for example, a cross-marketing deal: "I'll sell you advertising on my Web site in exchange for advertising on your Web site—and we'll both book the sale as revenue. How much is the advertising worth? My site is extremely valuable; can't say for sure, but I think you just bought $5 million in advertising. You say it's worth $10 million? OK." In a profit-driven world, since rise in revenue is offset by increased advertising cost, earnings stay the same and stock prices would not move.

However, if revenue-based valuation is deployed, since both companies' revenues increase, their stock prices could rise accordingly. In early 2000, almost 10 percent of all Internet advertising revenues came from barter deals.[2]

Some deals resembled random land grabs more than thoughtful business moves. Companies rapidly seized digital real estate on a partner's Web site in an effort to get marketing exposure without adequately thinking through how the deal would drive revenue or what profit results could reasonably be expected. A marketing executive from one of the many dot-com pet stores that mushroomed during this period likened his deal team to "cowboys," wildly riding around without giving consideration as to how a deal would be roped in and implemented. This haste may be partially forgivable, given the early Internet gold-rush frenzy.

But the era of quasi-rational whirlwind digital deals has ended. Stock prices do not remain linked to revenues alone in the long run. As markets solidify and companies mature, investors demand earnings and cash flow. By the summer of 2000, Internet companies needed to deliver profits sooner rather than later or suffer plunging stock prices. The only business model that seemed to count was sending out and collecting on invoices.

Firms need to structure meaningful partnerships that make real business sense. This chapter continues the discussion about how to craft a systematic deal strategy. Building on the last two chapters, which looked at ways to gather and analyze a market fact base, it explores how companies should select their own deal rationales and choose actual partners for digital deals (Steps 5 and 6 of the market modeling framework portrayed in Figure 1-2). With these two steps, market modeling moves forward from analysis to action.

## INTRODUCING SHATTUCK HAMMOND

In 1993 Shattuck Hammond Partners was formed by eight principals to provide financial advisory and bond underwriting services to hospitals and healthcare systems. During the mid- to late 1990s, the firm repositioned itself as a leading merger and acquisition advisor to the healthcare industry. In 1998, Shattuck Hammond was sold to Coopers & Lybrand

Securities and later became part of PricewaterhouseCoopers Securities after Coopers & Lybrand merged with Price Waterhouse.

By 2000, it appeared likely that PricewaterhouseCoopers (PwC) would break itself up, largely in response to SEC regulatory concerns. As part of PwC's Financial Advisory Services, Shattuck Hammond could be spun off with this arm of the company. Whatever the future, the group needed to position itself for new opportunities afforded by the digital economy.

Michael Hammond, CEO of PricewaterhouseCoopers Securities/ Shattuck Hammond, sensed that the Internet would eventually transform the bond market and wanted his company to play a significant role in the change. He understood that Shattuck Hammond would need an intelligent deal strategy to succeed. By June 2000 Hammond and Keith Dickey, his chief knowledge officer, were well along in developing digital deal rationales and identifying potential partners that could attack the "e-bond" space.

## Online financial services

Online financial services has been called "an industry made in Internet heaven." A Morgan Stanley Dean Witter study published in 2000 projected the brokerage subindustry of Internet financial services to grow from $2.5 billion in 1998 to $32 billion in 2003, reflecting a compounded annual growth rate of 67 percent. During 1999, online brokerage accounts increased 44 percent from 8.6 million to 12.4 million.[3] While growth dampened somewhat after the Nasdaq collapse of March 2000, financial services on the Web continued on a steady march.

The Internet was not only changing retail equity investing but it was also transforming investment banks. In one short year, Merrill Lynch had moved from a position that "Internet trading should be regarded as a serious threat to Americans' financial lives," to a strategy that embraced the Internet by offering $29 trades to match challenger Charles Schwab. Rarely had the business models of an industry changed so rapidly.[4]

Online investment bank HR Hambrecht, for example, sought to make share allocation for an initial public offering both democratic and scientific by creating a Dutch auction[5] process it had dubbed Open IPO. The idea was to try to avoid massive gains for investors on initial public offering issues at the expense of the company's owners.[6] Hambrecht also wanted to level the playing field between institutional and retail investors.

## E-bonding

Bonds have been characterized as an inefficient market of immense financial dimensions. Given the high costs associated with market-making activities, the investor community has frequently complained about the cost inefficiencies of fixed-income markets.[7] It was a market ripe for Internet efficiencies.

But in 2000, factors that might have spurred more rapid change in the e-bond market were still missing. First, traditional investment bankers and brokers, having created jobs and profits from an opaque, illiquid market, were reluctant to aggressively embrace the possibilities afforded by the digital economy. Second, there were fewer challengers to the established players in the bond market than in the equities market, where hypergrowth in the number of online retail investors had driven many of the changes. Incumbents had been able to maintain more control over e-bond market developments than was possible with equities. In a number of cases, traditional investment banks were hanging back and hoping that change in the fixed-income market would continue to be delayed.[8]

The traditional structure of the bond market, as well as the Internet's potential for transforming this space, bore a striking resemblance to the music market. Figure 4-1 shows a side-by-side overview of these two markets. Note that in both markets there are creators of product (artists and issuers) who establish relationships with managers (agents and financial advisors). These creators, together with their managers, develop, market, and distribute products through third-party organizations (record companies and underwriters). Both music and debt instruments are pushed through channels that include intermediaries (wholesalers and retailers for music, and broker-dealers and institutional investors for bonds). Finally, after a process that involves many hands taking pieces of the profit, product (music or fixed-income investments) reaches the consumer or retail investor.

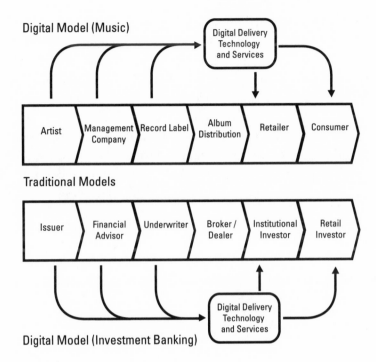

**FIGURE 4-1**
*Comparing online investment banking to digital music.*

There are other similarities. Large incumbents dominated both markets. As discussed in Chapter 2, the Big Five (Warner, EMI, Universal, BMG, and Sony) enjoyed oligopoly power in the music space. The likes of Goldman Sachs, Morgan Stanley Dean Witter, Merrill Lynch, and Salomon Smith Barney had a similar grip on the fixed-income market. Yet digital technologies were shaking up the structure of both markets by promising to offer new paths through the value webs for music and for investment banking. (The value web for an industry such as investment banking consists of all value activities—traditional, hybrid, and digital—together with all possible paths and partner combinations that a company can utilize in bringing a product or service to market.)

## Shattuck Hammond's deal rationales and partners

How could a smaller player like Shattuck Hammond reposition itself through digital deals to gain market share in the fixed-income market? Let's start by looking at the set of value activities involved in the e-bond market.

Figure 4-2 shows a market overview for the e-bonds with key value activities. Recall that developing a market overview such as this comprises the first step of market modeling. Note that through bond auctioning, an issuer such as a hospital or municipality could (at least in theory) sell directly to retail investors. Of course, intermediaries, including large or regional broker-dealers and institutional investors, could also participate in auctions.

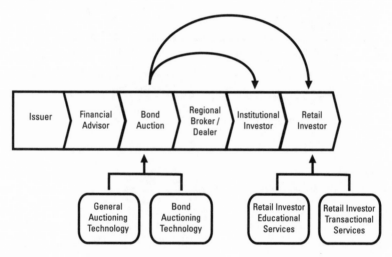

**FIGURE 4-2**
*Value web for the e-bond market.*

But what captured Shattuck Hammond's imagination was facilitating a direct auction relationship between issuer and retail investor. Retail brokerage firms like Charles Schwab had aggregated millions of such investors. Volatility in the stock market could cause these investors to acutely realize the need to allocate a greater portion of their portfolios to high-quality fixed-income investments. And tax-exempt issues (one of Shattuck Hammond's areas of expertise) were highly suited to retail investors because corporations could not enjoy many of the tax-shielding benefits that these investments afforded.

Having developed a market overview that identified key value activities, Shattuck Hammond went on to Steps 2 through 4 of market modeling. It identified major players in each value activity and companies associated with each activity. It studied online investment banking deals that had already occurred and analyzed the rationale behind each deal.

Shattuck Hammond was now ready to select its own deal rationales and target partners. The company identified strengths it brought to the table—core competencies that included a long history of relationships with healthcare issuers and rich experience in and knowledge of the fixed-income market. It then identified two key rationales for partnerships, each of which represented a vital complementary value activity to support Shattuck Hammond's strategy of creating a direct issuer to investor value path (see Figure 4-3):

◆ The need to partner with companies that had aggregated retail investors who were or could be educated about the bond market

◆ The need to develop a bond-auctioning Web site with the help of a technology partner

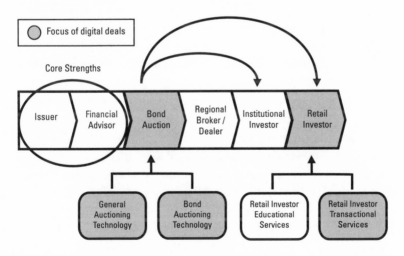

**FIGURE 4-3**
*Shattuck Hammond's digital deal focus.*

If Shattuck Hammond could build strong partnerships in these areas, the company would be able to offer issuers a new and compelling value proposition. It would provide a novel way to market tax-exempt bonds that could save issuers substantial interest costs through a direct-to-retail model. Retail investors could bid on these new issues at lower interest rates than broker-dealers or institutional investors, while still enjoying a higher interest rate than they would receive after purchasing such instruments after two or three channel markups.

What companies should Shattuck Hammond partner with to get access to retail demand? The company identified a player universe for this value activity that included dozens of companies, but a few quickly made the short list. For example, Charles Schwab, which had amassed more than 3.5 million online retail investors, was particularly attractive. Preliminary discussions with Schwab indicated that the company was gearing up its marketing efforts for fixed-income securities.

Shattuck Hammond also researched players developing auctioning technologies and found two types of players to consider. First, there were companies building sites that focused exclusively on auctioning municipal and tax-exempt bonds, such as MuniAuction. In November 1999, the city of Pittsburgh became the first municipal issuer to use MuniAuction's technology to competitively bid bonds directly to both traditional broker-dealer firms and to institutional investors (but not to retail!). Second, there were general auction-enabling technology companies such as Moai. Based in San Francisco, Moai was marketing its LiveExchange solution, which allowed companies to create public or private auctions and trading exchanges for business-to-business (B2B), business-to-consumer (B2C), and consumer-to-consumer (C2C) marketplaces on the Internet.

Shattuck Hammond signed an agreement to test MuniAuction's technologies. On September 20, 2000, Shattuck Hammond successfully conducted its first Internet bond auction, a $44 million revenue bond issued by the World Wildlife Fund. The bidders in the auction were broker-dealers, not retail investors, but Shattuck Hammond was moving up the Internet auctioning learning curve. The company was also considering partnership discussions with auction-enabling technology companies such as Moai, possibly structured on a risk sharing basis.

Let's review the steps that Shattuck Hammond took to develop its digital deal rationales and select partners. The company began by executing the first four market modeling steps:

◆ Develop a market overview that includes key value activities.

◆ Build a player database of companies in each value activity.

◆ Develop a deal database.

◆ Uncover deal rationales.

Next, Shattuck Hammond clarified the business model it would pursue, determining its core competencies and then identifying complementary value activities for which it needed to establish digital partnerships. If Shattuck Hammond wanted to build and control a new core competency—as opposed to outsourcing the activity to someone else—this preference would influence the structure of the digital deal. (Parts 2 and 3 of this book cover the relationship between deal rationale and deal structure.)

With deal rationales in mind, Shattuck Hammond started the process of sourcing and selecting partners in each of the key value activities it would need to execute its vision for a direct-to-retail e-bond market.

# STEP 5: SELECTING DEAL RATIONALES

*Within the context of a company's core strengths, select deal rationales that will contribute to a superior business model.*

Step 5 of market modeling involves developing a deal rationale strategy or, in other words, selecting the goals for digital deals. This step, like all strategic decisions, will be based on both knowledge and intuition. As a prerequisite, build a knowledge base that provides an understanding of market value activities (and how they are evolving), competitive players and potential partners, and the types of deals they are executing. This is what the first four steps of market modeling accomplish. Next, taking this information, an executive decides where and how in the market space to compete and which strategic partnerships will position the organization to build a superior business model.

There is no precise formula for selecting deal rationales. However, deals must be grounded in well-considered strategy, which, in turn, is rooted in exceptional market knowledge. Consider a three-part process for selecting deal rationales: (1) identify core strengths—value activities in a market where distinctive skills and capabilities are enjoyed; (2) select a guiding strategic vision for how and where to compete; and (3) explore how to buttress this strategy with deals in complementary value activity areas that support marketing, operations, finance, or organizational design.

For example, Shattuck Hammond identified its core strengths as privileged relationships with healthcare bond issuers and rich experience in the fixed-income market. From there it decided to pursue a strategy that would ultimately provide municipal bond issuers with the ability to conduct e-bond auctions using a direct-to-retail model. To execute this strategy, it would need to develop complementary partnerships in two critical value activity areas: auctioning technology and online retail customer demand. These partnerships would provide needed operational support for bond auctioning and necessary marketing support to reach a critical mass of Internet retail investors.

Let's look at each of the three steps in more detail.

## Taking stock of core strengths

Firms should begin selecting deal rationales by taking stock of existing core competencies that are relevant to the new economy. More specifically, where in a market's value web does an organization enjoy distinctive skills and capabilities? Clarifying core competencies will help identify deal rationales in two ways. First, it allows a company to identify areas of strength that make it valuable to a prospective partner. Firms can then promote these areas when sourcing and structuring deals, as competencies will attract partners and provide negotiating leverage. For example, Shattuck Hammond's long-term relationship with issuers of fixed-income instruments would entice both technology and online retail transaction partners.

Second, clarifying existing core competencies will uncover areas of weakness that need to be shored up with new economy partnerships. A digital deal can be a quick way to close skill gaps. For example, in 1999 CVS, one of the largest drugstores in the United States, wanted to rapidly establish an online drugstore presence. Acknowledging that it lacked the skills to move quickly, CVS acquired an existing online player (Soma.com) and rebranded the site as its own. Later in 2000, CVS received kudos for the integration of its Web and brick-and-mortar systems in support of customer needs.

Similarly, Staples, the office supply superstore, excelled at running physical retail stores selling office supplies and furniture to small business owners, but it came to the Web late. By 1997, its archrival, Office Depot, had already developed an ecommerce site that was selling office products and providing helpful services such as free tax form downloads. Staples knew that it needed help to craft an online response. To catch up quickly, Staples acquired Quill, a catalog marketer of office products that had also established a Web presence known as Quill.com. The Quill team went to work on Staples.com, and the site was successfully launched six months later.

In summary, an assessment of existing core competencies will bring to light partnership marketing and bargaining power as well as an organization's digital deal needs. As with CVS and Staples, extending core strengths into digital value activities often requires an acquisition, whereas other deal structures are often more appropriate for rationales associated with complimentary competencies. (The relationship between rationale and structure is examined in more detail in Chapter 11.)

## Selecting a strategic vision

Deal rationales must be grounded in a guiding strategic vision relating to how and where an organization will compete in the new economy. The strategy will strongly influence the types of deals to be pursued. Let's take a look at how three different strategies suggest different deal rationales.

### SPECIALIZATION

As discussed in Chapter 1, some firms are following a strategy of specialization by focusing on a single core strength or niche. A firm choosing this strategy needs to craft deals that team it with partners in other crucial activities of the value web. For example, in pursuing a specialization strategy built around tax-exempt e-bond offerings, Shattuck identified two other "choke points" in the value web where it needed key partnerships to succeed: auctioning technology services and access to aggregations of online retail investors.

Consider another example. Bamboo.com developed visual imaging technology that enables realtors to digitally film virtual 360-degree tours of properties, thereby reducing customer search cost for a home. Buyers can screen dozens of prospective houses from the comfort of their family rooms and then visit the handful of houses that make it to a second cut. It also enables realtors to show houses that have a higher likelihood of being sold. Bamboo.com decided to pursue a specialization strategy—concentrating on improving its visualization technology—and establish partnerships with other companies to reach online real estate buyers. Bamboo.com moved to lock up key relationships with real estate destination Web sites (Realtor.com and homes.com), Internet portals (Yahoo! and Excite), as well as with traditional real estate brokers (RE/MAX, Century 21, and Coldwell Banker). For example, Yahoo! agreed to incorporate the technology into its real estate Web pages.

In late 1999, Bamboo also structured a major partnership to bolster its core technology, merging with Internet Pictures (iPIX) to create immersive virtual tour technology for other industries such as travel and automotive. In 2000, iPIX rapidly grew revenues, but as with other Internet companies, saw its stock price hemorrhage. Later that year, the company announced it was developing plans "to accelerate profitability." Its deals made good business sense; the company now needed to execute.

## HORIZONTAL MASSIFICATION

Firms following a horizontal massification strategy seek to build scale in a particular market segment. They are likely to acquire other companies or competitors to consolidate an activity slice in a value web. In 2000, America Online's announced purchase of Warner Music/Time Warner and attempted control of EMI reflected AOL's desire to build mass in music content. (AOL was also doing digital deals in other areas of the music value web, simultaneously pursuing massification and vertical integration in this space.)

Firms selecting a horizontal massification strategy may also want to strike deals that stimulate demand for their activity slice of the value web. For example, in 1996 Microsoft wanted to move beyond its operating system and application software by building up mass in entertainment content. Microsoft's game division had already marketed several titles, including Flight Simulator and Monster Truck Madness. Although Flight Simulator and its sequels sold well, Microsoft's other games had failed to achieve the unit sales and hit status the company desired. Furthermore, the rise of online gaming made Microsoft question whether it was concentrating on the right segment of the gaming industry.

Microsoft decided to meet with a small company in Cupertino, California, named Electric Gravity. This company had established an online gaming zone that allowed multiple users to play games such as chess, bridge, and hearts over the Internet. Intrigued by Electric Gravity's existing visitor base, Microsoft purchased the company and renamed Electric Gravity's Internet Gaming Zone after itself. The online user base continued to grow, and by mid-1998 there were over 2 million registered users and 16,000 simultaneous gamers at peak times. The MSN Internet Gaming Zone continued to grow in popularity, reaching 10 million users by late 1999, and the number promised to rise even more as online gaming accelerated.

At the same time, Microsoft was investing heavily in independent computer game developers to spark demand for this market. It structured a deal with Digital Anvil, a company founded by former Electronic Arts employees. Funded by Microsoft, Digital Anvil would develop gaming content, and Microsoft would use its distribution to aggressively promote its games. (In fact, Microsoft announced plans to acquire Digital Anvil in late 2000.) Microsoft also signed a deal with Red Storm Entertainment, a gaming company cofounded by the author Tom Clancy to create war simulation games. Recognizing that gaming creativity flourishes within small organizations, Microsoft often structured noncontrolling deals (investments or minority-owned joint ventures) to build content mass in the online gaming market.

## VERTICAL INTEGRATION

A third strategy, vertical integration, seeks to assemble all major activities in a market value web under one umbrella. Often, the goal is to secure a competitive advantage through superior information. In essence, a vertical integration strategy allows a firm to iron out all the inefficiencies in the value web by controlling information at each activity area. Thus to succeed, a firm following this strategy needs to structure deals to gain a controlling end-to-end presence in the value web.

Blockbuster Video, facing competitive threats, decided to pursue a vertical integration strategy, focusing on digital value activities. Although the company would not own all value activities, it hoped to exert enough influence to achieve virtual vertical integration. Blockbuster had expanded rapidly during the 1990s to become the largest U.S. video rental company. But as broadband communications continued to increase Internet video transmission speeds, Blockbuster feared that its array of stores could become "dead-end assets." After all, few people would drive several miles to rent a videotape if they could just order a movie through the Internet instead. Blockbuster decided to explore a strategy where it would morph its well-known brand into a vertically integrated online video distribution system.

To execute this strategy, Blockbuster needed to form deals at both ends of the digital value web: securing more content and accessing an audience of viewers. First, Blockbuster formed alliances with studios, such as one with Metro-Goldwyn-Mayer that would allow customers to download MGM's extensive library of movies from Blockbuster's Web site. Next, Blockbuster formed alliances with AOL and TiVo—which makes devices that digitally record video for later playback—to help distribute digital movies into the home. In July 2000, it signed a deal with Enron Broadband Services to deliver entertainment over Enron's global broadband infrastructure network. (This highly touted deal was later dissolved.) A few months later, it brought in InterTrust to provide digital rights management technology for the service (this was a crucial step to assuage movie studios' fears about movie piracy and build a viable business model). In 2001, Blockbuster added Universal Pictures as a digital-streaming content partner. The Blockbuster brand was still strong. By establishing end-to-end deals in the digital video value chain, it hoped to make a winning strategic shift before it was too late.

## OTHER STRATEGIC VISIONS

A number of strategists have offered guiding visions for winning business models in the new economy. For example, Don Tapscott, David

Ticoll, and Alex Lowy suggest that five distinct "types" of organizations are emerging: agora, aggregation, value chain, alliance, and distributive network.[9] These organizations vary across the two dimensions of value integration and control. For example, an *agora* is characterized by low value integration and low control (eBay). In contrast, a *value chain* organization provides both high value integration and control (Dell). Such constructs can be useful in designing a vision for partnership strategy. Whatever the source of inspiration, a guiding vision will provide a context for integrating digital deal decisions.

## Supporting business functions

A third way to select deal rationales involves working through the four classic business functions mentioned in Chapter 2—marketing, operations, finance, and organizational design—and systematically identifying deals in value activity areas that bolster these functions. To start, one reviews the deal database for partnerships that other players (including competitors) have pursued to support each functional area. This will often trigger good ideas and help avoid mistakes. Here are some examples of how firms have established digital deals to bolster each of the four business functions.

### MARKETING

After launching Staples.com, Staples turned its attention to marketing deals designed to capture new customers. First, it made a $7 million equity investment in Register.com, one of the major Web site registries. In exchange for the investment, Staples gained access to Register.com's list of 1 million business customers. Armed with this database, Staples.com sent out emails containing helpful hints about how to run a new business using its computer equipment, office furniture, and online services.

Staples.com next decided to partner with a surprising ally—Ariba, a company famous for developing technology that runs business-to-business exchanges. Ariba got its start by offering "e-procurement software" that helps firms buy raw materials for less. Much of the savings came from cutting out retailers like Staples and buying products directly from the manufacturer. Ariba seemed an unlikely digital deal partner for Staples, but in the Internet economy, oblique pairings are not uncommon.

Staples signed a joint marketing agreement in which its catalogs would be offered in Ariba's software packages. It knew that Ariba's software ends up in front of corporate buyers with decision-making power. While buyers were using Ariba to save on major purchases, they might be willing to buy smaller items from Staples.

Another important marketing duty involves setting prices. Often just a 1 or 2 percent change in pricing can lead to significant swings in profitability. But the Internet has thrown the science of pricing into upheaval by providing greater price transparency. Customers can quickly shop around and compare prices to find the sellers with the lowest prices. Even better, they can use "shopbots," sophisticated search algorithms that scout the Web to find the lowest price on a specific item. For buyers, Internet price transparency is a windfall.

But for incumbent retailers seeking to build an ecommerce empire, price transparency creates pressure to offer lower prices on the Web. Start-ups with less-expensive cost structures (or less to lose) can charge low prices to gain critical mass. Unless an incumbent is willing to match (or beat) these lower prices, it stands little chance of gaining a significant user base. But incumbents also face pressure to keep prices high and avoid cannibalizing their physical stores. In some cases, incumbents give in to pricing pressure. For example, in the online pharmacy business, brick-and-mortar stores decided to sell the same drugs for a much lower price online. The largest chains—CVS, Walgreen, Rite Aid, and Eckerd—were undercutting their brick-and-mortar prices by 10 to 30 percent. Except to meet immediate need, why would people with Web access drive to a store when they can buy the same drug, from the same retailer, for 30 percent less? Price disparity can lead to significant channel conflict as Web sales take away profits from brick-and-mortar retailers.

Is there a better way? Possibly. Some incumbents have signed deals to sell their products through online retailers with another brand. The incumbent takes a significant equity stake and provides operational know-how, but otherwise keeps a low profile to avoid diluting its brand or causing channel conflict. It's basically a sophisticated fighting brand. Ideally the incumbent will also receive stock options, so if the Web site really takes off, it can increase its ownership in the venture.

Firms are also forming marketing deals to build their own brands. For example, the drugstore chain CVS signed a comprehensive five-year deal with Healtheon/WebMD, an online healthcare company. CVS.com would be the sole pharmacy promoted on WebMD's medical Web site, and visitors to CVS.com gained access to WebMD's content, including health information and chat rooms. In exchange, CVS would promote WebMD in its brick-and-mortar stores via signs, banners, shopping bags, and advertising circulars. CVS also agreed to switch all of its healthcare transactions—such as insurance verification—to Healtheon's network. With extensive cross-branding on both Web sites and in the brick-and-mortar world, this deal illustrates what has become a popular marketing-induced digital deal.

## OPERATIONS

The most successful operational digital deals reverberate through an entire company, changing the way it buys steel, makes cars, or ships products. Successfully executed, these deals create value by cutting costs and reducing the amount of working and fixed capital investment needed to run a business.

Toward the end of 1998, General Motors President G. Richard Wagoner didn't even have a computer in his office. A year later, he was leading GM into the Internet era. As Wagoner woke to the fact that the Internet could drive down prices across the entire supply chain, he commissioned a team to develop an online supplier portal. GM would buy all of its products through the site, saving billions of dollars by eliminating the elaborate network of personal contacts and forms that made up its purchasing department. Each purchase order—and there were hundreds of thousands of them—was costing GM approximately $100 to process.

There were other benefits. If GM could get its 30,000 different suppliers to make their purchases through the portal, they would be able to take advantage of GM's size to cut costs. Lower supplier costs would eventually flow through to GM. In addition, suppliers could sell products to other customers (besides GM on the site). The non-GM sales volume would serve as an independent confirmation that the suppliers' prices were low. If GM noticed that it was the only company buying from a particular supplier, it would search for a lower-priced source. (The benefits would be magnified if other automobile manufacturers, such as Ford or DaimlerChrysler, joined the supplier portal, which, in fact, they agreed to do in 2000.)

The team immediately looked for a partner to help them create the supply chain portal. After meeting with Oracle and several other software companies, GM decided to strike a deal with Commerce One, located in Northern California. Commerce One provided the ecommerce technology for the portal and would do much of the behind-the-scenes dirty work to build the site. As part of the deal, GM was granted options in Commerce One (vesting as the portal reaches revenue goals). GM's supplier exchange (then called TradeXchange and later renamed Covisant when Ford and DaimlerChrysler joined) went live with the automotive industry's first Internet-based business-to-business auction in late 1999.

Taking operational deals even further, automakers are searching for their own holy e-grail. They want to do for cars what Michael Dell did for computers—let customers drive the manufacturing process. In their ideal world, customers would order what they want directly, clicking though a series of menus to pick their car's color, horsepower, and transmission. Once the order was placed, the information would travel to Ford or GM, which would then make that specific car. This new manufacturing process would slash expensive inventory carrying costs—instead of shipping a car to a dealer's lot to sit around for a few months, the car would travel directly to its owner, saving Ford or GM billions of dollars in inventory investment.

To move closer to this dream, Ford made a minority investment in Microsoft's auto site, CarPoint. This site offers detailed automobile information for new car shoppers, and Microsoft hoped to possibly spin it off as a new company (following Expedia's lead). Ford would work with CarPoint to create a build-to-order online system. CarPoint provided technical expertise, customer access, and information on their desires. Ford would do the heavy lifting, retooling its auto factories to provide the flexible manufacturing needed for customers to have control over the options they can buy. If Ford and Microsoft can get the idea to work, the digital deal will trigger huge operational savings. (As an intermediate step, in 2000 Ford partnered with its nervous dealer network in FordDirect.com, an ecommerce initiative that would give consumers access to dealer inventories.)

Consider another example of a deal constellation designed to cut operational costs. Late in 2000, Boeing, Miramax Films, AMC Theaters, and others unveiled a new satellite-to-movie-screen distribution system.

The service, named Cinema Connexion, used Boeing's satellites (purchased earlier that year from Hughes Electronics) to beam digital movies directly to theaters. Boeing brought the technology, Miramax the content, and AMC the customer reach. Cinema Connexion could quickly send one movie to thousands of screens at a fraction of traditional costs and promised to change the economics of movie distribution.

## FINANCE

In the middle of 1999, Williams Communications Group (WCG) prepared to launch an IPO. WCG was a telecommunications company that had been spun off from Williams—a large energy company—in a strategic move to leverage skills in natural gas pipelines to fiber-optic pipes. Williams had constructed a vast fiber-optic backbone, and now sold capacity to telephone carriers and Internet service providers.

Needing more money to expand its optical network, WCG decided to file an IPO to sell 14 percent of the company. On the side, WCG signed an agreement with Intel to sell $200 million in stock—no small amount even for cash-rich Intel. Intel would make a private investment in the Class A common stock of WCG simultaneously with Williams' upcoming IPO. From Intel's point of view the deal was strategic; it was creating a data-services business and Williams would provide key transport services for Intel. WCG was doing the deal to land Intel's business, but also to show Wall Street that its stock was worthy of Intel's investment. Such an endorsement would increase the chances of a strong IPO debut. Financial endorsement deals, whether in the form of large private placements or dot-com minority investments, have become common. By taking funding from a prestigious technology company, firms seek to improve Wall Street's reaction to future financings. Chapter 8 analyzes these investments in detail.

## ORGANIZATIONAL DESIGN

Many partnerships are created for organizational reasons. As discussed earlier, Microsoft elected to build a network of alliances with online gaming companies in addition to designing and programming the games in-house. It knew that some talent did not work well inside corporate confines and trying to do so would stifle developers' creativity.

Likewise, recruiting and retaining key personnel is driving digital deals such as spin-offs. For example, a large factor in Microsoft's spin-off of Expedia, the Internet travel site, into a separately traded company was the desire to create an entity that could attract and retain employees with the potential for stock price appreciation. Indeed in late 1999, Expedia went public and rose 382 percent on its first day of trading. Deals such as Expedia's IPO were important not only in unlocking the value of Microsoft's Internet properties but also in retaining key personnel within the general Microsoft fold. (Expedia's stock tumbled in the Internet downturn of 2000, creating another complex wrinkle in maintaining employee commitment.)

There are numerous methods for selecting deal rationales. This chapter has explored three different approaches: clarifying existing and possibly expanded areas of core competence, selecting a guiding strategic vision, and buttressing strategy with deals in complementary value activities that support business functions (marketing, operations, finance, and organizational design). However an executive chooses which deal rationales to pursue, the next step involves picking a specific partner for the deal.

# STEP 6: TARGETING PARTNERS

*Choose target partners.*

After an organization identifies which deals to pursue, the next step involves selecting specific partners. For example, recall that Shattuck Hammond decided to structure deals in two primary areas: e-bond auctioning technology and online retail investor access. An initial list of potential targets is sometimes obvious. Yet, in almost all cases, a good player database will add additional candidates, while a deal database will add value to a manager's thinking as subtleties such as potential partnership conflicts are considered.

A list should be culled to generate an A-list of partners that (1) bring the specific "assets" that meet needs in each activity area; (2) are likely to consider a deal; and (3) will not generate excessive conflicts with preexisting partnerships on either side. Looking at retail brokers, for example, Charles Schwab provided services for more than 3.5 million online retail investors in 2000. Significantly, Schwab was gearing up its marketing efforts for municipal bonds and was not locked into any investment bank for sourcing debt issues. The company appeared to be a good fit for Shattuck Hammond.

In some respects, selecting target partners becomes easy if a manager has done a good job of developing a fact base. For example, a player database can be queried to reveal the universe of companies for every activity in a market value web that needs to be covered or for every business function that needs bolstering. Likewise, by reviewing a deal database, managers can determine firms that have already entered into similar deals, eliminating them from consideration or identifying conflicts that need to be resolved.

In other respects, partnership selection is highly complex, with significant and subtle organizational and human dimensions to consider. This is where digital deal making becomes more intuitive and opportunistic. Basic questions rise to the surface as a result of phone calls, emails, and meetings. Are counterparts liked? Can they be trusted enough to handle sensitive information? Will they be able to execute and will they have staying power? These soft factors become increasingly important in Steps 7 and 8, which involve structuring and implementing the deal.

There is much more to say about selecting partners throughout the case studies in Part 2. These chapters explore how different deal rationales—ranging from knowledge of local markets to fueling an industry value web—drive partnership selection and ultimately deal structure.

## Identity and intimacy

Erik Erikson was a psychosocial theorist who suggested that human experience consists of eight critical events or nuclear crises. Erikson's fifth and most important event, which occurs during adolescence, is identity versus identity confusion. During this crisis an individual must determine the extent to which he or she is (1) like all other people, (2) like some other people, or (3) like no other person.

Erikson's work has been contrasted with the interpersonal theory of psychoanalytical theorist Harry Stack Sullivan. Sullivan stressed the need for close relationships in clarifying identity. In other words, much of self-identity comes from relationships and interactions with other people. By contrast, Erikson insisted that a solid self-identity is not the result of intimacy, but, in fact, is a prerequisite to intimacy.[10] In other words, before intimate relationships with others can be developed, "you must first know yourself."

Enough psychobabble. This issue, however, is a key consideration in determining deal rationales and selecting partners. Should a company establish identity in a market before reaching out for partner intimacy? Or is it better to be supported by a portfolio of partners right away? There's no universal answer. As stressed in this chapter, an organization's special solution can only come through consideration of present and evolving core competencies, strategic vision, and an acute sensitivity regarding which business functions should be supported through partnerships.

While the first four steps of market modeling involve collecting outside information by analyzing markets, this chapter focuses on turning analysis into action. Step 5 involves selecting deal rationales, the underlying goals that partnerships are expected to accomplish. Step 6 involves selecting target partners by reducing a relevant universe of players down to a short list of prospects that are positioned to fulfill each rationale. The next chapter moves on to the final steps of market modeling: structuring and implementing digital deals.

# EDEL'S DEAL RATIONALES AND TARGET PARTNERS

As seen in Chapter 3, throughout its history Edel Music has used partnerships and deals to expand its business and position itself as a leading independent label. But by 2000, facing unprecedented transformation of the music industry, Edel struggled to design and execute a digital deal strategy. What deal rationales would unlock key value activities that could give the company a leg up in the new ways that music would be promoted and distributed? And which partners should the company select?

Recall that in 1999, Edel bought 80 percent of RED, an independent distribution company, from Sony. While negotiating the deal, Edel's chairman, Michael Haentjes, met Ron Urban, a senior VP at Sony Music. Haentjes liked what he saw and hired Urban as president and CEO of Edel

North American. In August 2000, Urban set a goal for Edel to grow into a major music company or at least become the largest independent.[11]

Edel enjoyed two core strengths: (1) an outstanding A&R group that stayed close to music customers, spotted key trends, and sourced hot content; and (2) distribution efficiencies, which resulted in a lower distribution cost structure and the ability to attract artists with better deals.

Given these competencies, the following is a deal rationale strategy that could provide Edel with a superior new economy business model. (Future events—including a sale of Edel—could swamp this analysis; the case is used only to illustrate partnership selection.)

Figure 4-4 shows the framework for a business model and digital value web that could guide Edel in selecting deal rationale and value activities. In this model, Edel builds on its established ability to spot music trends and source talent through promoting its distribution efficiencies. In particular, Edel establishes a digital artist center, marketing directly to consumers.

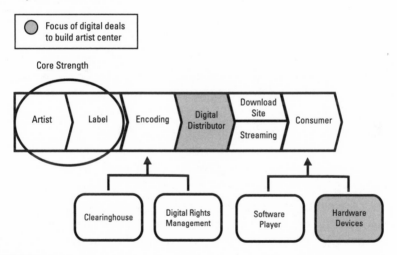

**FIGURE 4-4**
*Edel's core strengths and digital deal focus.*

The appeal of Edel's new model to artists is based on both cost efficiency and reach, and aggressively builds on its tradition of offering musicians better deals. Edel develops a mobile music portal—an artist center that is specifically tuned to promoting musicians to consumers with digital players. To make this case convincingly, Edel needs to establish part-nerships at two complementary choke points in the music value web:

◆ Aggregators of consumer demand such as manufacturers of digital music devices. Companies like Sony or Nokia are on a partner A-list.

◆ A digital distributor. Edel needs to leverage digital distribution resources to deliver its content to users of mobile devices.

There are a number of partner possibilities for the second choke point. For example, Edel already has a licensing and distribution alliance with News Corp., the media conglomerate run by Rupert Murdoch. In 2000, Edel formed an alliance with News Corp.'s Mushroom Records, Festival Records, and Rawkus Records units. News Corp. would license its repertoire to Edel outside of Asia, and the two companies would develop a joint-venture company to market Edel's repertoire in Australia and New Zealand. Edel could expand the relationship by having News Corp. provide Edel with digital distribution through direct satellite con-nection to a large consumer base in Asia and elsewhere around the world.

These digital deals could lead to channel conflict with Edel's tradi-tional distribution outlets. Furthermore, there would be an initial chal-lenge in providing enough music to appeal to a significant number of consumers. However, if Edel did not address these issues and move for-ward with digital distribution, the company would not only lose any first-mover advantage, but could also fall behind on how the majority of music was destined to be marketed.

Edel wanted to aggressively grow its market share. Being a small, but significant player in the music space, it had more to gain than lose by pushing the digital music envelope. In fact, in early 2001, Edel became the second music company (after giant BMG) to agree to distribute music over a legal version of Napster that was being explored.

Should Edel become even more aggressive in attracting new and established talent by offering artists digital deals that included distinctive promotion through a dedicated artist center and attractive revenue splits buoyed by superior back-end demand aggregation and distribution? Answers to questions such as these are at the heart of selecting deal ratio-nales and key partners.

# CHAPTER 5

# Structuring and Implementing Deals

In 1969 the first computer-to-computer Internet transmission was sent from UCLA to Stanford University.[1] Thirty years later, as part of commemoration events, UCLA sponsored a panel to discuss how the Internet was transforming business. The discussion came around to the topic of partnerships and how executives on the panel were structuring and implementing deals. There were few set rules or common protocols. Perhaps Ken Goldstein, then general manager of Disney Online, summed it up best when he said, "During every deal negotiation there comes a pregnant pause when each side tries to figure out which way cash is going to flow."

Structuring a deal has always been a subtle affair. There are endless possible twists to each variant of deal structure: acquisition, joint venture, minority investment, alliance, spin-off, and license. Now however, as Goldstein's comment illustrates, even fundamental negotiating principles had become up for grabs in dynamic market landscapes associated with digital deals. Historically, partners rarely questioned something as basic as who would pay for the deal. Coke bought sponsorship time from ABC. Ford paid Goodyear for tires in a simple purchaser-supplier relationship. In the new economy, both parties in a deal often benefit in complex ways. Yahoo! gets new financial content for its Web portal, while

TheStreet.com gains exposure on Yahoo!. Who should pay? Negotiating postures change over time as a company builds prestige and power. For a while, AOL paid generously for online content that would attract additional users to its network. Yet eventually the typical deal structure reached a tipping point. In 1999 and 2000, AOL demanded millions of dollars from content providers seeking to tap into AOL's vast audience.

This chapter focuses on the final two steps of market modeling: structuring and implementing deals. These last two steps are critical. All the research, analysis, and planning become useless unless a firm can execute a deal successfully and make it work after the papers are signed.

Structuring and implementing deals are topics requiring extensive treatment. In this chapter, the goal will be limited to introducing five of the most common deal structures and key issues that commonly come into play with each structure. In Part 2, the discussion will be expanded with case studies designed to explore how firms have successfully (or unsuccessfully) executed five different deal structures—mergers and acquisitions, joint ventures, minority equity investments, advertising and commerce alliances, and spin-offs and tracking stocks.

# STEP 7: STRUCTURING DEALS

*Structure the partnership or investment.*

Digital deals will often take on one of five forms, with each form conveying different levels of control, risk, and duration. While there are other ways to structure deals, the focus here will be on these five structures, each of which, in turn, has a wide range of variants. Let's take a closer look.

## Five common deal structures

Mention the word *deal*, and many people immediately think of *mergers and acquisitions* (M&A). It's not surprising that M&A is the first deal structure to jump to mind—these deals grab newspaper headlines. They often involve large, permanent bets with tremendous risks and consequences. At the same time, successful mergers and acquisitions allow immediate control and rapid growth. An M&A deal involves any business combination where two firms come together, joining forces to operate as a single entity. In Chapter 6, Cisco (which has completed over 60 acquisitions) will be used as an example of the effective use of mergers and acquisitions as a digital deal structure.

The second deal structure is a joint venture (JV), which classically has been defined as "a cooperative business activity, formed by two or more separate organizations . . . that creates an independent business entity and allocates ownership, operational responsibility, and financial risks and rewards to each member, while preserving their separate identity/autonomy."[2] The hallmark of a joint venture is that the deal creates a new, independent business entity. Joint ventures rarely allow as much control as mergers because two or more partners must work together to collectively make decisions or at least influence strategy and operations. But at the same time, JVs can often be structured to involve less risk than mergers—if the deal fails to create value, it's easier for the partners to dissolve the JV and walk away. The JV as a digital deal structure will be examined in Chapter 7, using Microsoft as a lighthouse case.

Third, a minority investment deal structure is used when a firm invests money or services in another company in exchange for an equity interest, and possibly a management role, in the target firm. As the name suggests, a minority investor receives a noncontrolling block of equity, but also assumes much less risk. Chapter 8 will examine the range of new economy deal rationales a firm might pursue through minority investments. This chapter will examine how Intel—the granddaddy of minority investing—has used this deal structure to weave a vast web of minority investment positions, some of which have become mutually supporting.

The fourth deal structure is an advertising and commerce alliance. Similar to a joint venture, a commerce alliance allows firms to work together to reap benefits that neither party could easily achieve alone. But unlike joint ventures, such alliances do not create a separate business entity. The partners work within existing corporate structures. While some firms think that advertising and commerce alliances are easy to structure—just set it up over lunch—smart firms pay painstaking attention to detail because these types of deals are hard to implement successfully. For example, by 2000, advertising-commerce ("adcom") deals received much more scrutiny because revenue generation was no longer a sufficient deal rationale. Advertising and commerce alliances often lead to heated disagreements because no one commands clear decision-making control. They also can fail for lack of management attention. The flip side is that alliances usually involve less risk and greater flexibility. When done right, these deals create significant value for the partners, bringing together strengths in a highly fluid arrangement. Chapter 9 will explore the rationales and methods associated with AOL Time Warner adcom deals, taking the perspectives of both AOL and its vast portfolio of partners.[3]

Finally, a fifth type of deal structure, the spin-off, will be explored. Unlike other structures, a spin-off does not involve teaming up with another company. Instead, one firm carves off a specific division or cluster of assets to form a new, independent business entity. In one sense, it's the opposite of a merger—a firm gives up control assuming that the parts will create more value than the whole. Why might this be true? Chapter 10 will illustrate how spin-offs can allow assets to be used more flexibly by unlocking conflicts of interest. Moreover, there may be organizational or human resource reasons for spinning off divisions. Spin-offs have stirred both interest and debate in the new economy. AT&T and Microsoft are featured as cases to tease out key issues associated with this form of digital deal.

To recap, here are the differences between the deal structures. If two firms become one, it's a merger; if one becomes two, it's a spin-off. If two or more firms jointly create and own a third, it's a joint venture. If a firm gains partial ownership in another, it's a minority investment. And a collaborative, nonequity partnership between two firms is a commerce alliance.

## Selecting a deal structure

How should a firm decide which structure to use for a particular deal? Chapter 11 explores the relationship between deal rationales and deal structures. The rationale for a deal may, in fact, dictate structure. For example, Cisco has often pursued a strategy of staged acquisitions to acquire promising technology. Initially, Cisco structures a minority investment in a start-up, giving the young firm advice, capital, and space to develop a new technology in an entrepreneurial environment. Later, if the firm shows signs of success, Cisco will step in to acquire the company. Taking complete control, Cisco then uses its powerful marketing and sales skills to bring the new technology to market. At the time each deal is structured, Cisco's goals govern whether it prefers a minority investment or an acquisition.

Apart from deal rationale, there are other factors to consider when choosing structure. What degree of control is required for the deal to succeed? How much risk is a company willing to bear? What is the desired duration of the partnership? How much time does an organization have to get the deal done? What resources will be devoted to the deal? At one extreme, an acquisition provides complete control, but also can involve great risk, permanent duration, and a drawn-out execution. At the other end of the spectrum, a commerce alliance may provide little control, but involve limited risk and can be formed in days or even hours. And consider organizational resource requirements. While Intel has been able to execute 100 or more minority investments per year (no small feat!), Intel's joint ventures can be counted on one hand. In fact, in 2000 Intel shut down Pandesic, one of its most significant JVs formed with SAP America. A JV is a resource-hungry animal and to work well, it requires high levels of organizational and financial attention from partners.

Legal considerations, including antitrust or tax issues, can determine digital deal structure. For example, facing an intense antitrust investigation in 1999 and 2000, Microsoft structured many joint ventures, which, unlike acquisitions, often did not attract the same regulatory scrutiny. Chapter 7 shows, however, that even the JV structure will not always work to satisfy regulators, and "lesser" forms of partnerships must be considered.

Politics and personalities play a large role here. On the macro level, trade policies between countries sometimes force firms to establish a joint venture or alliance instead of making an outright acquisition. A country may mandate that a foreign company own less than 50 percent of a local company, making an acquisition impossible. Not unlike postwar foreign-ownership restrictions in Japan to protect sectors under reconstruction, local governments may nurture nascent, digital economy sectors.

On the micro level, executive personality and corporate culture can also impact deal structure. For example, a control-oriented CEO may insist that the deal be structured as an acquisition when a joint venture would work better. On the other hand, Sony, which often has operated under a "not-invented here" handicap (relying exclusively on internal technology) is reconsidering the use of more cooperative digital deal structures to gain access to technology and extend its market presence.

# STEP 8: IMPLEMENTING DEALS

*Implement the deal successfully.*

The deal is done. Papers are signed, champagne is on the side table, glasses are raised, and press conferences are called. What's next? Actually, most of the work! Step 8 of the deal strategy framework involves successfully implementing the deal.

Historical studies report that a high percentage—sometimes over 60 percent—of deals fail during implementation.[4] They cite reasons such as overoptimism, poor communication, lack of shared benefits, or slow results and/or payback. The age of digital deals does not appear to be any different. In fact, given the increased number and types of potential partners and the urgency that often accompanies digital deal decisions, the failure rate is likely to increase.

In the new economy, the pressure is increasing to do the right deals guided by well-designed rationales. An executive must also do deals right. Leadership skills that cut across organizational boundaries are more important than ever. Part 2 of this book illustrates successful deal implementation for each digital deal structure—merger and acquisition, joint venture, minority equity investment, advertising and commerce alliance, and spin-off and tracking stock. For now, consider two overarching principles.

First, consider adopting a life-cycle approach to deal implementation. According to Robert Spekman and Lynn Isabella, deals characteristically pass through life-cycle stages: engagement, valuation, coordination, investment, stabilization, and renewal and/or conclusion. At each stage in the life cycle, managers must engage in different implementation tasks.[5]

In the early stages of engagement and valuation, firms develop a shared vision for how the deal will work, what the partners will accomplish, and what respective duties will be. At this stage, successful implementation requires partners to bring a collaborative spirit, creative thinking, and high energy to bear on identifying how they can maximize the value of the deal. Next, they move into the coordination stage.

Implementation now takes on more of an operational focus, requiring clear communication, division of labor, and back-end integration. Some deals then move into an investment (reevaluation) stage where change is required to make the deal work. Successful implementation now requires managers to make hard choices about the ultimate level of resources they are willing to commit to the deal, possibly broadening the degree of risk and commitment. If the partners weather this phase, they move to the stabilization stage, where the deal settles down and proceeds as planned. The major implementation efforts now involve measuring the performance of the deal against targets and milestones and making minor adjustments. Finally, many deals eventually pass into a renewal or termination phase as working relationships deteriorate or market needs change. The deal becomes less productive, and managers must decide whether to terminate a declining venture or meaningfully restructure the deal.

Firms adopting a life-cycle approach to implementation recognize that the nature of the implementation challenge changes over time. They identify the critical skills needed for each phase of implementation and assign the right managers to do the job. This approach also suggests that firms should rotate their implementation teams over the deal life cycle, bringing in new skills as appropriate.

Sometimes a firm is successful at implementing one form of digital deal, but struggles or even fails with another. As previously mentioned, Intel has successfully implemented a vast strategic portfolio of corporate minority investments. However, Chapter 8 will demonstrate how Intel has struggled with its joint ventures. For example, in 1997 Intel and SAP America formed Pandesic, a JV to offer Internet commerce solutions to small- and medium-size businesses. In the summer of 2000, citing the inability to make the business profitable, Intel and SAP announced that they would shut down Pandesic and lay off all 400 of the joint venture's employees. Intel and SAP were criticized for being too hands-off in supporting their "child" at critical stages of development.

Second, successful implementation of many digital deals requires a tight relationship between a firm's deal team and functional departments. Close internal ties can help avoid both overly optimistic and meaningless deals. With many deal structures, including business commerce alliances and minority equity investments, an organization will want to involve functional managers as early as possible.

For example, when marketing heads are not adequately involved in advertising and/or commerce partnerships, the side effects can be disastrous. As the marketing VP of an ecommerce pet product company stated, "Our business development group consists of a bunch of deal junkies. They don't think implementation. They don't think test campaigns. They don't think placement. They're caught up in an orgy of deal making and have little sense of what happens after the deal is done. We need a level of deal granularity in our commerce deals that will produce actual results. Our business development team has been caught up in a land grab mentality."

Firms need to run quickly to avoid losing opportunities. But at the same time, they should improve the odds that they are running in the right direction by including functional area managers as early as possible. This will make deal implementation much easier by smoothing the transition from the business development group to appropriate business departments.

When done correctly, deal implementation fluently translates into competitive advantage as measured by critical variables such as retention of technical talent. For example, Cisco has implemented over 60 acquisitions, with many successes. As soon as it closes a deal, a dedicated, full time implementation team (known in some circles as the "clean-up crew") swarms in to integrate the company. Cisco moves fast. In August 1999 Cisco acquired Monterey Networks. According to Lori Smith, the human resource director at Monterey, "We closed the deal at 11 p.m. on a Wednesday. When I walked in Thursday morning, we all had Cisco tags on our doors and a banner on the front of our building. And they had this huge Cisco art thing on the wall in the lobby. I saw someone in here putting bottled water in the fridge to replace our coolers. They really don't mess around."[6]

## SUMMARY

The entire eight-step framework for designing a thoughtful partnership strategy has now been presented. Chapters 2 and 3 covered the first four steps, building a robust fact base around the market, players, and deals. Chapter 4 moved the discussion from analysis to action as firms select their own deal rationales and partners within the context of a business model.

The final two steps of market modeling—structuring and implementing deals—are the capstone elements of digital deal strategy. This chapter has only introduced the topics. The best way to learn how to structure and implement deals is to study how successful firms are doing it. (Failed deals will also be highlighted, given that understanding failure can breed success.) Part 2 of this book is organized around the five major deal structures—mergers and acquisitions, joint ventures, minority equity investments, advertising and commerce alliances, and spin-offs and tracking stocks. Each chapter draws on extensive case studies to explore the mechanics of the different deal structures, analyzes when a particular structure is appropriate, and identifies how firms are successfully implementing each form of digital deal.

# Structuring Digital Deals

Part 1 of this book presented an eight-step market modeling framework for crafting a digital deal strategy. The first four steps require a careful analysis of markets, players, deals, and deal rationales. The next four steps move from analysis to action, as a firm selects deal rationales and partners within the context of its business model, and then moves on to structure and implement partnerships. Chapters 2 through 5 in Part 1 each focus on two steps in the market modeling framework. Taken together, the chapters provide a process for tackling complex strategic issues in a systematic, structured manner.

Part 2 will flesh out the market modeling framework through the use of case studies. Exploring how other firms do it (or fail to do it) will help an organization execute its own deal strategy. Each chapter begins with an overview and description of a featured player and then explores rationales often associated with a specific deal structure. Across different markets and industries there are many similarities in when to use a deal structure and how to make it work. By taking a closer look at how lighthouse firms have developed and implemented a particular deal strategy, executives can glean lessons that are relevant to specific partnerships they are considering. (The term "lighthouse" characterizes an organization that provides clear guidance on the use of deal rationales and structures.)

To that effect, this part of the book is organized around five primary types of deal structures. Each of the next five chapters focuses on a company that has been active (often, but not always, successful) at a particular form of digital deal: Cisco and acquisitions, Microsoft and joint ventures, Intel and minority investments, AOL Time Warner and advertising and commerce alliances, and AT&T and spin-offs and/or tracking stocks. Examples are also used from other companies that have succeeded or failed in structuring each type of deal. In all five chapters the same two questions will be answered: (1) What are key rationales associated with each deal structure? and (2) How can an executive succeed in effectively using each structure? Examination of why and how lighthouse companies establish and execute each type of partnership or investment will provide insight and guidance and help executives successfully craft digital deal strategies.

# CHAPTER 6

# Mergers and Acquisitions

*"The companies who emerge as industry leaders will be those who understand
how to partner and those who understand how to acquire."*
—John Chambers
President and CEO, Cisco Systems, Inc.

Early in 1998, Solomon Trujillo, CEO of regional phone company
US West (later purchased by Qwest), called up John Chambers, the head
of Cisco. He asked if Chambers had heard of a company named Net-
Speed over in Austin. NetSpeed had developed some outstanding DSL
(Digital Subscriber Line) products both for US West's central offices and
for end users. (DSL technology gives customers simultaneous high-speed
Internet and telephone connections over existing copper telephone
lines.) Mr. Trujillo thought the DSL market could take off and wanted
to use NetSpeed's products to offer DSL to his customers. But US West
was reluctant to rely on a small company in Texas. Trujillo insisted that
this company was a perfect fit with Cisco's DSL business and asked
Chambers to take a look at them. US West wanted to buy their DSL
products from Cisco.

Chambers promised to check NetSpeed out. He called up Mike
Volpi, then vice president of business development, and explained the sit-

uation: US West wanted to write out a purchase order immediately. He told Volpi that we have to buy these guys. Two months later the deal was signed; Cisco agreed to acquire NetSpeed for around $250 million in stock.[1]

NetSpeed was Cisco's seventeenth acquisition, but by no means its last. It went on to buy over 40 companies during 1999 and 2000, spending more than $25 billion (see Table 6-1). Cisco's purchases spanned a dozen different markets including cable modems, wireless networks, Internet telephones, DSL, network security software, call center software, and optical networking. Although Cisco's pace of acquisitions slowed in early 2001, the company asserted that such deals would continue to play a role in its strategy after the economic downturn.

**Table 6-1 Summary of Cisco's Acquisitions**

**2000**

| Date | Company | Price at announcement ($millions) |
|---|---|---|
| December 14 | ExiO Communications | 155 |
| November 13 | Radiata | 295 |
| November 10 | Active Voice | 296 |
| October 20 | CAIS Software Solutions | 170 |
| September 28 | Vovida Networks | undisclosed |
| September 28 | IPCell Technologies | undisclosed |
| August 31 | PixStream | 370 |
| August 1 | IPmobile | 425 |
| July 27 | NuSpeed Internet Systems | 450 |
| July 25 | Komodo Technology | 175 |
| June 7 | Netiverse | 210 |
| June 5 | HyNEX | 127 |
| May 12 | Qeyton Systems | 800 |
| May 5 | ArrowPoint Communications | 5700 |
| April 12 | Seagull Semiconductor | 19 |
| April 11 | PentaCom | 118 |
| March 29 | SightPath | 800 |
| March 16 | infoGEAR Technology | 301 |
| March 16 | JetCell | 299 |
| March 1 | Atlantech Technologies | 180 |
| February 16 | Growth Networks | 335 |
| January 19 | Altiga Networks | undisclosed |
| January 19 | Compatable Systems | undisclosed |

**Table 6-1 (Continued)**

**1999**

| Date | Company | Price at announcement ($millions) |
|---|---|---|
| December 20 | Pirelli Optical Systems | 2100 |
| December 17 | Internet Engineering Group | 25 |
| December 16 | Worldwide Data Systems | 26 |
| November 12 | V-Bits | 128 |
| November 10 | Aironet Wireless Communications | 799 |
| October 26 | Tasmania Network Systems | 25 |
| September 22 | Webline Communications | 325 |
| September 15 | Cocom A/S | 66 |
| August 26 | Cerent | 6900 |
| August 26 | Monterey Networks | 500 |
| August 19 | MaxComm Technologies | 143 |
| August 16 | Calista | 55 |
| June 29 | StratumOne Communications | 435 |
| June 18 | TransMedia Communications | 407 |
| April 28 | Amteva Technologies | 170 |
| April 13 | GeoTel Communications | 2000 |
| April 8 | Sentient Networks | undisclosed |
| April 8 | Fibex Systems | undisclosed |

Cisco also prides itself on deal implementation. While typical technology acquisitions suffer a 40 to 80 percent employee attrition rate within two years, Cisco reports losing only 6 or 7 percent of its acquired employees per year. It develops clear criteria for whether or not a deal has been successful and closely monitors key data. How many managers have left? Engineers? What is the acquisition's current run rate (annualized estimate of revenues and earnings based on the current quarter's performance)? As soon as it closes a deal, a dedicated implementation team swarms in to integrate the company. Often keeping a full-time human resources team in place (with an open door policy), Cisco makes newly acquired employees feel comfortable by working through a new-economy rendition of Maslow's hierarchy of needs—water, food, safety, belonging, and esteem. They really don't mess around, putting needed resources in place and leaving little to chance in integrating an acquisition. However, in 2001 Cisco's ability to motivate and retain key employees would receive a major test, as the company faced macroeconomic pressures to trim costs.

This chapter examines mergers and acquisitions as a digital deal structure. The focus will be on how Cisco and other competitors in the optical networking industry, such as Lucent Technologies and Nortel Networks, have pursued an "acquire and absorb" strategy, continually buying young companies with promising technology to feed through their manufacturing, distribution, and sales pipelines. Other reasons why many new economy firms are pursuing mergers and acquisitions will also be examined. Finally, this chapter discusses what it takes to get a deal done in today's world—what are some typical steps and key considerations behind a merger or acquisition and what are potential pitfalls.

## M&A RATIONALES OF CISCO AND OTHERS

For decades economists have sought to explain why firms choose to acquire or merge with another firm. In the early twentieth century, most corporate managers explained their motivations for a merger in vague terms, citing a reason such as "expanding operations," or "achieving economies of a larger size," or "meeting the competition more effectively." It's likely that the real reason behind many of these early acquisitions was a monopolistic attempt to control the market.

However, by the 1940s, academics undertook more detailed analyses of M&A rationale. One research team spent eight years performing extensive case studies on more than 100 mergers. They discovered that the motives for the mergers differed between buyers and sellers. Buyers were interested in acquiring a new product or plant capacity, achieving a greater degree of vertical integration, or enjoying financial advantages, such as a stock price boost. On the other side of the deal, sellers wanted to save taxes, cash out their investment, or solve a management problem.[2]

As research continued, studies on M&A activity refined the notion that a larger company would enjoy lower cost structures. Economists suggested that "avoidance of duplicate selling and distributing organizations may result in appreciable savings."[3] Similarly, spending on advertising, research and development, and other fixed expenses and investments can be spread over a larger base of operations. Mergers and acquisitions commonly represent the fastest way to obtain these economies of scale. Likewise, executives have justified their mergers with revenue synergies, asserting that combining two firms will boost revenues through cross-selling opportunities, better promotions, and the like. Regardless of the specific motivation for the deal, most mergers and acquisitions have been grounded in the general belief that bigger is better.

Much remains the same today. Firms routinely pursue mergers with the intent of cutting costs or the unstated goal of controlling markets. However, it is worth examining a few acquisition rationales that have become especially important in the new economy. Specifically, this chapter will explore four types of acquisitions: (1) controlling new technology, (2) dramatically transforming a business model, (3) consolidating competitors in the wake of market turbulence, and (4) locking up synergies before it's too late.

## Rationale 1: Controlling new technology

New economy acquisitions often work differently than old economy deals. Companies are bought fairly early in their life cycle—sometimes with products or technology still in the trial phase—mostly for their future potential. For example, in December 1999, Nortel Networks bought a company named Qtera for $3.2 billion in stock. Qtera was a tiny Florida company less than two years old with no revenue and technology that was still being tested by potential customers. But Nortel was betting that it could keep Qtera's engineers and use their brains to develop superior optical networking technology.

Many of Cisco's acquisitions have followed a similar strategy. According to John Chambers, "When we acquire a company, we aren't simply acquiring its current products, we're acquiring the next generation of technology through its people. If you pay between $500,000 and $3 million per employee and all you're doing is buying the current research and the current market share, you're making a terrible investment."[4] Deal rationale for Cisco almost always involves what is yet to be.

In the early 1990s, while other networking companies were focusing on technology, Cisco perfected its relationship with customers. Chambers made customer focus the firm's top priority. Cisco listened to customer needs and provided them with exceptional service. As the Internet grew in popularity, Cisco moved early to establish online systems that customers could use to order and monitor product flow, keeping

Cisco close to its customers. Strong customer relationships provided a bedrock strength that allowed many of Cisco's later acquisitions to succeed.

As its stock continued to appreciate, Cisco was able to use this strong currency to buy new technology. Essentially, it was outsourcing its R&D department. It pushed the best technology through the rest of the value chain, continuing to drive up revenues and stock prices. Strong share price was the key—almost all of Cisco's deals were stock swaps, and it grew so large that the dilution resulting from any single deal was practically meaningless. It quickly brought a new company into the fold and then went after the next acquisition. Going forward, Cisco is likely to expand its internal R&D activities and emphasize other deal forms (alliances and minority investments), but acquisitions will continue to play an important role in Cisco's overall growth.

Cisco's strategy of using acquisitions to tap into new technology is best illustrated by its moves in the optical networking industry. To set the stage, by 1999 Cisco had fallen behind competitors in this market, which was becoming tremendously important. This is the story of how Cisco followed its serial acquisition strategy to gain a foothold in the optical networking market. Let's begin with a market overview.

## UNDERSTANDING OPTICAL NETWORKING TECHNOLOGY

Optical networks use light instead of electricity. They convey digital 1's and 0's as pulses of light that travel over thin fiber optic cables. Since light moves much faster than electricity, more information can be transferred per second. But it gets even better. Optical scientists have developed technology called dense wave division multiplexing (DWDM), which divides each beam of light into a different color (or wavelength), allowing many channels to be transmitted simultaneously. Each channel, carrying a different stream of information, is combined into a single beam of light that is transmitted through the fiber. At the back end, the channels are split out again and sent off to the right destination. DWDM networks are lightning fast, delivering over 6 terabits (the equivalent of about 4 million T-1 lines) of information per second.

The pace of technological progress in fiber optics is astounding. Moore's law successfully predicted that computer processing power would double every 18 months. Optical networks may move even faster. So far, the amount of information that can be transmitted over a strand of glass is doubling every nine to twelve months. As engineers are able to split light into more and more channels, the same beam of light can carry larger amounts of information. In 1996, a company named Ciena introduced optical technology that could split light into 16 channels. By 2000, firms were able to break light into 128 channels, and Lucent Technologies was experimenting with equipment that could handle 1024 channels. As this rapid progress continues, optical advances are emerging as the driver of change in the new economy.

A complete optical network solution travels through several different network layers: (1) long-haul transmission, (2) short-haul transmission (metropolitan), and (3) access. Each layer of the network presents different challenges and requires different technology.

Long-haul transmission moves data hundreds or thousands of kilometers at a time. This layer is the freeway of optical networking; bits fly through fiber optic glass across the United States or around the world. As a signal travels from San Francisco to Boston, for example, it begins to weaken around Denver. Therefore, a particularly important challenge involves amplifying a signal periodically to make sure it arrives at its destination with the same intensity and integrity as when it was sent. Historically, special regeneration equipment was needed about every 400 km, but new technology has made this process much more efficient. By carrying 128 streams of data on a single beam of light, telecoms only need one set of regenerators to amplify the light in Denver, not 128. Other technological advances are also improving regeneration. For example, Qtera (purchased by Nortel Networks late in 1999) has developed technology that allows optical signals to travel up to 4000 km without needing regeneration. As data arrives in Boston, some of it may need to be directly switched down to Atlanta. Wide area optical switches are used to direct signals between long-haul segments. Rapid long-haul transmission speeds require special wavelength routers to send each stream of light to the right destination.

Short-haul optical networks transmit data tens of kilometers. In dense cities with heavy data demands across town, it often makes sense to establish short-haul optical networks to manage local demand. Think of the long-haul carriers as 747s that travel from Chicago to Los Angeles, and the short-haul networks as American Eagle flights, taking passengers to smaller destinations like Santa Barbara. This type of optical networking presents its own challenges—a carrier no longer needs to worry about amplifying fading signals, but it must now route data to many more end users. While long-haul optical networks can concentrate on point-to-point delivery, short-haul networks need to weave a finer web that connects many different points in the city.

Finally, end users need to access optical networks. It's rarely economical for smaller customers to lay fiber optic connections directly to their computers. Instead, they will typically access short-haul optical networks with Ethernet, wireless, or another technology. These different access technologies all need a way to hook into the optical network, and many companies are developing solutions. In addition, a few players are preparing for the day when end users will hook up directly to optical networks, transmitting and receiving light instead of electrical pulses.

## OPTICAL NETWORKING VALUE ACTIVITIES

The optical networking market is expected to soar from $18 billion in 1999 to $50 billion or more by 2003.[5] Let's turn to examine the value activities that were competing for shares of that enormous market in 2000. (See Figure 6-1.) First, component manufacturers produce the raw materials for optical networking products. Telecommunications market research firm RHK estimated that the component market exceeded $5 billion in revenue in 2000. Specialized optical companies, such as JDS Uniphase, make chips, laser transmitters, and the other basic building blocks of optical networks. Other well-known electronics companies (Corning, Siemens, Ericsson, NEC, Hitachi, and Fujitsu) also make optical components.

In the second major value activity of this market, optical equipment makers combine basic components with R&D and engineering to develop the complex equipment that will encode, send, amplify, and receive optical signals. This stage is the heart of the market, with dozens of companies competing to develop different technologies for long-haul, short-haul, and access equipment.

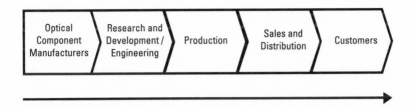

**FIGURE 6-1**
*Optical networking value activities.*

After completing the development and engineering process, optical equipment companies enter a production phase, running their products through a manufacturing, testing, and assembly process. Large companies, such as Lucent, typically do their own manufacturing, while others rely on specialized contract manufacturing firms, such as Celestica and Teradyne. Either way, they end up with finished optical equipment, ready for customers to buy.

The fourth value activity involves sales and distribution to optical telecommunications customers. At least three types of customers buy optical networking equipment. Broadband wholesalers, such as Williams Communications and Global Crossing, are large customers in the race to encircle the planet with fiber. Other telephone and data carriers—including AT&T, Qwest, and Level 3—are also big buyers of optical networking equipment. Finally, some of the largest enterprise customers are also buying their own optical networking products to quench bandwidth thirst.

These broadband wholesalers and carriers then compete to provide high-speed information to businesses and consumers. Communication networks have traditionally been used for phone calls and data transfers. Now, new forms of content, applications, and services—including digital video and hosted software—are flowing through communication networks, exploding the demand for high-speed transmission. Fueled by this enormous demand, optical networking has become a pivotal market.

## MAJOR OPTICAL NETWORKING PLAYERS

Not surprisingly the optical networking space is crowded. Three major players—Cisco, Lucent, and Nortel—battle throughout the value chain, while a host of other firms have focused more narrowly. Let's take a look at some of the players.

### Cisco

In 1984, Leonard Bosack, a computer scientist at Stanford, kept tinkering with a device that would link his PC to his wife's computer lab at the business school. When he finally got it to work, his wife, Sandra Lerner, thought they had a winning idea for a business. Bosack and Lerner mortgaged their house to raise Cisco's seed capital and bought a mainframe computer for their garage. They hired friends and relatives, promising to pay them later, if and when the company took off. Cisco sold its first network router—a machine that decodes the address of a piece of data and sends it to the intended recipient—in 1986. Cisco focused initially on sales to universities and various government agencies, but it soon started chasing large corporate customers.

Two years later, Cisco received a much needed cash infusion from venture capitalist Donald Valentine at Sequoia Capital. Valentine bought a controlling stake in the company and became Cisco's chairman. He soon hired John Morgridge, an executive at laptop maker GRiD Systems, to be CEO. Sales grew steadily, and Morgridge took the company public in 1990. That same year, Cisco suffered from a major internal rift. Morgridge and Lerner could not agree on Cisco's future strategy, and their clashes soon led to a battle for control of the company. Morgridge secured Valentine's support (as controlling shareholder), fired Lerner, pushed out Bosack, and consolidated his power.

Over the next few years competition intensified, and Cisco realized that it would need to offer more than just routers. Cisco decided to buy other companies. It acquired Crescendo Communications and Kalpana to launch a network switching division (network switches steer data to its intended destination). Cisco was still fairly small, and these deals changed the company quickly. Not every acquisition succeeded. Cisco's third acquisition was a company named LightStream. It couldn't get the product to work as planned and ended up buying StrataCom for $4.7 billion two years later to replace LightStream's products. Steady deal execution continued to broaden Cisco's menu of networking equipment, and by the mid-1990s Cisco reached $4 billion in sales.

John Chambers had been hired in 1991, after selling computers for 14 years at IBM and Wang. From the start, Morgridge groomed Chambers to be Cisco's CEO, and he finally took over in 1995. Chambers worked hard to successfully shift Cisco's focus from developing "cool technology" to delivering impeccable customer service. By the end of 1998, Cisco had emerged as the dominant player in data networking equipment, becoming the fastest company in history to reach a market capitalization of $100 billion (a record later supplanted by Qualcomm).

But toward the end of the 1990s, Cisco needed to shore up its long-term strategy. A massive shift in the communications industry was coming as voice, data, and other information networks began to converge. Traditionally, voice calls were sent over expensive, but highly dependable, circuits, while data was transported through packet-based systems—much cheaper but much less reliable. This new generation of communications technology promised to combine the best of both industries: a single optical network would transport voice, data, and video quickly and reliably. To capture its share of the new market, Cisco needed to move fast.

Cisco trailed its competitors in key technology areas. It lacked serious positions in the optical technology that telecommunications companies—such as Sprint, Qwest, and AT&T—craved to build their new economy networks. Two of Cisco's toughest competitors, Lucent and Nortel, had grown up on the voice side of communication networks. Since telecom companies had used optical technology for years to connect long-distance phone calls, Lucent and Nortel were positioned to improve the capabilities of fiber optics to support new economy needs. At the same time, they had built great relationships with telecom customers by supplying reliable equipment for decades. Undaunted, Cisco once again executed a series of acquisitions in an attempt to catapult it to the top of the industry. Cisco's moves into the optical networking market richly illustrate its classic acquire and absorb strategy.

### Nortel

In 2000, Nortel Networks was a dominant optical player, owning nearly 40 percent of all optical networking markets. Nortel has proved an extremely adept competitor, willing and able to move quickly to execute acquisitions. Indeed, one could argue that Nortel's strategy was to protect and expand its early lead by buying niche optical players before Cisco could get them. For example, in late 1999 it outbid Cisco, paying $3.2 billion to buy a start-up company named Qtera. Although Qtera had no revenues and no product on the market, it had developed long-haul technology that could send a signal 4000 km without regeneration. Nortel's high-priced stock—which quadrupled during 1999—had allowed Nortel to compete "stock-to-stock" with Cisco for optical networking acquisitions. Nortel has used this currency to grab a dozen optical start-ups, including component makers CoreTek and Photonic, and equipment makers Xros and Qtera. In July 2000, Nortel entered into talks with Corning to buy its fiber optics division for $100 billion. The deal collapsed, however, after two weeks of negotiations.

### Lucent

Lucent Technologies, having historically supplied communications equipment to AT&T and the Regional Bell Operating Companies, was a leader in the optical networking market. Spun off from AT&T in 1996, Lucent was restricted for two years from acquiring other companies. So it relied primarily on internal R&D rather than tapping into new technology acquisitions. To that effect, Lucent was plowing 11 percent of its revenues back into research and development, making optical technology a top priority. On the way it collected over 2000 optical technology patents. Freed from the deal-making restrictions in late 1998, Lucent began to augment its internal product development with some targeted optical acquisitions. Lucent's largest optical deals include Ortel, which supplies optical products for cable TV networks, and Chromatis, a maker of short-haul equipment. Lucent also announced construction of new optical networking labs, including two in China, one in Germany, and one in North Carolina. It doubled the capacity of its manufacturing plant and released over 18 new optical products in 1999. The year 2000 was a tough one for Lucent: it repeatedly missed earnings, lost its CEO, and saw its stock price drop from $80 to $15 per share. Early in 2001 Lucent announced that it was laying off more than 16,000 employees. Nevertheless, Lucent promised to compete fiercely in the optical networking market.

*Other players*

Not surprisingly, the optical networking market has also attracted fleet start-ups, such as JDS Uniphase, Sycamore, and Ciena. JDS Uniphase, which focuses on optical components, was moving aggressively to acquire other large component makers. Sycamore, which makes optical transport equipment and intelligent optical switches, launched an IPO in October 1999. Its stock rose 533 percent on the first day of trading, and soon the company was worth $25 billion. Later that year, it signed a $400 million contract with Williams Communications. Sycamore's top executives, Gururaj Deshpande and Daniel Smith, vowed not to sell this company early, unlike their prior venture, Cascade Communications (which they had sold to Ascend Communications). They were gunning for the three majors.[6] Another aggressive company, Ciena, focused on the long-haul market by developing DWDM technology that splits optical signals into hundreds of different channels. In addition to these players, dozens of other firms sprang up, attracted by the promise of industry revenue growth and Wall Street's willingness to reward optical networking companies. Table 6-2 lists some major players in each part of the market.

**Table 6-2 Selected Players in the Optical Networking Market (c. 2000)**

| Components | Long Haul | Metropolitan | Access |
| --- | --- | --- | --- |
| Lucent | Lucent | Lucent | Lucent |
| Nortel | Nortel | Nortel | Nortel |
| JDS Uniphase | Ciena | Ciena | Amber Networks |
| Corning | Corvis | ONI Systems | Geyser Networks |
| Alcatel | Alcatel | Alcatel | Kestral Networks |
| SDLI | Sycamore | Tellabs | Quantum Bridge |
| Pirelli | Cerent | Qeyton | PipeLinks |

## CISCO'S ACQUISITIONS IN OPTICAL NETWORKING

The optical networking market was important to Cisco for several reasons. First and foremost, it represented a huge revenue opportunity as demand for increased bandwidth pushed broadband wholesalers and carriers to buy more optical equipment and upgrade often. Second, Cisco needed to protect its relationships with telecom customers; if Cisco could not offer these customers the optical technology that they craved, then Lucent, Nortel, and others would keep infringing on Cisco's best customers. While Cisco enjoyed strong distribution and sales channels, it needed the optical technology to run through this established infrastructure. As before, Cisco elected to buy its way in.

It started small, acquiring a California company named PipeLinks late in 1998. PipeLinks had developed an optical access router, which could hook up end users to optical networks and carry both circuit and packet traffic. It gave Cisco entry into the access market, but PipeLinks was just the beginning.

By 1999, Cisco knew that it needed to make a more aggressive move. That May, John Chambers flew down to a technology conference at the Laguna Niguel Ritz Carlton to meet Carl Russo, the CEO of Cerent. Cerent made a product called the 454 that sat between long-haul optical transport and local access. The 454 connected several types of traffic and technologies, breaking a major bottleneck. Most importantly, customers did not have to tear out existing networks to use Cerent's cross-connect. Over 120 telecom service provider customers had bought the 454, including Frontier, Qwest, and Williams. With a sheepish grin, Chambers asked Russo how much it would cost to buy Cerent.

Russo did not want to sell the company to Cisco. He had been working hard on a public filing scheduled to take place in just a few months. His bankers at Credit Suisse First Boston were confident that Cerent's IPO would sizzle, and his managers were excited about going public. So Russo laughed off the offer. He continued to push the IPO forward over the next couple of months, filing Cerent's S-1 with the SEC in July. The IPO would launch in two months.

Chambers was relentless. On August 13 he came back to Russo with an alluring proposition: Cisco would match Cerent's expected IPO value by paying almost $7 billion for the company. According to one insider, this deal was valued with a single sentence: "CS First Boston had a gut feel that the IPO would give Cerent a $7 billion market cap."

This decision perplexed Russo. Many of Cerent's executives wanted to go public, and he had already filed SEC paperwork. Yet Cisco's massive offer—nearly $7 billion in stock—seemed too good for Russo to pass up. It wasn't just about money. An IPO was highly volatile and brought on new pressure, while a sale to Cisco was a sure thing. There were also several market factors that led Cerent to accept Cisco's proposal: accelerated access to existing markets, access to markets Cerent had not been pursuing previously, faster integration of other technology into the Cerent platform, and the ability to offer customers end-to-end solutions. By becoming part of the Cisco family, the doors to many decision makers' offices would be thrown open in North America—as well as outside the United States, where Cerent had not been targeting its sales efforts. The deal also gave Cerent ready access to Cisco's team of related technology experts—resources that Cerent otherwise would have had to find by partnering with another company or by developing internally. A deal with Cisco would probably create more value than an IPO, given how well the two companies complemented each other.

Russo realized that the deal made sense at this price: Cerent would enjoy Cisco's distribution and sales prowess and accelerate its access to key markets. It would receive a lofty valuation but be shielded from volatile public markets. Finally, Cisco promised that it would build an end-to-end optical network solution. When Chambers agreed to give Russo veto power over any employee layoffs, he agreed to the deal.[7]

Cerent's products offered a way to connect long-haul backbones with access networks, but Cerent used older SONET optical technology. Cisco also needed a product that it could use with long-haul DWDM equipment. While he was negotiating with Russo, Chambers had his eye on yet another optical company, Monterey Networks in Texas. Monterey had developed a router that could take each wavelength of light directly to its appropriate destination. As a less mature company, Monterey would command a much lower price than Cerent, $500 million.

Cisco announced both acquisitions on the same day: August 26, 1999. The Cerent deal stunned Wall Street; analysts were astounded at such a high price for a private acquisition. Yet Cisco never looked back, confident that the deals made sense for everyone. By purchasing both companies at once, Cisco could offer a breadth of products to customers, spanning both old and new optical technologies. Instead of assembling sales and distribution forces, the start-ups could leverage Cisco's distribution and sales support. On top of it all, Cisco got R&D expertise to create new optical technology.

Cisco was not finished—it still needed a position in long-haul optical technology. Late in 1999, Cisco announced that it would buy an optical division of Pirelli, an Italian tire and cable company for over $2 billion in stock. Pirelli was a leader in long-haul multiplexing—it sold the machine that could combine and split light into 128 channels, greatly multiplying the amount of data that could be carried over a single strand of fiber. Why did Cisco choose Pirelli? In short, the acquisition was a good fit with Cisco's other product lines. A carrier could eventually hook up Pirelli's long-haul products to Monterey's and Cerent's routers and use PipeLink's equipment to provide customer access, all backed by Cisco sales and service. Cisco was almost finished putting this puzzle together.

But at least one piece was missing: Cisco needed to acquire a short-haul optical player. Late in 1999, a company spokesman acknowledged that Cisco needed to address a lack of transmission products designed for networks encircling large metropolitan areas. He said that the company will "eventually decide if it makes better sense to build or acquire technology to fill this gap." It's not hard to guess which option Cisco chose. In May 2000, Cisco announced that it was acquiring Qeyton Systems for $800 million. Qeyton had developed a DWDM product for short-haul, metropolitan markets. It would be integrated with Cisco's other optical networking products to offer customers an end-to-end solution.

The optical networking market offers a textbook example of how Cisco taps into enabling technology companies to feed its sales and distribution pipelines. By purchasing Pirelli's, Cerent's, and Monterey's long-haul technology, Qeyton's short-haul technology, and PipeLink's access technology, Cisco acquired all layers of the optical network (see Figure 6-2). Cisco still had a long way to go. It would not be easy to cobble together these diverse technologies (and, in fact, Cisco retreated from Monterey's products in 2001, citing technical problems). It needed to digest these acquisitions, leverage its strong manufacturing and sales capabilities, and develop new customers, to aggressively grab market share from the other optical players.

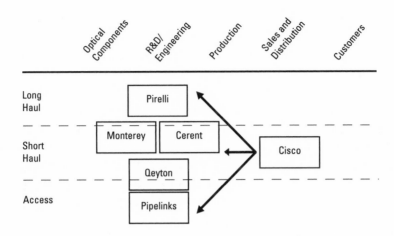

**FIGURE 6-2**
*Selected Cisco optical networking acquisitions.*

## Rationale 2: Transforming a business model

In addition to controlling technology, let's examine a couple of other acquisition rationales that have become increasingly important in the new economy. A second reason why firms are doing M&A transactions is to dramatically transform their business models. As competitive markets change at a fast pace, many companies find it necessary to execute a "right turn" in strategy. "Bet-the-company" acquisitions allow firms to immediately transform their business models.

In the middle of 1999, Carly Fiorina stepped in to become the new CEO of Hewlett Packard. She moved quickly to launch an aggressive marketing campaign—invoking the memory of HP founders Bill Hewlett and David Packard's obsession with homegrown invention. She spun off several businesses and executed a major internal reorganization that replaced dozens of autonomous product-focused business units with a handful of new divisions focused on customer needs.

But perhaps Fiorina's grandest vision was to transform HP's business model from a low-margin computer systems supplier to a higher margin e-services firm. The strategy carried a lot of risks. It assumed that value in this market would continue to migrate toward services instead of remaining with technology products. Sun Microsystems was betting the other way, insisting that it was first and foremost a technology company and resisting making major investments in building up services.

However, there was precedent for HP's strategic focus on higher margin services. IBM had built up an enormous global services business during the 1990s, which grew to account for roughly 40 percent of its profit by 2000. Even though IBM continued to lose nearly $1 billion per year on its PC business, it followed up many of these sales with consulting services. HP, seeking to copy this success, began to hire up to 200 consultants each month, although analysts criticized the firm's lack of a real game plan for business model transformation.

In September 2000, word leaked out about a major acquisition that would allow HP to execute its right-turn business model shift—HP was in talks with PricewaterhouseCoopers to purchase its massive consulting arm. If executed, the deal, valued at nearly $20 billion, would give HP 30,000 additional consultants. This increase in consulting horsepower would allow HP to help its customers optimize computing systems to meet individual needs. It would instantly transform the firm into an e-services provider. Two months later the deal fell through as HP badly missed fourth quarter earnings and saw its stock fall to a 52-week low. In particular, investors were spooked by HP's lack of warning on the poor earnings, which its CFO blamed on a new internal reporting system. HP called off the deal, needing to get its current business under control before it could swallow such a large acquisition. The deal with PricewaterhouseCoopers may have made sense, but the timing was wrong.

Buying another company can be the most effective way to transform a business model. While these types of deals often involve substantial risk, they also provide immediate assets that can be marshaled. On top of that, these deals can galvanize current employees to action. For example, after Nortel announced that it had decided to become an "Internet company," it took a $7 billion acquisition of Bay Networks to really get the company moving. As many firms struggle to reinvent themselves in light of the new economy, a major acquisition that signals directional shift may make sense.

# Rationale 3: Consolidating in turbulent waters

In April 2000, the stock of many Internet companies plummeted. As the Nasdaq continued to fall, analysts claimed that their long-predicted market shakeout was finally here. Internet executives and venture capitalists lay awake at night asking themselves, "What now?" In a number of cases, the answer would involve mergers and acquisitions.

Hard economic times have traditionally led to mergers, as companies band together to share resources and gain financial strength. In the new economy things were no different—perhaps only happening faster. Facing crowded competitive landscapes and unnerving market turbulence, weaker firms sought to get out alive. Stronger firms looked to purchase choice assets at bargain prices. Consolidating or "rolling-up" market competitors became a popular acquisition rationale in the hard-hit business-to-consumer Internet space, and other spaces followed. And marginal firms combined fixed assets in hopes of achieving economies that would yield a workable business model.

The online grocery delivery business is an excellent example. Louis Borders became famous for devising a complex inventory tracking system that enabled the rise of the mega–book store chain Borders. But Mr. Borders decided to jump from books to the much larger $475 billion grocery industry. He joined the Webvan Group, and used his inventory tracking background to develop a complex grocery distribution warehouse for online grocery purchases. These grocery warehouses contained 330,000 square feet of temperature-sensitive rooms for fish and milk and over 4 miles of conveyor belts for cereal and soup. Borders insisted that the model could transform the industry's economics—potentially even boosting profit margins from 4 to 16 percent. Hoping to redefine the way consumers buy groceries, Borders lured George Shaheen of Andersen Consulting (now Accenture) to run the venture.

But Borders and Shaheen had a problem. Webvan's economics were not working as they had hoped. Shaheen began to expand the company's market vision, pitching Webvan not as a grocery delivery company, but as a "last mile ecommerce infrastructure player" that would deliver books, videos, and more. As the numbers for the second quarter of 2000 surfaced, Shaheen realized that the company would lose nearly $60 million on sales of $30 million.

Part of the problem was due to rapid expansion. Facing competition from a host of other online grocery companies—including HomeGrocer, Peapod, Streamline, and Pink Dot—Webvan was spending millions of dollars to quickly set up infrastructure, promote its services, and capture key markets. Everyone else was doing the same thing, resulting in P&L hemorrhaging. Peapod nearly went out of business, and HomeGrocer lost around $50 million during the second quarter of 2000. As Webvan's stock price fell from the mid 30s down to well below $10 per share, Shaheen knew that industry consolidation was needed.

One day in May 2000, Shaheen picked up the phone and called HomeGrocer CEO Mary Alice Taylor about merging the companies. Webvan would issue 138 million shares of its stock—worth around $1.2 billion at that time—and keep most top management jobs. Six weeks later the deal was announced, and it closed in early September.

Although the combination did not guarantee success, it provided hope. The merger consolidated the two strongest players in the online grocery space, providing a national footprint and a presence in 13 markets. It eased the capital crunch that both companies were facing and allowed them to concentrate on proving unit center profitability instead of chasing rapid market expansion. Shaheen expected the merger to save the firms $200 million in capital investments and $20 to $30 million in marketing and other costs. Over the next few months, the industry continued to consolidate, with Peapod—a smaller online grocer in the Eastern United States—purchasing select assets of cash-poor rival Streamline in the Chicago and Washington, D.C., areas a few weeks later.

Firms in other markets have also pursued acquisitions to consolidate competition. For example, in the crowded online pet store space, Pets.com bought the assets of rival Petstore.com. Pets.com saw its stock languish from a February 2000 offering price of $11 down to $2 per share by the middle of summer. While "value compression" hurt Pets.com, it was perhaps worse for other pet store e-tailers hoping to raise capital in public markets. Launching a wave of market consolidation, Pets.com purchased most of Petstore's strategic assets, including key relationships with Discovery.com (affiliated with TV networks

Discovery and Animal Planet) and Safeway. Unfortunately, market consolidation could not save the firm, and Pets.com shut down late in 2000.

Expect to see continuing (and rapid) waves of consolidation as crowded new economy markets are later combined under financial or market pressure. By late 2000, "re-incubators" had formed to purchase distressed Internet companies—at bargain prices, of course. This new breed of digital acquirers sought to inject new management talent into these companies, rerig their business models, and put them out to sea once again with a more certain direction.

## Rationale 4: Locking up synergies before it's too late

In early 2000, Cynthia Ringo, CEO of CopperCom, needed to move quickly. Focusing on the voice over DSL market, CopperCom had developed technology that enabled service providers to transport 24 phone lines plus high-speed Internet access over a single copper pair. Ringo, however, wanted to do more than mere transport.

DTI Networks had built a "softswitch" solution for local telephony services. In fact, Ringo believed that DTI had built the only Class 5 switch (enabling local exchange switching, standard voice calling features, as well as new personalized calling features) other than Nortel, Lucent, and Siemens.

Both Ringo and Dennis Chateauneuf, CEO of DTI, felt that combining their two companies could change the business model for "voice over DSL" by allowing them to deliver integrated local telephony services, high-speed Internet access, and innovative calling features at a greatly reduced cost. A merger made a lot of sense.

There were two problems, however. Both companies were private, and neither could use cash or stock as a liquid currency to smooth the transaction. Furthermore, if Ringo and Chateauneuf waited until after one of the companies had completed an IPO, the odds were high that the other company would not be available.

Somehow, CopperCom and DTI needed to move quickly to lock up synergy before it would be too late. The CEOs started by getting relative valuations from five different investment bankers, although they had little intention of using an investment bank to negotiate and close the deal.

The process enabled them to establish value ranges for both companies within which the executives would feel comfortable.

The executives then met on neutral turf near the Dallas Airport with two board members from each company to hammer out final details. Not atypically, the board members postured, puffed, and then stalled at 1 percent difference in ownership of the combined entity. Ringo and Chateauneuf quickly huddled and agreed each would meet with their respective boards and tell them the deal was off. The CEOs heard the same response back from each board: "Are you crazy, we can't blow off this great combination."

The 1 percent difference was split down the middle, and Ringo and Chateauneuf had their pre-IPO merger. A driving rationale had been to get the deal done now, or get it done never.

# DIGITAL DEAL INSIGHTS

What lessons can executives learn from these companies? Let's conclude this and each of the next four chapters by summarizing key insights and takeaways from the cases. With that in mind, here are a few suggestions for a company's merger and acquisition deal strategy.

## Before you close . . .

Once a target acquisition is identified, what questions should an executive ask to determine whether or not to close the deal? As with marriage, it's not an exact science. But the odds of success can be increased with a mindful approach. For example, Cisco's John Chambers offers a five-step guideline to use in sizing up a deal:[8]

1.  Do the companies enjoy a shared vision with complementary roles? It will rarely make sense to buy a company that thinks the industry is moving in a different direction. Both companies should be excited about moving forward together. And each should bring something distinctive to the table.

2.  Can the companies create short-term wins for acquired employees? Since so much value in digital deals comes from retaining the talented employees, look for ways that the newly acquired employees

can feel good about the deal. New stock options, new responsibilities, quicker product-to-market time. Something right away.

3. Does the company's strategy provide a good fit that creates a win for all key stakeholders (shareholders, employees, customers, business partners)?

4. Are the organizational cultures similar? This is not an objective, but rather an intuitive, "sniff" test. Does the target feel right? Can top executives at both companies see eye to eye? Does the due diligence team feel good about the way the place works? Is the chemistry right?

5. Is there geographic proximity? For example, Cisco traditionally preferred to buy companies that are nearby to simplify integration. More recently, Cisco has relaxed this guideline—out of a set of 25 deals in 1999 and 2000, only 10 targets were headquartered in California. And the optical networking firm Pirelli may the toughest of all to integrate into the fold—it's a long way from San Jose to Milan.

Chambers insists that deals meet at least four out of the five criteria, and he claims to have killed as many acquisitions as he's made. While each company's deal closing factors may be different, it pays to develop a clear formulation.

## Use M&A for the right deal rationales

Acquisitions are complex deal structures that require enormous effort to succeed. It's almost always worth asking whether the deal has to be structured this way to work. For some deal rationales, such as controlling new technology, building new divisions, or consolidating competitors, acquisitions are probably the way to go. But in some cases, the underlying goal of the deal can be achieved much more easily through a minority investment or joint venture.

From the seller's point of view, valuation obviously becomes a compelling rationale for an M&A transaction. As discussed earlier, Cerent made the tough choice to sell its optical networking technology to Cisco just weeks before its IPO was supposed to hit the market. Other firms have come to the same conclusion. In October 1999, Sandpiper Networks, which develops software to accelerate Web page transmission, had already picked Goldman Sachs to underwrite its IPO. But Goldman soon found itself ousted, as Credit Suisse First Boston advised Sandpiper on a proposed acquisition by Digital Island, a San Francisco web hosting service. The deal initially valued Sandpiper at about $630 million, but by the time the market finished driving up Digital Island's shares following the acquisition's announcement, the deal was worth almost $1.2 billion.

Being on the sell side of an acquisition can be a smart way to go, even if a company has a chance to gain liquidity through an IPO. Of course, uncertainty in the future direction of an acquirer's share price adds to the complexity of this decision. Of Cisco's 27 acquisitions during 1998 and 1999, 23 of them were paid for with Cisco common stock (the others were paid for with a combination of stock and cash).

## Buy companies at the right time

Like plucking an apple from a tree, Cisco tries to wait until the company is ripe for acquisition. Too early, and the company gets overwhelmed by Cisco's corporate structure looking over its R&D shoulder. Too late, and the start-up has already established sales channels and customer relationships and becomes harder to integrate with Cisco's own channels.

One way to monitor when the time is right for an acquisition is to establish early relationships through a minority investment (which is discussed in Chapter 8). Cisco commonly invests in start-up technology companies, and future acquisitions can sometimes be predicted by looking at its minority investments. This is known as a staged-acquisition strategy. Consider its optical networking acquisitions. Cisco first invested in PipeLinks in 1997. It also held minority positions in Cerent and Monterey prior to acquisition. Sometimes at the initial minority investment Cisco has been able to obtain an option to buy the company in the future (at substantial premium to the initial investment valuation). In any case, timing is a critical variable—if at all possible, Cisco wants to acquire a company at exactly the right stage in the company's life cycle.

Once it is time to do the acquisition, move quickly. Cisco has been known to pay a premium so a target company won't feel compelled to shop the deal. Cisco's seasoned deal team and its reputation for paying the best price often leads to a fast transaction. When Cisco bought Lightspeed International, a network software company, negotiations mimicked the company name and took only three hours. Lightspeed did not even bother to tell other suitors it was for sale. The company did not feel the need to go anywhere else.

## Whiteboards that spell m-e-r-g-e-r

Recall how CopperCom's Cynthia Ringo and DTI's Dennis Chateauneuf locked up "now-or-never" synergies in a pre-IPO merger. There's a little more to the story that must be told.

Before the two executives and two board members from each company met to hammer out relative valuations, Ringo and Chateauneuf met together at a retreat in an attempt to harmonize what would be their respective postmerger roles. They started by going to whiteboards on opposite walls and writing down what each liked to do. The moment of truth came as each CEO turned around and went to examine the other whiteboard.

Ringo was ecstatic. "You mean you actually like to do budgets?" Chateauneuf was thrilled. "You mean you actually like to meet with investors?"

The two CEOs had devised a process that would meld people as well as technology. In a mid-size merger of relative equals, market synergy is important, but human synergy is vital.

## Flawless implementation in deal cleanup

After a deal is closed, the real work begins. The success or failure of a deal really depends on the implementation. Product lines need to be merged, sales forces need to be combined, and operations need to be streamlined. Key employees must be retained. Let's take a quick look at how Cisco has been able to implement so many of its acquisitions successfully.

The first step in successful implementation is knowing what a company wants out of the deal. Cisco starts by developing clear criteria for success; it knows the key variables to measure in the out years. For example, Cisco usually sets employee retention goals, both for engineers and the management team. Simultaneously, it sets revenue or earnings goals—such as "this acquisition should contribute revenues equal to purchase price within three years."

The second crucial step is to make the incoming employees feel welcome. Cisco has established a corporate culture that thrives on diversity and change. Over 20 percent of all employees come from companies that have been acquired. Former CEOs are usually left in charge of a core group (product development, engineering, or marketing), while sales and manufacturing are folded into existing Cisco departments. It is vital to get incentives right. Cisco has shunned golden parachutes, preferring to pay new employees with Cisco stock vesting over several years. (The economic downturn of 2001 pressured Cisco to consider passing out new option grants.) Clear communication is crucial throughout the process.

Finally, Cisco moves quickly. Companies establish patterns of behavior that are hard to change. Make the difficult calls early. Avoid the temptation to say what the target wants to hear, as an organization will pay for that later. Figure out executive roles before the deal is done. After buying a company, Cisco moves in the next day to change signs and make its presence known. The company often retains creative freedom, but it knows that things have changed. The importance of being direct and implementing change quickly cannot be overemphasized.

If a company is a serial acquirer, it has much to gain by emulating Cisco and having full-time professionals dedicated to making acquisitions work. Analysts, engineers, and managers assess deals, conduct due diligence, and close the transactions. Then, a full-time integration unit swarms in to reissue stock options, hang new signs, and make new employees feel comfortable.

# CHAPTER 7

# Joint Ventures

"We are very excited to expand our strategic alliance with NBC and with GE, whose tradition of technological innovation dates back to Thomas Edison. We have great respect for the quality of NBC's international newsgathering organization. Microsoft will contribute on the technology side—in understanding software platforms and the need for new graphical interfaces and tools."
—Bill Gates, Chairman, Microsoft, on formation of the MSNBC joint venture

The joint venture as a business structure long predates the digital era. In the 1700s, for example, international joint ventures targeted at North America involved English venture merchants partnering with banks, trading companies, or the crown to further common commercial interests relating to the colonies.[1] Throughout the twentieth century, joint ventures were used as a vehicle for international expansion and to pool and manage risk. Mining and petroleum exploration companies frequently structured JVs.[2]

Joint ventures remain a common deal structure in the new economy. This chapter examines how and why firms are using the joint venture structure to execute digital deals.

# MICROSOFT JVS

By the end of 2000, Intel may have made over 500 minority equity investments, but Microsoft was no business development laggard. In fact, Microsoft's corporate investment portfolio was valued at some $20 billion.

Microsoft was active in all types of digital deal structures—from acquisitions to minority investments to spin-offs. It acquired companies in diverse markets, ranging from Internet advertising (LinkExchange) to wireless communications (OmniBrowse) to traditional applications software (Visio). Microsoft made large-scale minority investments in cable giants—including AT&T ($5 billion) and Comcast ($1 billion)—as well as taking dozens of minority equity positions in smaller companies. It spun off Internet properties, such as its Web travel site Expedia. And in 2000, Microsoft faced another externally imposed corporate development "opportunity" arising out of a possible antitrust-related breakup.

This chapter tells a lesser-known story of the software giant's corporate business development activities—Microsoft was growing adept at forming joint ventures. By 2000, it had announced more than twenty joint ventures, making it a leading user of this digital deal structure.

Establishing a JV involves creating a separate entity in which two or more companies invest cash or other resources in return for equity stakes in the new entity. A JV usually builds its own management team (although it may "borrow" executives from the parent companies) and develops its own organizational resources. Although a joint venture investment may look a lot like a minority investment, the JV can signal a deeper level of commitment. When companies put assets and management time—as well as money—into a separate, shared entity, their commitment to the venture is likely to be greater.

In some cases, a joint venture may be a viable alternative to an acquisition, which arguably demands the highest level of effort and commitment. Sometimes a company is not for sale—lock, stock, and barrel. In other cases, antitrust or national laws relating to foreign ownership limitation may prohibit an outright acquisition. Even when a company is for sale, a suitor may not want to make the purchase, fearing postmerger integration side effects.

So as a rule of thumb, JVs signal less corporate development commitment than acquisitions, but more than minority investments. Of course, as anticipated rewards (or problems) associated with a deal change, the level of organizational commitment relating to any form of deal can ratchet up or down. A digital deal is like a mobile, with many moving parts that change over time. As soon as a deal closes (or even before), factors such as changing market conditions, technology surprises, or poor personal chemistry can alter the commitment level.

The previous chapter used Cisco as a lighthouse company to study the acquisition as a digital deal form. This chapter focuses on Microsoft's broad collection of joint ventures, while also discussing select JVs of other companies, to illustrate rationales commonly associated with the JV structure.

# MICROSOFT BACKGROUNDER

The history of Microsoft is well known[3]—so this backgrounder is painted with broad strokes featuring the company's business development activities. Bill Gates and Paul Allen, high school friends, founded Microsoft in 1975 to sell a version of the BASIC programming language. Gates moved Microsoft to Redmond, Washington (near Seattle), in 1979 and began developing operating system (OS) software.

Microsoft started business development activities early in its history with an acquisition and a licensing deal. In 1980, IBM chose Microsoft to write the operating system for its new line of personal computers. Gates acquired QDOS (Quick and Dirty Operating System) for $50,000 and rechristened it Microsoft Disk Operating System (MS-DOS). Personal computer manufacturers wanted to be compatible with IBM, and MS-DOS emerged as the standard operating system for the PC. Microsoft retained licensing rights for MS-DOS and began making application software to run under the OS.

In 1985, Microsoft, mimicking Apple's Macintosh graphical interface, introduced the Windows operating system. The dominance and ubiquity of Windows would become the most important driver of Microsoft's success. In 1993, the company launched Windows NT and signaled its intent to compete with UNIX, an operating system running on enterprise platforms. Microsoft's operating systems controlled an estimated 80 percent of the world's PCs, and its Windows NT/2000 server technology would slowly but steadily extend the company's reach from desktops to corporate networks.

In 1995, although late to the Internet party, Microsoft rushed in with an "embrace and extend" policy that impacted every area of the company. In the same year, the company launched MSN (Microsoft Network), an AOL-like service that would morph and remorph over the next five years. In 1996, Microsoft unleashed a browser war with Netscape by introducing the Internet Explorer based on technology licensed from Spyglass. Spyglass had exclusively licensed Mosaic (an early Internet browser) from the National Center for Supercomputing Applications at the University of Illinois.

Microsoft remained eager to move beyond the PC and engaged in an extraordinarily wide range of business development activities to meet this goal. It moved into interactive television by acquiring WebTV, developed television programming through the MSNBC joint venture, built wireless Internet appliances through a joint venture with Ericsson, and developed computer games by teaming up and investing in companies such as Red Storm and Digital Anvil. Microsoft also placed large minority investments in cable companies around the world to help position its software in the set-top box market.

Meanwhile, clouds of litigation hovered over Redmond. In perhaps the most widely watched antitrust case ever, U.S. District Judge Thomas Penfield Jackson ruled that Microsoft had monopoly power in the PC operating system market. Judge Jackson found that Microsoft had used its monopoly power to stifle innovation, hurt competitors, and harm consumers. In June 2000, handing down a decision with the potential to rival the significance of the breakups of Standard Oil in 1911 and AT&T in 1984, Judge Jackson ordered Microsoft to split into an operating system company and an applications company. Microsoft continued to fight, with company executives characterizing the ruling as an unwarranted and unjustified intrusion on the marketplace.

On an upbeat note, in 1999 Microsoft (together with Intel) was added as a "new economy" stock to the thirty listings comprising the Dow Jones Industrial Average (DJIA). This was the first time that stocks from the Nasdaq were included in the classic index. Paul Steiger, managing editor of *The Wall Street Journal*, remarked, "The changes we are announcing today will make the Dow Jones Industrial Average even more representative of the evolving U.S. economy, as the average—and the nation—enter a new century."[4]

Independent of any judgment or settlement that would emerge from its contest with the U.S. Justice Department, in 2000 Microsoft moved forward to reinvent itself on many fronts. Many of its actions repositioned the company with a robust array of digital deals. For example:

◆ Microsoft repeatedly tinkered with its organizational structure to retune itself to the new economy. For example, in August 2000, the company reorganized for the third time in eighteen months. It would now consist of five groups, three of which targeted distinct customer segments—consumers, business users, and software developers. The two remaining groups focused on platforms—one on the company's traditional Windows systems and the other on an emerging .NET architecture, which Microsoft held out as the future of the company.

◆ The mantra "software as services" reverberated around the Microsoft campus, suggesting that MSN and other groups would morph into an enabler of business and consumer services that could be run on any Internet device—even those not running a Microsoft operating system. MSN was becoming both a provider of specific content or services and a provider of software that would enable others to offer services.

◆ Expedia (Microsoft's Web travel service) was partially spun off in November 1999, going public and rising 382 percent on its first day of trading. Over the next year, Expedia's stock price followed a general downward slope, mirroring the performance of many consumer Internet stocks. Nevertheless, deals such as Expedia's IPO were seen as important not only for unlocking the value of Microsoft's Internet properties but also for retaining key personnel within the general Microsoft fold.

◆ Microsoft actively supported its proprietary technology for streaming audio and video. For example, the Windows Media Broadband JumpStart initiative encouraged providers of Internet audio and video services, as well as high-speed Internet-access providers, to support

Microsoft's Windows Media technology. Companies in the 35-member consortium included broadband providers such as Road Runner and content delivery technology companies such as Akamai. Microsoft had made minority investments in many of these companies.

◆ Microsoft launched the Microsoft TV Platform Adoption Kit (Microsoft TVPAK), a system that allowed network operators to merge Internet and television technologies. Microsoft TV (client software) would operate TV-connected devices ranging from Internet terminals to digital set-top boxes and digital TVs. Microsoft TV Server was targeted at network operators and would help manage enhanced television service.

◆ Microsoft would manufacture and market a video game console, dubbed XBox. In doing so, Microsoft was taking on major video game producers including Sony, Sega, and Nintendo. The console, which is planned to be released in time for Christmas 2001, will be built around a PC-based Intel Pentium III microprocessor, and will contain a hard drive and a DVD-ROM drive.

◆ Microsoft introduced MSN Mobile, a version of its online service designed to deliver customized information to interactive pagers and mobile phones. The launch was related to the company's acquisition of OmniBrowse. Microsoft decided to make a significant commitment to wireless Internet technologies.

◆ In June 2000, Microsoft formally announced a new computing platform, dubbed Microsoft.NET. The platform—which the company claimed was as significant as its previous move from DOS to Windows—was billed as core technology for next-generation Internet services. The move also signaled a potential business model shift where many Microsoft offerings (including its application software, for example) would be rented as a service.

# JOINT VENTURE RATIONALES

Part 1 of this book described market modeling as a system for analyzing and taking action relating to a company's deal strategy. Steps 3 and

4 involve building a deal database and analyzing the rationale behind each deal. Among other things, a deal database should include information relating to structural market-related dimensions such as: [5]

◆ Product or service vertical

◆ Geographic scope

◆ Customer segment

◆ Value web activity

Tracking this information provides a rich context for competitive intelligence and partnership analysis. To illustrate, let's use these four dimensions as an organizing framework for analyzing Microsoft's joint venture activity (see Figure 7-1, where the ventures appear in alphabetical order). Although many of these joint ventures could be classified under all four market-related dimensions, certain variables are featured in each deal. Take a closer look at how Microsoft has used JVs to penetrate new product and service markets, support geographic expansion, reach new customers, and stake out positions in technology-driven value activities.

## Penetrating vertical markets

Joint ventures can be a good vehicle for developing new products and services. Microsoft has established joint ventures to explore Internet-related service and product offerings in areas that include finance, automotive, cable programming, gaming, and even possibly gambling.

### FINANCIAL SERVICES

In May of 1999, Microsoft took a 2 percent interest in InsWeb Japan. This joint venture was created in 1998 by Softbank (a Japanese media and investing group) and InsWeb (an online insurance shopping guide) to bring Internet insurance products to Japanese consumers. Simultaneous with Microsoft's investment, Marsh & McLennan, a New York insurance broker and investment company, took a 20 percent stake in the venture. InsWeb Japan launched its Web site in November 1999 and offered auto insurance in the spring of 2000. Microsoft decided to join the venture because it wanted to develop and support financial service applications on the Web. As part of this deal, Microsoft could offer its

| Joint Venture | Market Dimension | | | | Deal Rationale | Deal Facts / Status |
| --- | --- | --- | --- | --- | --- | --- |
| | Product / Service | Geography | Value Web Activity | Customer Segment | | |
| Asia eBusiness | | Taiwan | | Enterprises | Provide regional business-to-business computer services | Microsoft (25.1%); Compaq (25.1%); Systex (49.8%) |
| Asia Global Crossing | | Asia | | | Influence broadband infrastructure in rapidly growing region | Microsoft (3.5%); Softbank (3.5%); Global Crossing (93%) —prior to IPO |
| BET.com | Online service | | Content creation and aggregation | Blacks | Gain access to demographic segment | Microsoft and partners (49.9%); BET Holdings (50.1%) |
| CarPoint | Automotive | | Extending ecommerce to factory floor | | Penetrate vertical market (automotive); participate in new value web activities | Microsoft (75%); Ford (25%) |
| CarPoint Japan | Automotive | Japan | | | Penetrate regional vertical market (automobile) | Microsoft (40%); Softbank (50%); Yahoo! (10%) |
| DreamWorks Interactive | Games | | | | Penetrate vertical market (gaming) | Microsoft (50%); DreamWorks SKG (50%); venture sold to Electronic Arts |
| Ericsson JV | Wireless communications | | Wireless application services | Corporate users | Beachhead hardware partner | Microsoft (30%); Ericsson (70%) |
| InsWeb Japan | Financial services | Japan | Retail insurance | | Penetrate vertical market (financial services); Develop partner for future deals in Japan (Softbank) | Microsoft (2%); Softbank (53%); InsWeb (25%); Marsh & McLennan (20%) |
| Liberty Media Group and UPC | | Europe | | | Regional market expansion; create market for products (services/set-top boxes) | Microsoft (25%); Liberty Media (25%); UPC (50%) |

| Name | Industry | Country | Function | Target market | Rationale | Ownership |
|---|---|---|---|---|---|---|
| Mobimagic | Wireless communications | Japan | Content creation and aggregation | Corporate users | Learn from Japanese wireless market; migrate applications back to United States | Microsoft (50%); NTT DoCoMo (50%) |
| MSN Israel | | Israel | Content creation and aggregation | Hebrew-speaking | Regional market expansion; sourcing of local content and services | Microsoft (49.9%); Internet Gold (50.1%) |
| MSNBC | Cable programming | | Assembly/aggregation: news portal | | Penetrate vertical market (news); support expanded role in digital TV | Microsoft (50%); NBC-TV (50%) |
| NineMSN | Online service/gambling? | Australia | Content creation and aggregation | | Learn about emerging market (gambling); expand geographical reach | Microsoft (50%); ecorp/PBL (50%) |
| SpeedNet | Wireless Internet access | Japan | | Consumers | Stimulate ecommerce and other Internet services in regional market | Microsoft (31%); Softbank (31%); Tepco (31%); Yahoo! (5%); others (2%) |
| Telmex JV | | Mexico | Content creation and aggregation | | Regional market expansion (Mexico) | Microsoft (50%); Telmex (50%) |
| TransPoint | Financial services | | Bill presentment services | | Penetrate vertical market (online bills); establish technology standard | Microsoft, FDC, and Citibank were partners in TransPoint; JV later acquired by CheckFree |
| Wireless Knowledge | Wireless communications | | Services for mobile workers | Corporate users | Positioning in a rapidly growing market | Microsoft (50%); Qualcomm (50%) |

**FIGURE 7-1**
*Microsoft's joint venture deal rationales.*

asset management software and .NET technology to the joint venture. It also allowed Microsoft to continue building a relationship with Softbank, a conduit into Japanese markets.

In another financial services move, Microsoft and First Data Corporation (FDC) created TransPoint, a joint venture to provide a system for electronic presentment of richly formatted bills over the Internet. The JV would also develop electronic payment and remittance capabilities. Initially, TransPoint was owned equally by Microsoft and First Data, but in 1998 Citibank joined the venture. The JV would help Microsoft incorporate electronic bill presentment and remittance capabilities into its operating systems.

By early 2000, TransPoint faced stiff competition. The venture had successfully signed up 27 companies—including MCI, Mobil Oil, and GTE—to offer e-bills through its service. However, aggressive competitors continued to develop electronic billing capabilities. A few months later, in a move reflecting industry consolidation, an Atlanta financial services company named CheckFree acquired TransPoint. As part of the deal, Microsoft and CheckFree entered into an exclusive five-year partnership for electronic billing and payment technology whereby Microsoft guaranteed a minimum of $120 million in revenue for CheckFree. Microsoft received a seat on CheckFree's board, along with an 11.3 percent stake in the company. Microsoft now had a smaller piece of a larger player in a deal form that morphed from JV to minority equity investment. The JV, however, had been Microsoft's entrée into the electronic billing space.

AUTOMOTIVE

In 1999, Ford Motor became the first partner in a new MSN CarPoint joint venture designed to "create a simpler, better way for consumers to design and order the car they want, when they want it." Ford was the world's largest producer of trucks and the second-largest producer of cars and trucks combined. Microsoft and Ford formed the venture to develop an online build-to-order system to link consumer order configurations directly with automotive manufacturers' supply systems. Consumers would ultimately be able to order a car model built to their specifications on CarPoint, Ford.com, and other automotive destination sites. They could also receive feedback on a car's availability and schedule delivery or service at a dealership. Microsoft would hold the majority stake in CarPoint, although Ford took a significant minority interest (25 percent) as the lead partner. Other automakers would later be offered positions in the venture.

Although the Microsoft-Ford relationship was not new (Ford had been a Microsoft customer for over 10 years and was part of the Microsoft Office Advisory Council), the CarPoint joint venture took their association to a new level. This partnership represented an attempt at nothing short of transforming the auto industry. It signaled a shift in the Internet's role in auto purchasing. To date, the dominant model had been for automakers and car-buying sites to use the Web to connect buyers to dealers (directly or indirectly) or to provide buyers with consumer research on cars. The new venture represented an effort to bring the Web onto the factory floor or "couple consumers to the back end."

A year later, however, Ford decided to hedge its bets. In August 2000, it launched an ecommerce initiative (FordDirect.com) with its 4200 dealers, enabling consumers to choose, price, finance, purchase, and schedule the delivery of a new vehicle. Ford would be an investor, but the dealers would have 80 percent voting control. The venture sought to eliminate the need for third parties by providing consumers with direct access to dealer inventories. Ford appeared to be responding to dealer concerns about being minimalized in the auto-purchasing process.

Microsoft also pursued the automotive market overseas. Before creating the joint venture with Ford, Microsoft had set up another JV with Softbank and Yahoo! to build an online car-buying service in Japan. The venture, CarPoint Japan, adapted Microsoft's CarPoint Web site for the Japanese market. Microsoft owned 40 percent of the new company, while Softbank owned 50 percent and Yahoo! 10 percent. Initially capitalized with $7 million, CarPoint Japan was another point of entry for Microsoft into Internet commerce in the Japanese market. Allying with Japanese-based Softbank, a major force in the digital information industry, gave Microsoft added credibility. CarPoint Japan continued to expand its services, adding used cars, financing, and insurance to its Web offerings. The site also provided used car assessment services.

In both domestic and international markets, Microsoft was establishing a toehold in the trillion-dollar automotive market through the use of joint ventures.

## CABLE PROGRAMMING–INTERNET NEWS

In 1995, Microsoft and NBC-TV, a unit of General Electric, part-nered to establish a 24-hour cable television news channel. Microsoft paid $220 million for a 50 percent share of MSNBC Cable. The two companies would spend $200 million over the next five years to expand the cable venture and create MSNBC.com, an online news service that utilized NBC's network of correspondents and video clips archive. NBC would operate the channel, relying on its network news organization and its affiliate news service.

The joint venture allowed Microsoft to stake out a news content posi-tion on the Internet. Although Web connections were slow initially, Microsoft was betting that rapidly increasing bandwidth connections would enable delivery of a richer form of media than was practical in 1995. In fact, Microsoft was actively stimulating the creation of addi-tional bandwidth, including, as mentioned earlier, billion-dollar-plus investments in cable providers AT&T and Comcast.

By 1998, MSNBC.com became the leading Internet news site, according to Media Metrix. MSNBC.com moved to form partnerships of its own. In late 1999 it partnered with iBeam, a streaming media dis-tributor, to offer live news feeds and archived video clips to broadband Internet users. (Microsoft had earlier made a minority investment in iBeam.) That same year, MSNBC.com expanded its interactive televi-sion to include polls, chats, and online reports during broadcasts of *Date-line NBC, NBC Nightly News with Tom Brokaw,* and the *Today Show.* MSNBC.com also introduced PencilNews—a news service for children that presented daily news coverage and current events in age-appropriate language—and launched MSNBC Russia, a Web site that provided news derived from Russian translations of top headline stories from MSNBC.

Microsoft had used the joint venture structure to make a major move into news services.

## GAMES

Chapter 4 discussed how Microsoft had been active in business development efforts to establish itself as a major player in online games. Among other things, Microsoft had aggressively expanded its Internet Gaming Zone, purchased from Electric Gravity in 1996. Microsoft also made minority investments in game content developers (for example, Digital Anvil and Gas Powered Games) and acquired Fasa, NetGames, Bungie, and others. (In late 2000, Microsoft announced plans to acquire Digital Anvil in a staged acquisition.) Microsoft also formed one prominent gaming joint venture, which fell well short of its planned potential.

In 1995, Microsoft and DreamWorks SKG established DreamWorks Interactive, a joint venture to create multimedia software for families, including adventure games and interactive stories. Each company put up $15 million in initial funding for the venture. Titles were based on motion picture and television concepts produced by DreamWorks. The venture's goal was to combine the creative expertise of DreamWorks with the distribution clout of Microsoft. In 1997 when Microsoft cut back on creating in-house entertainment content, it still remained firmly committed to gaming.

DreamWorks Interactive released games such as Warpath Jurassic Park, which featured head-to-head dinosaur fights, and Medal of Honor, a World War II–themed action game inspired by Steven Spielberg's film *Saving Private Ryan*. But the venture failed to live up to its potential, and in February 2000, Electronic Arts (EA) acquired DreamWorks Interactive from Microsoft and DreamWorks. Estimates of the purchase price were as low as $10 million. Over five years, DreamWorks Interactive produced just eight games, and only Lost World: Jurassic Park and Medal of Honor achieved hit status. Electronic Arts and DreamWorks had been working together on console games, and DreamWorks Interactive would become a unit of EA.

DreamWorks Interactive clearly failed as a Microsoft-Dreamworks joint venture. But why? Some analysts cited the adage that a good film often does not beget a good game. Or perhaps DreamWorks had not viewed games as a core business. It appeared unlikely that Microsoft, which was ratcheting up its efforts in content development in anticipation of its Xbox game console launch in 2001, would be eager to leave the JV. But perhaps DreamWorks Interactive was spending too much time thinking about Sony's PlayStation.

ONLINE GAMBLING?

NineMSN was established in 1997 as a 50-50 online joint venture between Microsoft and ecorp, a division of Publishing and Broadcasting

Limited (PBL), Australia's largest magazine and television company. NineMSN combined technology and content from Microsoft with content from PBL's Nine Network and Australian Consolidated Press. The site also featured homegrown versions of Microsoft's services such as CarPoint (automotive), Expedia (travel), and Investor (money).

Apart from the expansion opportunities into Australia, Microsoft may have entered the NineMSN venture for another reason: to learn about online gambling. Online gambling is extremely controversial in the United States, and, given Microsoft's legal problems, controversy was something that Microsoft did not want to associate with its brand.

Nevertheless, the NineMSN JV and its relationship with ecorp could provide a distant safe haven for Microsoft to learn about this "service." In May 2000, in the face of a proposed online gambling moratorium by the Australian government, ecorp announced plans to build a global online gambling enterprise on the island of Tasmania. There was no indication that Microsoft or NineMSN would be involved. Australian residents would not be permitted to gamble on the site nor would residents from jurisdictions where online gambling is prohibited. Instead, ecorp appeared to be targeting select Asian countries, which were fast becoming the hottest Internet gambling markets. For example, online betting on horse racing in Hong Kong was poised to emerge as a huge business.

Australian (and U.K.) companies began to position themselves as Internet betting capitals that some day could challenge Las Vegas casino brands. The Island of Gibraltar was becoming a "rock of wagering." Analysts estimated that online gambling revenues could surpass $3 billion by 2002, compared to the $10 billion Nevada casinos garnered from gamblers in 1999.[6] Internet gambling was a market Microsoft might want to learn about, albeit from a distance. Although this was not the stated intent of the deal, the NineMSN joint venture could be the teacher.

In sum, Microsoft has actively used the joint venture structure to enter, or learn more about, new markets including financial services, automotive, cable-news programming, games, and possibly even gambling. Most of Microsoft's partners were already established players in these verticals, increasing, but by no means guaranteeing, the chances of a successful Microsoft JV.

# Extending into new geographies

In addition to targeting vertical product or service markets, Microsoft has also used joint ventures to expand its geographic reach. This deal rationale is not new; classically, international joint ventures (so-called IJVs)[7] have been used to move rapidly into overseas markets. Microsoft has structured many regional initiatives to pursue the same motives.

## AUSTRALIA

The NineMSN joint venture with ecorp/PBL, a company with stakes in Australian broadcasting, magazine, and newspaper operations, provided Microsoft an entrée into Australian markets. As discussed earlier, the deal also offered Microsoft a relatively safe testing ground to observe developments in the Internet gambling market.

## ASIA

As previously discussed, Microsoft joined InsWeb Japan and CarPoint joint ventures in the Japanese market. In addition, the company has been active in several other Asian joint ventures.

Together with Global Crossing and Softbank, Microsoft established Asia Global Crossing, a joint venture company to provide network-based telecommunications services to businesses and consumers throughout Asia. The venture would construct a network called the East Asia Crossing to link Asian countries—including Japan, China, Singapore, Hong Kong, Taiwan, South Korea, Malaysia, and the Philippines—to Global Crossing's broadband network in the Americas and Europe. Global Crossing initially held 93 percent of the venture, while Microsoft and Softbank each contributed $175 million for a combined 7 percent stake. After Asia Global Crossing's IPO in October 2000, Microsoft owned about 16 percent of the venture. This Microsoft investment reflected a continuing bid to establish its place in broadband services as the Internet began to provide services ranging from phone calls to digital television. Microsoft saw Asia as a rapidly developing market.

Microsoft and NTT Mobile Communications Network (NTT DoCoMo) also established a joint venture in Japan. NTT DoCoMo was Japan's largest cellular phone company, having over 30 million subscribers in 2000. In August 2000, NTT DoCoMo's market capitalization stood at $260 billion, which made it the most valuable mobile phone company in the world. NTT DoCoMo offered wireless Internet-based services that allowed customers to make financial transactions and airline reservations. And the company's i-mode lime-gold handsets had become a fashion statement for Tokyo teens.

Microsoft and NTT DoCoMo took equal stakes in their venture, dubbed Mobimagic. The venture hoped to develop services for NTT DoCoMo subscribers, initially targeting corporate users with mobile telephones. However, when DoCoMo's services rapidly developed apart from Mobimagic, the venture needed to rethink what additional value-added services it would offer. Mobimagic was expected to play a role in third-generation mobile phones that offered multimedia content via the Web.

Microsoft saw Japan as fertile soil to learn about wireless technology. While announcing the Mobimagic venture in 1999, Steve Ballmer, then Microsoft's president, remarked that "the U.S. is the most far-behind major wireless market in the world." He wanted to establish a direct pipeline into Japanese technological developments and trends. Japanese consumers were using cell phones (and not PCs) to access the Internet. Microsoft intended to develop wireless services in Japan and then transplant appropriate technology and applications to the United States and elsewhere. However, DoCoMo had many eager partners, and Microsoft would have to work to get its fair share of attention.

In another Japan-centric JV, Microsoft, Softbank, and Tokyo Electric Power (Tepco) launched SpeedNet to provide low-cost, wireless Internet access to Tokyo-area consumers. The venture would use wireless technology to link users to Tepco's network of optical-fiber lines and then to the Internet. Each of the three partners held a 31 percent stake in the JV, which was seeded with start-up capital of $52 million. Other investors (including Yahoo! Japan) held 7 percent. The JV made a commitment to provide free Internet access to all schools in the service area for 10 years.

SpeedNet represented potential competition for Nippon Telegraph & Telephone (NTT), the former Japanese phone monopoly, which in 1999 had reorganized into three units. Given that DoCoMo (another NTT subsidiary) was Microsoft's partner in the Mobimagic JV, the SpeedNet deal certainly reflected an element of coopetition. SpeedNet would offer users a way to connect to the Web without using the phone lines of NTT East, a unit of NTT that charged for local telephone calls. Softbank and Microsoft also hoped to partner with other regional power companies to offer Internet access outside Tokyo. Microsoft was not looking for direct profits to come out of the ISP business, but wanted to stimulate the development of the Internet in Japan in order to generate ancillary application and service revenue streams.

Asia eBusiness was yet another Microsoft JV in Asia. Microsoft Taiwan, Systex (a systems integration company in Taiwan), and Compaq Computer Taiwan invested $100 million to establish Asia eBusiness. Microsoft and Compaq each held a 25.1 percent position, while Systex owned the remaining 49.8 percent. Asia eBusiness would provide Internet business services in Taiwan, developing and marketing business-to-business ecommerce applications, with an emphasis on the emerging Application Service Provider (ASP) market. Microsoft hoped to solidify its position in Taiwan, which had more than 4 million Internet users and significant manufacturing and software capabilities.

## EUROPE

Across the globe, Microsoft continued to structure JVs in several European markets. For example, in 1999, Microsoft formed a joint venture with Liberty Media Group and United Pan-Europe Communications (UPC), a Dutch cable company. Through this venture Microsoft, Liberty, and UPC planned to hold minority stakes in European cable companies and jointly invest in the broadband space. Microsoft and Liberty each owned 25 percent of the JV, with UPC holding the remaining 50 percent. Microsoft wanted to be the dominant provider of server and set-top box technology for the European broadband market, envisioning a new era for entertainment, information, and commerce services. It viewed cable as a key horse to ride in bringing broadband interactive services to Europe because most European telecom companies were working through deregulation issues and moving slowly.

One of the classic reasons for creating joint ventures is quick access to international markets. In 2000, however, even though Microsoft used several complex joint ventures to invest in cable assets, the company suffered from a regulatory pushback. For example, in a deal with head-spinning convolution, the Microsoft-Liberty Media JV sought to take control of Telewest, a large cable provider in the United Kingdom. However, the European Union antitrust authorities recommended against the Microsoft investment, insisting that the deal threatened competition in the digital TV market. In response, Microsoft agreed to cap its investment in Telewest at 23.7 percent and break structural links with Liberty Media.

## MEXICO

In 1999, Microsoft and Telefonos de Mexico (Telmex), Mexico's dominant phone carrier and Internet access provider, signed a joint venture agreement to create and operate what was planned to be the largest Spanish-language Internet portal. Microsoft and Telmex made a joint investment of $100 million and each owned 50 percent of the venture. In 2000, the portal was named T1msn.com and initially targeted Mexico, with plans to branch to other Latin American countries, including Argentina, Venezuela, Colombia, Chile, Peru, and Central America.

With the Telmex JV, Microsoft attempted to gain ground in the rapidly growing Spanish-speaking Internet market. Although the Microsoft Network was already available in Spanish, Telmex had regional knowledge that could generate superior local content. Telmex also brought other assets to the venture, including over 10.5 million phone lines, 4.1 million wireless customers, and 150,000 Internet subscribers.

## ISRAEL

In 2000, Microsoft and Internet Gold, an Israeli Internet service provider, launched a joint venture called MSN Israel, a Hebrew-language Web service based on the Microsoft Network. Internet Gold would hold 50.1 percent of the joint venture and Microsoft 49.9 percent. The companies planned to initially invest around $7 million over two years in the service, which would represent Israel's first international portal. Internet Gold had more than 40 percent of the Internet user market in Israel, and, in addition to local content, could provide business development and technical support for the joint venture. Furthermore, users of a Hebrew-language portal would extend beyond Israel. Microsoft provided technology and distribution rights to the MSN brand.

In sum, Microsoft had structured a number of joint ventures to extend its reach around the world. Some JV partners were major corporations such as NTT DoCoMo in Japan. Others were new players, such as Internet Gold in Israel, that had rapidly built market share in a regional market. Through its extensive web of joint ventures, Microsoft intended to expand its MSN, digital TV, and other services and technologies throughout the world. Recruiting and selecting the best JV partners were central to this effort.

## Reaching customer segments

The Internet has enabled and engendered combinatorial communities. Driven by the mathematics of Metcalfe's law (the overall value of a network rises exponentially with the number of users), groups of all kinds—from football fanatics to culture critics—have established gathering places. Ventures have targeted almost every customer segment and demographic, from life-cycle stage to ethnicity. A number of Microsoft joint ventures seek to penetrate important customer segments. Here are some examples.

### RACE AND ETHNICITY

In 1999, BET Holdings established a joint venture with Microsoft, USA Networks, and the interactive divisions of Liberty Media and News Corp. to create BET.com, a Web portal aimed at African-Americans. The group planned to invest $35 million in the JV, which offered email, sports, news, shopping, and travel services. BET owned 50.1 percent of the site. The African-American Web demographic was highly sought after (Blackvoices.com and NetNoir.com were other competitors targeting this space), as it was expected to grow from 2.8 million to almost 4 million households over the first year of the JV. BET's previous Web site, MSBET.com (an earlier BET and Microsoft JV), failed to attract desired traffic levels and was folded into BET.com. By June 2000, BET.com was ranked first in unique visitors among African-American sites. In November 2000, Viacom announced it would purchase BET Holdings (including the company's position in BET.com) for $2.5 billion in stock and assume $500 million in BET debt. This deal is a good example of how Microsoft uses JVs to access ethnic groups (another example is MSN Israel, the Hebrew-speaking portal).

## CORPORATE OR CONSUMER?

Joint ventures can also be targeted primarily toward either consumer or corporate users. For example, contrast two Japanese deals mentioned previously.

Mobimagic, the Microsoft and NTT DoCoMo JV, planned to initially target corporate users by offering mobile telephones that remotely access and update information at the office, such as work schedules and email. Over time, Mobimagic services may be made available to DoCoMo users.

In contrast, SpeedNet—the Microsoft, Softbank, and Tokyo Electric Power (Tepco) joint venture—would provide low-cost, wireless Internet access to Tokyo-area consumers. Microsoft was not looking for immediate profits (evidenced by the JV's promise to provide free Internet access to all schools in the service area for the next 10 years), but wanted to stimulate the broad development of the Internet in Japan (and generate ancillary revenue streams).

As stated in Chapter 3, using customer segment as a structural dimension for classifying companies and relationships is a good way to model markets and analyze partnership possibilities. This chapter shows how Microsoft deploys joint ventures to target customer segments at various levels of granularity.

## Value web activities

Microsoft's joint ventures can also be characterized by an activity in a market value web.

### PORTALS

Many of Microsoft's JVs concentrate on portal-centered activities, defined by geography, demographics, content, or technology: NineMSN (Australia), MSN Israel (Israel), Telmex (Mexico), BET.com (African-Americans), MSNBC.com (news), and Mobimagic (wireless). Microsoft viewed "portals" as a choke point in the online value webs of many market segments.

### INFRASTRUCTURE

In addition, Microsoft's JVs frequently sought to advance communications infrastructure and technology. Consider, among other deals,

Microsoft's involvement in the Asia Global Crossing joint venture that provided telecommunications services throughout Asia. This investment and many others in infrastructure reflected Microsoft's goal of enhancing its position in markets from set-top boxes to gaming.

### WIRELESS

Like many other companies Microsoft viewed wireless communications as a particularly attractive market. Microsoft formed a joint venture with Ericsson, a Swedish provider of wireless telecommunications equipment and solutions. The two companies would develop mobile email solutions for network operators. By combining their technologies—Ericsson's wireless application protocol (WAP) systems and Microsoft's Mobile Explorer (a scaled-down Web browser)—the firms planned to create handsets aimed at the corporate market. Ericsson obtained a majority share (70 percent) of the venture, which would initially provide email for cell phones.

In another deal, Microsoft and Qualcomm established Wireless Knowledge, a 50-50 joint venture created to meld computing and wireless communications. The venture hoped to provide wireless access to enterprise data and applications for mobile workers.

Through these joint ventures with Ericsson and Qualcomm, Microsoft was able to work with mature partners at the center of the attractive wireless market to test new services and business models.

## SUMMARIZING MICROSOFT'S JV ACTIVITY

By stepping back from Microsoft's long list of joint ventures, the following observations can be made:

♦ Microsoft's joint ventures involved international markets and partners more than 60 percent of the time. Regional expansion and exposure to developments in foreign markets were major drivers for Microsoft's venture activity.

♦ In almost every case, Microsoft became involved at the outset of the joint venture. In rare circumstances where Microsoft came in after a JV was established, the company commonly took a very small position in the venture. For example, Microsoft took just a 2 percent position in InsWeb Japan after joining the venture a year after it was established. Why do the deal at all? In part, because Microsoft was interested in building its relationship with Softbank for future deals in Japan and elsewhere.

◆ Although its ownership percentages varied widely, Microsoft rarely assumed control of its joint ventures. As seen in the InsWeb Japan deal, if Microsoft came in late, it might own as little as 2 percent. On the other hand, when Microsoft spun off an internal business to form a JV (as was the case with CarPoint), it kept a majority share. Many of Microsoft's JVs were 50-50 equity splits with one other partner. In a few cases (as with MSN Israel), Microsoft's partner took a slight controlling interest. Ownership percentages are influenced by foreign ownership caps that apply in some markets.

◆ Microsoft focused on pivotal activities in a value web, such as developing a regional portal (Telmex JV, for example) or demographic portal (as in the case of BET.com). In most cases, the JV partner brought distinct assets to the venture that Microsoft could not easily duplicate. Consider MSN Israel, where Internet Gold brought local Hebrew content as well as broad customer access.

◆ Microsoft often used joint ventures to quickly develop new technology or position itself to offer new services. For example, by 2000 Microsoft had entered at least four joint ventures involving wireless technology and communications.

## DIGITAL DEAL INSIGHTS

Having structured over 20 joint ventures, Microsoft offers a rich case study in how and why to use this deal form. To be sure, some of Microsoft's predilection for the JV may have been caused by antitrust problems—it's harder to get an acquisition cleared when a company is constantly lambasted for being too powerful already. However, much of the strategy behind Microsoft's joint ventures is applicable to both large and small companies. What are the key takeaways from this chapter?

## Smaller companies use JVs for international expansion

International joint ventures are not only for giants like Microsoft. Smaller companies can also use IJVs to quickly expand their global reach.

In December 1999, Ask Jeeves, a Web site answering plain-text questions, formed Ask Jeeves International (AJI) to deliver country-specific versions of its service. AJI would pursue global expansion by structuring a number of joint ventures with strategic partners to create a series of language-specific sites. For example, in February 2000, AJI established Ask Jeeves UK in partnership with Carlton Communications and Granada Media Group (the two U.K. commercial television companies). Ask Jeeves International owned 50 percent of Ask Jeeves UK. Carlton and Granada Media Group formed a new entity to hold the other 50 percent and contributed $62.5 million in cash and advertising to fund the development, launch, and operations of the IJV.

Later that year, AJI formed additional joint ventures, including Ask Jeeves en Espanol with Univision (a leading Spanish-language media company in the United States) and Ask Jeeves Japan with Trans Cosmos, a Japanese business-to-business network services company.

Rob Wrubel, CEO of Ask Jeeves, described what Ask Jeeves International was looking for in a JV partner: "We will focus on forming joint ventures with strategic partners that provide access to mass audiences, powerful knowledge of a country's consumers, and a keen understanding of the rapidly developing Internet marketplace."[8] Through these joint ventures, Ask Jeeves gained access to local markets, knowledge of local customers, cash, and media exposure.

## Selecting the right JV partners

In the predigital economy, the subtlety associated with selecting the right joint venture partner was often compared to that of selecting the right spouse.[9] As was discussed in Chapter 2, in the digital economy the number of players involved in a market (and options for partnership selection) have become much more complex.

Using the market modeling methodology outlined in Part 1 of this book, JV partners should be selected against the background of a market overview that identifies traditional, hybrid, and digital value activities, together with the players and existing deals relating to each of these value activities. Microsoft, for example, in selecting partners for regional portal joint ventures (Telmex, MSN Israel, NineMSN, and so on) wanted players in regional markets that could provide specific value activities such as local content creation and customer capture.

The softer issues of joint venture partner selection in the predigital world remain valid for digital deals.[10] For example, partners should bring complementary skills and resources and have a mutual dependency or need. Not everything is the same, however. Many joint ventures in the digital economy have ignored a classical warning against "the elephant and the ant" complex, which argues that partners should be of comparable size and sophistication. For example, while some of Microsoft's JV partners are large, others are less experienced, smaller players that have rapidly established positions in the new economy. At least within the context of a JV, the elephant has rarely squashed the ant.

## Why 50-50 JVs?

As noted earlier, many of Microsoft's joint ventures have been structured as 50-50 partnerships. This may be surprising, given Microsoft's traditional penchant for control.

In some cases antitrust or foreign-ownership caps may have limited Microsoft's ownership position. However, there are additional reasons for a 50-50 split. As indicated by the adage "A good marriage is not 50-50, it's 100-100," a successful JV requires extremely high levels of commitment by both parties. Equal power can reinforce and enhance commitment, because each venture partner assumes equal responsibility for success. Equal power can also support the autonomy of the venture's management team. The joint venture is different from most other deal structures in that management activity is often handed off to a separate entity. (This does not mean that in 50-50 ventures all aspects of control are handed off. NBC, for example, insists on editorial control and independence from Microsoft in the MSNBC joint venture.)

In the new economy, as in the old, a joint venture must be tuned to garner sustained commitment from partners. Sometimes a 50-50 split keeps everyone in the game.

# What a JV needs from its parents—anatomy of a failure

A robust joint venture adequately considers both the parents' and the child's perspectives.[11] Taking the parents' perspective implies that each partner appreciates the other's reasons for establishing the venture, how the investments are valued, and how the returns are distributed.

Taking the child's perspective includes assuring that the JV has the resources and support necessary for success. Sometimes parents can become too distant. In 1997, Intel and SAP America (a unit of German software company SAP) created Pandesic, a joint venture that offered hardware and software solutions for Internet commerce to small- and medium-size businesses. Pandesic's solutions were based on both parents' assets; it used Intel servers and a scaled-down version of SAP's R/3 business-management software, which was used by larger organizations.

In the summer of 2000, citing the inability to make the business profitable, Intel and SAP announced that they would shut down Pandesic and lay off all 400 of the joint venture's employees. The companies stated that adoption of business-to-consumer ecommerce solutions had been slower than expected.

Industry analysts also questioned whether Intel and SAP had provided the venture with the critical resources it needed from its parents. One Pandesic postmortem asserted that failure came from the parents' remote management styles. Pandesic may have had money, but not enough "love." One former Pandesic manager stated: "Intel and SAP were very hands off. In fact, we were trying to figure out how to leverage those partnerships."[12] Perhaps Intel was better tuned to providing the level of commitment required by a minority equity investment (discussed in the next chapter) than that required by a joint venture—at least this JV.

# When not to structure as a JV

Recall how Microsoft expanded its CarPoint auto-shopping Web site into Japan through a joint venture with Softbank and Yahoo!. In 2000, CarPoint wanted to continue its international expansion by opening operations in Canada and select European countries.

In Europe, Microsoft decided to reject JVs in favor of other deal structures. According to Gwen Weld, director of international business development for CarPoint: "I'm looking at different types of partnerships as well as different types of partners."[13] In Europe, dealer groups are the major players in the auto market. Multiple joint ventures would be awkward, and a single JV could not easily accommodate a very large set of partners. When the structure of a market is not concentrated and is highly decentralized, a joint venture may not make sense.

## JVs for nonblinking giants

In November 1996, ESPN (Walt Disney) and STAR TV (News Corp.) created a 50-50 joint venture called ESPN STAR Sports. In pooling content and distribution assets, the venture brought sports ranging from badminton to basketball to some two dozen countries of Asia, including India and China. Why did these historic competitors agree to work together?

For STAR, based in Hong Kong, sports content was critical as it sought to establish itself as the dominant player for entertainment programming, technology, and distribution throughout Asia. By 2000, James Murdoch, CEO of STAR, wanted to control the services offered via an interactive set-top box and digital television. Bruce Churchill, President and Chief Operating Officer for STAR, described the rationale behind creating the joint venture with ESPN as: "Both ESPN and STAR were going after the sports audience in Asia, and neither one of us would blink." Head-to-head competition would have led to enormous and redundant investments.

Joint ventures can be a good solution for two industry leaders who decide it's time to emphasize cooperation more than competition.

## Cultural rationales for JVs

This chapter has shown that many of Microsoft's international joint ventures sought partners that could provide cultural context, including regional knowledge and content. STAR TV as it expanded into regions such as India and China would learn just how important such a partner could be. When STAR began beaming programs such as *Baywatch* into India, local media warned of "cultural erosion." Reportedly (and curiously), Indians were less concerned about the exposure of cleavage than that of legs. An Indian court was even persuaded to issue an arrest warrant for Rupert Murdoch, News Corp. CEO.

As the 1990s progressed, STAR became much more sensitive to cultural dimensions of its programming. As part of a plan to enter the vast Chinese market, STAR established Phoenix, a joint venture with Today's Asia and China Wise International, to produce high-quality Mandarin-language entertainment, news, and sports programming. STAR would own 45 percent of Phoenix, which developed a number of locally produced programs. STAR had learned the power of joint ventures to help it be "culturally unobtrusive" as it pursued global expansion.

# CHAPTER 8

# Minority Equity Investments

*"We offer a certain halo effect when a leading company in the business says, 'Hey, we think this technology is important and we think this management team may be able to do something interesting . . . '"*
—Les Vadasz
President, Intel Capital

Corporate venture capital is not new. Long before the dawn of the new economy, companies such as GE's Equity Group were actively investing in other firms. So what's new about minority investing as a form of a digital deal?

What's new is the number of companies investing. By mid-2000, according to the Corporate Venturing Report, 350 companies around the globe were regularly making minority equity investments. Corporate venture capital was at an all-time high in 1999, reaching $6.3 billion, compared to $1.7 billion in 1998.

The number of deals completed by many of these investors has also multiplied. Consider Intel. In the early 1990s, Intel started a group that became known as Corporate Business Development (CBD), and each year invested modest amounts (rarely more than $1 million) in a half dozen companies. However, by the end of the decade, Intel had dramatically stepped up the pace of its venture activities, with the annual number of its investments exceeding 100.

In January 2000, CBD was rechristened Intel Capital, appropriately dignifying the vigorous investing activity that had been going on for the past three years. In April 2000, Intel announced it would invest an increasing share of its venture capital in international markets. Les Vadasz, president of Intel Capital, stated that deals outside the United States were about one-third of all investments in 1999, but could grow to be as large as 50 percent. At that time, Intel had invested in over 425 companies, a portfolio valued between $8 and $10 billion (although this value would fluctuate significantly during the remainder of 2000 as Intel's portfolio was not immune to the Nasdaq downturn). By the end of 2000, Intel had invested in a cumulative total of over 500 companies. During the year, Intel had arguably become the world's largest venture capitalist, having made over 200 investments.

By and large, Intel picked winners, although the Internet bubble of 1999 and early 2000 was a factor in this success. Companies such as Ariba, Broadcast.com, Broadcom, CMGI, Covad, eToys, GeoCities, Inktomi, iVillage, StarMedia, Red Hat, and VA Linux had more in common than just their triple-digit initial public offering price "pops." All twelve firms (and hundreds more) were companies in which Intel made a minority equity investment. Such investments were almost always made prior to the company's IPO. While a number of these firms saw their stock prices crash during 2000, others continued to enjoy impressive market caps.

Why did Intel build this huge portfolio of venture investments? Was it primarily looking for opportunistic financial gain tied to the new economy? Or were there strategic deal rationales underpinning Intel's minority investment constellations?

Although financial return clearly played a role in Intel's investment decisions, it often executed these deals for strategic reasons as well. This chapter studies Intel's partnership strategy by querying a database of Intel's minority investments and building deal constellations that elicit underlying rationales behind Intel's deals. Given the unparalleled scale of Intel's investment portfolio, large, medium, and small companies can learn a lot by studying this best-of-breed corporate VC in action. This chapter probes the who, why, and how of Intel Capital's investments.

# INTEL BACKGROUNDER

Intel researchers, under Gordon Moore, coinvented the integrated circuit (IC) and produced the world's first commercial microprocessor (the 4004) in 1971. The IC enabled computer manufacturers to miniaturize room-size computers that had relied on vacuum tubes for processing. Intel initially focused on developing silicon memory storage chips, designing microprocessors on the side. But as Japanese memory chip manufacturers intensified price competition, Intel began to lose money on memory chips.

IBM introduced its first line of personal computers (PCs) in 1981 and spawned the "Intel-Microsoft duopoly" by incorporating the two companies' products—Intel's 80086 microprocessors and Microsoft's DOS—into its initial PC design. PC industry standards quickly converged around Intel and Microsoft products, providing a foundation for what became market domination.

Demand for Intel microprocessors skyrocketed as more and more consumers demanded PCs. On the other hand, Intel's memory chip business continued to suffer, leading the company to exit the memory product business by closing factories and laying off thousands of workers. The company underwent what former CEO Andy Grove described as a "strategic inflection point" and transitioned completely from memory chips to microprocessors. Intel thrived during the next 15 years by focusing on PC microprocessors.

## Expanding the vision

By 1996, Intel was approaching yet another strategic inflection point. According to its annual report for that year:

"We know we can't wait for growth to come to us. We are responsible for our own future and work to make it as successful as possible by removing roadblocks to PC platform growth, developing preference for

Intel Inside® among PC users and supporting emerging PC markets around the world. Together, these strategies build value for our stockholders, which is, after all, our most important goal."

Intel intended to stimulate market growth for PC products, and minority equity investments were destined to play a major role. As the Internet blossomed, Intel's vision grew progressively grander, moving from a focus on the PC, to "visually connected PCs," to the "developer of building blocks for the Internet economy."

In November 1999, Andy Grove stated that although processors for PCs remained Intel's major product, over 50 percent of Intel's R&D was now spent on technology and applications relating to Internet servers. Grove listed other key strategic imperatives for Intel: network and communications applications, online services, Intel's own ecommerce activities, and a minority investment portfolio which, as mentioned earlier, would grow to more than 500 companies by 2001.

Intel continued to expand its product line. In 2000, its microprocessors included multiple brands such as Itanium (an emerging 64-bit architecture), Pentium III Xeon (servers), Pentium III (PCs), Celeron (low-end PCs), and XScale (low-power devices). Intel wanted to extend its reach beyond the PC to provide building blocks for new economy hardware including servers and mobile devices. Networking chips for digital communications and ecommerce services were also an increasingly important dimension of Intel's strategy.

Intel would execute its "building-block" vision through both internal and external resources. Internally, it created corporate groups to move into new markets. Externally, Intel's business development activities included many hundreds of investments, as the company became one of the world's largest venture capitalists.

## Intel's internal groups

Intel supported its expanded vision by building new corporate groups that included:

◆ Wireless: Intel positioned itself in the rapidly developing wireless market through silicon, software, and other technologies to respond to the clarion call for anytime, anywhere services.

◆ Online services: Intel invested over $1 billion in data centers, which would use thousands of servers to provide data processing, storage, and other computing services for companies that connect users to the Internet. Intel itself did not plan to become an Internet Service Provider (ISP), but would provide outsourcing services for ISPs.

◆ Communications products: Intel charged this group with bringing coordination and focus to a stable of communication-systems products including computer telephony and call center applications.

◆ Network communications: This group was responsible for developing network equipment chips to be used with communications products directing traffic across the Internet.

New corporate groups were almost always fueled through acquisitions. For example, Intel Online Services had been supported by the acquisition of Corollary, a supplier of multiprocessing technology based on the Intel Architecture. The Communications Products Group's momentum was accelerated by the purchase of Dialogic and Shiva. The Network Communications group was built around network equipment chips acquired through the purchase of Level One and Giga. However, minority investments also played a significant role in stimulating these groups.

## Building external ecosystems

From its start, "VC Intel" was designed to ensure strong market pull for the microprocessors churned out by new plants. Intel wanted to create demand for its own products.

The explosion of commerce, entertainment, and other activities on the Internet became a major focus of these efforts. In 1996, Intel began to dip into its "war chest" of cash reserves to make investments in new ventures that could stimulate Internet commerce and innovative digital content creation. By 2000, Intel had invested hundreds of millions of dollars in companies at the forefront of ecommerce and entertainment trends.

In his 1996 book, *Only the Paranoid Survive*, Andy Grove extended Michael Porter's "five forces" strategic analysis framework[1] by postulating a sixth force: the "power, vigor, and competence of complementors."

Grove defined complementors as companies whose well-being is tied to your own activities—"fellow travelers" with common interests. Analysis of this sixth force must include an assessment of whether each complementor would mutually benefit from market successes.[2]

Despite widely reported tensions between Microsoft and Intel, the two companies had been a classic example of complementor companies. Microsoft's software advances required more processing power from Intel's products, and Intel's microprocessors allowed for more compelling software that would, in turn, induce customers to demand more processing power. Each company's efforts drove demand for the other's products in a virtuous spiral. Grove commented to Intel executives that the day this spiral stopped would be the day he would start losing sleep.

That day eventually came. However, an expanded Intel vision for corporate development, involving a myriad of minority investments, would push its partnership strategy far beyond the notion of a dyadic complementor. The term ecosystem would become a catch phrase used inside Intel to describe an ever-expanding set of business development constellations.

## IMPLEMENTING A MINORITY INVESTMENT PLAN

There were prerequisites for executing a strategy where Intel would make hundreds of minority investments. Near the top of the list was cash or other currency.

Fortunately, spare cash was no problem for Intel. At the end of 1997, as Intel accelerated the pace of its investments, it reported net income of $6.9 billion on revenues totaling $25.1 billion. The company had generated nearly $10 billion in operating cash flow. Not only did Intel have an existing cash cache, it also had built a cash machine that for the balance of the 1990s would typically generate multiple billions of dollars of operating cash flow each year. With 80 to 85 percent of the worldwide PC processor market, the company had achieved dominant market position and fat (albeit shrinking) profit margins by taking billion-dollar production capacity expansion risks. No other microprocessor manufacturer in the world could reliably supply the volume of processor chips that PC manufacturers needed.

Intel, through its corporate business development–Intel Capital group—sought to stimulate continuing processor demand by going after what some viewed as far-afield pursuits. Nevertheless, Intel Capital had overarching goals for selecting minority investments and for extending Intel's ecosystem of companies beyond traditional suppliers, customers, direct competitors, and complementors. In addition to obtaining atmospheric financial returns (at times), Intel would make minority investments to:

♦ Get a continually fresh view into new technology developments.

♦ Establish new supply chain linkages.

♦ Broaden its "gene pool."

♦ Stage future acquisitions (a stated goal, although this would rarely happen).

♦ Move select R&D off its corporate balance sheet.

♦ And, above all, grow its marketplace.

On the other hand Intel offered numerous benefits to firms in which it invested:

♦ Marketing channels

♦ Relationships in an Intel family of companies with keiretsu-like support

♦ R&D

♦ Visibility

♦ Future financing support (possibly leading to an IPO)

♦ Endorsement

Even more important than providing VC-like money, Intel argued that an investment by the company would signal that an investee's technology, services, or content had a promising future. Les Vadasz, Intel's Senior VP for Corporate Development and later President of Intel Capital, commented on the company's investments: "I don't want to sound arrogant but we offer a certain halo effect when a leading company in the business [Intel] says, 'Hey, we think this technology is important and we think this management team may be able to do something interesting.'"[3] Vadasz went on to articulate the enlightened self-interest philosophy of investing that Intel promoted: "We work hard to try to convince everybody by example that what we're trying to do is a win-win equation. We're not trying to rob anybody of their opportunity; we're trying to help them. And that helps us."

Immersion, a San Jose, California, gaming company that developed force-feedback joysticks, received a less than 10 percent investment from Intel in 1997. Immersion president Louis Rosenberg testified to the approach that Intel took when making the investment:

"We were first very nervous about taking an investment from a corporate partner, especially because we're in a business of licensing our technology to many companies. But . . . Intel is so neutral [that] it's never been an impediment to us. In fact, it's been very positive to have some endorsement from Intel because they're so powerful in the industry . . . And they give us insights so we can make sure we're on the right track."[4]

Microsoft was also making minority investments in Internet-related companies, although the breadth of its portfolio did not approach that of Intel's. (See Chapter 7 where Microsoft was used to illustrate digital deals structured as joint ventures.) In contrast to Intel, Microsoft, at least during the 1990s, was viewed as a more controversial partner. Marc Gorenberg, a partner at Hummer Winblad Venture Partners, suggested that Microsoft could be a good partner for start-ups, with its market clout, capital, and huge distribution channel, but some in Silicon Valley likened an investment from Microsoft to making a deal with the devil. Neil Weintraut, another venture capitalist, said that "there are precious few instances in which Microsoft has invested in a company in a healthy way." He suggested that Microsoft often "borrows" ideas from the start-ups it invests in or undermines their business.[5] In 1997, a San Mateo start-up, Inktomi, accepted a $2 million investment from Intel and rejected the same from Microsoft. Inktomi CTO Eric Brewer reflected on Microsoft's tendency to scare potential partners more than Intel does. (However, later as a public company, Inktomi showed itself to be adept in building, losing, and regaining a relationship with Microsoft that involved licensing search technology to Microsoft's MSN.)

Not everyone viewed Intel's investment and growth practices favorably. A May 1997 *Wall Street Journal* article quoted Alexandre Balkanski, CEO of chip-designer C-Cube Microsystems: "They've [Intel's] got an incredible ability to take the value out of a market and suck it into Intel. They commoditize everything except the microprocessor itself."[6] Others (inside and outside of Intel) questioned whether Intel's investments fundamentally supported emerging companies or whether its burgeoning portfolio was more driven by financial return.

## Inside CBD–Intel Capital

Corporate Business Development managers at Intel had dual reporting responsibilities—directly to the head of CBD, as well as a dotted line relationship to the operating business unit that the manager supported. Operating business units included areas such as the Broadband Lab, the Laptop Group, the Server Group, the Telephony Group, and the Network Communications Group.

Aware of their operating unit's needs, CBD managers would source potential investments by attending trade shows or by building relationships with traditional venture capitalists in hopes of participating in their deal flow. (Intel's relationship with the venture capital community became complex, since the company was sometimes viewed as more competitor than partner. The fact that Intel rarely made investments as part of a staged acquisition—where Intel later bought the company—also hurt some VC relationships.)

Intel also launched a public relations campaign to get the word out that it was actively investing and would be a valuable corporate partner. In particular, Intel promoted the halo effect that could come from its investment. Around 1997, Intel became eager to reduce what it felt was a perception gap that Microsoft was much more active in corporate investments. So Intel cranked up its PR machine. While Intel had been relatively quiet about its investment activity, now almost every press release by an Intel-funded company featured a quote from an Intel executive. New deals flooded in from grassroots networking by CBD managers. At the same time, start-ups began to call in directly to Intel corporate offices as a result of its public relations campaign. By 2000, Intel Capital also aggressively promoted itself on Intel's Web site.

After finding a worthy investment candidate, a CBD manager would ask for a Deal Concept Meeting (DCM). Senior executives of CBD as well as an attorney would join the manager at the meeting. The manager provided a briefing on the target investment company, and if senior management liked what they heard, approval would be given to proceed. They assigned a three-person team to the deal: the CBD manager, an analytic support person from Intel's treasury group, and outside legal counsel.

The team then conducted due diligence on the company. If it continued to support the investment, then the larger group would reconvene for an Investment Proposal Authorization (IPA) meeting. During this meeting, the deal manager would present an overview of the company's strategy and competitive positioning. Treasury commented on why the valuation was reasonable, providing analysis such as metrics on comparable companies. Every investment was supposed to have both strategic alignment and financial viability for Intel. If investment authorization was obtained, Intel moved forward with the deal.

Intel invested in companies at all stages of the corporate life cycle— from early start-ups to publicly traded companies—both inside and outside North America. For private companies, Intel typically invested between $1 and $10 million and preferred to coinvest alongside other venture groups. It would rarely lead a deal, preferring to let another venture capital company take front position. Intel worried that if it led the deal, the investee company would push for a higher valuation, given the giant's deep pockets. Intel wanted a third party to negotiate price.

In July 2000, Intel stirred analyst controversy by including a $2.1 billion one-time gain from security sales as part of ordinary income for its second quarter. A significant part of the company's gain came from the sale of Micron Technology shares. Intel clearly sat on large capital gains, but the value of its portfolio would not always increase. For example, over three months ending July 1, 2000, Intel's investment portfolio declined from $10.8 to $7.5 billion, caused equally by the sale of financial assets and a decline in share values. Undaunted, Intel continued its aggressive deal making, assembling dedicated investment pools, such as a $250 million fund created to promote Intel 64-bit-related technologies. Boeing, Enron, and other companies participated as investors in this fund.

# INTEL'S INVESTMENT RATIONALES

Using both direct deal and constellation analysis, let's explore some significant deal rationales underpinning Intel's minority equity investments. This analysis is based on a deal database containing over 400 Intel minority investments. In particular, notice how Intel has selected deals involving complementary value activities that support its business model (recall that these are Steps 5 and 6 of the market modeling framework depicted in Figure 1-2). Another company can often replicate the strategic rationales behind many of Intel's investments even if it lacks the investment capital of an Intel (see Figure 8-1).

| Deal Rationales | Sample Investments |
|---|---|
| 1. Build indirect demand for core product through digital content | Quokka and SportsLine.com |
| 2. Replicate U.S. success elsewhere in the world | Sports.com |
| 3. Obtain home run financial returns | VA Linux, Immersion, Silicon Image |
| 4. Whip competitive horses for Intel's benefit | Covad, Northpoint, @Home |
| 5. Fuel an industry value web | Abaton, ChannelPoint, Communihealth, HealthAxis, Healtheon/WebMD, iVillage |
| 6. Achieve self-determination and exploit new market opportunities via coopetive investments | VA Linux, Esoft, TurboLinux, Red Hat |
| 7. Extend brand—downstream to the consumer | Eastman Kodak, Mattel (alliances); PictureIQ, MyFamily.com, eToys |
| 8. Extend brand—upstream in the enterprise | Extricity Software, Monterey Design Systems, SpeechWorks International, TimesTen Performance, Webline Communications |
| 9. Stimulate technology ecosystems to drive demand | 3Dlabs, Evans & Sutherland, Think3, Lernout and Hauspie, Nuance, SpeechWorks, eOriginal, Veridicom |
| 10. Build multibillion-dollar divisions through staged acquisition or outright purchase | NetBoost, Trillium Digital, Giga |

**Figure 8-1**
*Intel's deal rationales for minority investments.*

# Rationale 1: Building indirect demand through content

In 1995, Intel formed a Content Group charged with accelerating the growth of PC users' needs for advanced computer processing power. Ron Whittier, head of the group at that time, succinctly expressed the raison d'être of this group: "We want the entertainment and software industries to add an interactive component to their films, music, games and programs." Intel sought to spur creative development because it felt that content industries were slow in embracing new interactive technologies.

In the years that followed, Intel made a large number of investments in sports, entertainment, and other digital media. Many of these deals were intended to indirectly increase demand for high-end microprocessors and other Intel core technology. The goal was to create an irresistible pull for Intel semiconductors by amassing rich media. Sometimes, investees agreed to work with Intel to tune emerging products and services to developing Intel technology. In other cases, Intel was content to grow an overall market in which it enjoyed dominant market segment share. (Intel preferred the term market segment share as opposed to market share for antitrust-avoidance reasons.)

For example, consider some of Intel's sports content investments. In 1998, Intel invested in Quokka Sports to develop a framework for delivering sports-related content via broadband connections. Quokka was attempting to pioneer a "sports immersion" concept, hoping to change the way people experienced sports by using interactive programming delivered over the Internet. Quokka went public in 1999, and over the next year it strengthened its relationship with NBC (another investor) by coproducing NBCOlympics.com, a site that provided interactive digital content for the 2000 Sydney Olympic Games. By late 2000, Quokka, like other Internet companies now driven by a new metric for success, hoped to accelerate its path to profitability. The company faced an uncertain future.

Intel was also an early investor in SportsLine.com, a provider of sports news, programming, and merchandise on the Internet. The company's offerings included CBS SportsLine, GolfWeb, Soccernet, and Web sites for athletes such as Michael Jordan, Tiger Woods, Shaquille O'Neal, and Pete Sampras. CBS was a major investor in SportsLine. In 1999, Intel reduced its stake in the company, taking money off the table and locking in some of the gains from the investment. It was also confident that the site enjoyed adequate resources in CBS's arms.

## Rationale 2: Replicating United States success elsewhere in the world

In 1999, SportsLine.com formed a new subsidiary, Sports.com, which would provide content and ecommerce to sports enthusiasts throughout Europe. SportsLine bought one of Europe's leading sports Web sites (Sportsweb.com) from Reuters and incorporated this site into Sports.com. SportsLine would lend its resources and experience to accelerate the development of Sports.com. By October 1999, Sports.com averaged 1 million page views per day, reaching the mark in less than 100 days. In March 2000, Sports.com launched country- and language-specific Web sites in Spain, Germany, and Italy.

By investing in Sports.com, Intel hoped to stimulate the European Internet market. It felt that new content providers, such as Sports.com, would widen the appeal of the Internet and fuel explosive growth in Europe. Sports content had been a major driver of Internet growth in the United States. Through this deal, Intel planned to repeat the act in Europe, replicating success in another geographic region.

## Rationale 3: Obtaining home run financial returns

During the 1998-1999 period and into early 2000, Intel earned huge returns on its corporate venture capital initiatives. Many of its investments benefited from wildly successful IPOs. Although a number of these companies experienced substantial price downturns after the 2000 Nasdaq massacre, Intel still enjoyed large capital gains in its portfolio. It periodically cashed in these gains by reducing its position in a company. Some initial paper returns were staggering. For example, here's a sample of Intel's investments that went public during the last quarter of 1999:

◆ December 1999—VA Linux, a provider of Linux-based hardware, software, and services, set a record for the largest first-day IPO gain. The stock, initially priced at $30, opened at $299 a share and closed at $239.25. The gain was 698 percent. (VA Linux stock plummeted later in 2000.)

◆ November 1999—Immersion develops force feedback products, which take virtual information and then provide physical sensations to computer users—including realistic feel to joysticks, wheels, and other gaming peripherals. Immersion went public at an IPO price of $12 per share. By the end of the first day of trading, shares closed at $18.625, a gain of 55 percent.

◆ October 1999—Silicon Image develops semiconductors that enable high-speed transmission of digital video from PCs and set-top boxes to display devices. Its share price more than doubled to almost $27 per share on the first day of trading, leaving Intel (which owned 4.5 percent of the company) with a handsome paper return. It had purchased the shares via warrants exercisable at $0.35 and $3.50 per share.

Intel also held many of these investments for strategic reasons. For example, VA Linux added value to the Linux operating system, an emerging Windows alternative that Intel wanted to promote. Nevertheless, Intel's desire to achieve home run returns cannot be overstated. Without this carrot, undoubtedly Intel would not be as active in venture activity.

## Rationale 4: Whipping competitive horses

One of Intel's many strategic efforts sought to accelerate the use of broadband networks. To that effect, it took a minority position in a host of companies that stimulated broadband infrastructure and technology. Surprisingly, a number of these companies directly or indirectly competed with each other. For example, Intel invested in Covad and North-Point Communications, both of which provided Digital Subscriber Line (DSL) services for high-speed Internet access over phone lines. Intel also invested in @Home (later named Excite@Home), which provided high-speed Internet access over cable, DSL, and a proprietary network.

Why invest in competing companies? One reason was that Intel intended to whip all horses in a bandwidth infrastructure race, which included companies that supported any or all combinations of DSL, fiber, cable, wireless, and satellite technologies. It didn't really care which horse won the race in any market, as long as greater bandwidth drove demand for Intel's microprocessors (Rationale 1). Intel's broadband investments were global, running throughout North America, Europe, Asia, and elsewhere, and involved a range of broadband value activities.

## Rationale 5: Fueling an industry value web

The U.S. healthcare market is huge, comprising over $1 trillion or about 14 percent of the Gross Domestic Product (GDP). The market is also fragmented, inefficient, and deeply dependent on information exchange. Theoretically, it is well suited to benefit from Web technology. Intel wanted PCs and other devices running on its microprocessors to reshape the healthcare industry.

Figure 8-2 shows Intel's healthcare partnerships in traditional, hybrid, and digital value web activities. Among others, its investments included: Communihealth (technology for healthcare organizations

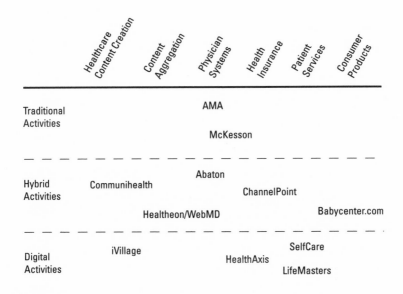

**FIGURE 8-2**
*Intel's partnerships across health care.*

involving consumer empowerment and e-health commerce); iVillage (women's health content); Abaton (applications for physicians to access clinical information, medication history, and to make prescriptions); HealthAxis (insurance using a digital insurance agent); ChannelPoint (solutions to streamline the insurance distribution cycle); and Healtheon/WebMD (Internet provider of information and services to doctors and consumers).

Why did Intel involve itself so deeply in health care? Here's the rationale as stated on its Web site in late 1999:

Quite simply, Intel is interested in helping consumers to find new ways to use personal computers, and increasing the number of people who purchase a PC to help manage their health. Today, personal computers are used for a huge array of applications: word processing, accounting, games, networking, email and the Internet; they are hardly used for health. The winds of change are looming: demanding consumers, the Internet, and an ailing health system are driving this revolution. In a consumer segment that amounts to 13.6% of the US GDP, Intel recognized the potential for growth of personal computers and launched the Internet Health Initiative . . . As consumers collect information, they turn to others to better understand how to use that information. In many cases, they take a printout to discuss it with their doctor. In most cases, they turn to interactive online communities to talk with other people that have experienced the same issues and more importantly the same emotions. These virtual fellows, who understand and sympathize with them, can share their experiences and provide them with support. Similar to accounting, personalization adds a new value dimension to online health seekers . . . Finally, consumers can attain the highest value when their physicians are connected at the other end of the wire. As physicians see that consumers are expecting more collaboration, using the Internet, many will also begin to use the Internet as a tool . . . [7]

This rationale spans virtually all activities of the healthcare value web—and so have Intel's investments.

## Rationale 6: Exploiting coopetive investments

*Coopetition* means simultaneously cooperating and competing with another business entity.[8] Sony signs a pact with Microsoft to link PCs and consumer electronics and then partners with Sun on a competing standard. AOL continues to use Microsoft's Internet Explorer browser long after it acquires Netscape. Harvard Business School's publishing arm sells case material to other business schools.

As mentioned earlier, Intel and Microsoft grew their businesses by being complementors—mutually benefiting from each other's market successes. Intel and Microsoft are also coopetitors; they compete while they partner. As coopetitors struggle to divide up total gains in a market, they may be able to extract a greater personal share by securing leverage over their partner. Intel's set of investments in companies promoting Linux-related technologies is a prime example.

Linux is an operating system (OS) that gained momentum with companies partly as a result of its reputation for being bulletproof—relatively free from system crashes. The software emerged as an alternative to Microsoft's proprietary Windows OS, which, of course, was running on a majority of the desktop PCs in the world.

Intel has actively invested in Linux-related firms. In 1999, it took a position in VA Linux Systems, a manufacturer of Linux-configured systems. Although VA Linux's IPO provided Intel with large paper gains, Intel also had strategic rationale for the deal: VA would port Linux to Intel's 64-bit architecture. In addition, Intel invested in ESoft, a developer of Linux-based Internet applications for small- and medium-size businesses, and took a stake in TurboLinux, an Asia-based distributor of Linux expanding into the American market. Furthermore, Intel invested in early shapers of Linux commercialization, including Red Hat Software.

In 2000, to further accentuate its commitment to Linux, Intel (together with IBM, Hewlett-Packard, and others) created the Open Source Development Lab in Portland, Oregon. The companies would each invest millions of dollars over several years in Web and application servers, database systems, and transaction servers. The lab would enable open-source developers to test programs for demanding enterprise environments.

Even though the Intel-Microsoft complementary relationship was decades old, Intel did not hesitate to put both technical and financial support behind Microsoft's competitors in its business development efforts. These coopetive investments were driven by an assortment of motivations, ranging from Intel's desire for self-determination to financial opportunity in emerging markets and platforms.

## Rationale 7: Extending brand—downstream

For Intel, brand extension meant taking product identification beyond its *Intel Inside*® ingredient branding. The company had launched the Intel Inside cooperative advertising program in 1991 to grow its brand equity and generate demand pull from consumers for PCs with Intel processors. As Grove described in *Only the Paranoid Survive*, the aim of the program was to "suggest to the computer user that the microprocessor that's inside his or her computer is the computer."

The Intel Inside advertising campaign was wildly successful. Under the cooperative program, Intel paid original equipment manufacturers (OEMs) roughly half of their advertising costs when they displayed the Intel Inside logo on their ads. The characteristic Intel Inside "bong" accompanied OEM television advertising and became widely recognized by consumers. Although Intel sold its microprocessors to OEMs—not to end users—it was able to increase bargaining power with OEMs by running the Intel Inside ads. Customers demanded Intel CPUs in their PCs. The Intel Inside program was described by the company as "the largest and one of the most successful marketing programs in the history of the electronics industry." Grove asserted that Intel's name recognition was on par with Coca-Cola or Nike.[9] By 1997, more than 60 OEMs participated in the advertising program, and Intel Inside spending had increased to an estimated $1 billion.

Grove lavished praise on Dennis Carter, one of the creators of Intel Inside: "With just two words—Intel Inside—Dennis has been able to simplify the complexity of microelectronics and create a level of comfort in our technology for millions of personal computer buyers. This is an awesome communications accomplishment." Indeed, the Intel

Inside program, along with NutraSweet's advertising program, became recognized as a classic example of successful ingredient branding. Intel's marketing prowess joined its operational expertise as a key corporate strength.

By the late 1990s, Intel wanted to take the Intel Inside campaign a step further. The company debated the extent to which it made sense to extend Intel's brand downstream into consumer products bearing the Intel name. To explore this further, Intel established business development deals with traditional consumer product players in markets such as imaging and toys. For obvious reasons, these digital deals with large companies, including Eastman Kodak and Mattel, were structured as alliances and not minority investments.

Intel and Eastman Kodak agreed to develop industry specifications for digital imaging within the computer environment. The agreement was aimed at making digital cameras easier to use and better at storing images. In 1999, Eastman Kodak introduced its Kodak Picture compact disc software product, codeveloped with Intel. The product integrated software with consumer photographs and, for example, let users combine personal photos with photographs of major twentieth-century events.

Similarly, Intel and Mattel formed a partnership to make "new generations of high tech playthings" based on computer technology. Mattel designers would work with Intel engineers to deliver play experiences incorporating toy-to-personal computer connections. The alliance demonstrated Intel's desire to explore alternative markets for its processor technology. Intel and Mattel developed the X3 Digital Video Microscope, which projected magnified objects onto a computer screen, as well as the Me2 Cam, a digital camera that placed content captured by a child into a cartoon environment on a PC.

Although the Kodak and Mattel deals were structured as product development and marketing alliances, Intel also took minority equity positions in companies that could help bring its name closer to consumers. For example, Intel invested in several companies in the imaging and toy space, including PictureIQ (digital imaging applications), MyFamily.com (online imaging communities), and eToys (online retail toys). Not all efforts were successful. By late 2000, eToys was running out of cash, and with investors unwilling to pony up more, eToys was forced to explore the sale of the company. In 2001, eToys announced it would file for bankruptcy protection.

## Rationale 8: Extending brand —upstream

As Intel positioned itself as a developer of building blocks for the Internet economy, it needed to extend its brand in commercial settings. Advertising campaigns began to convey a higher-end message than "Intel Inside your PC." Intel wanted to move its brand upstream, and as always, the company launched several investments and initiatives to start paddling in this direction.

Intel created a venture-capital alliance, the Intel 64 Fund, a $250 million investment vehicle to promote 64-bit technologies. Corporate coinvestors in the Fund included Compaq, Dell, Hewlett-Packard, and others. The fund's goal was to promote technology that supported solutions for Intel's IA-64 processor family (introduced in 2000). The Intel 64 Fund initially invested in five companies: Extricity Software (business-to-business application integration), Monterey Design Systems (physical design solutions), SpeechWorks International (speech-activated transactional services), TimesTen Performance Software (technology accelerating relational databases), and Webline Communications (customer service technology).

Intel selected the name Itanium for its first 64-bit chip to join Xeon, Pentium, and Celeron as Intel's heavily promoted brands. Intel expected that Itanium would help establish the company's position in the market for high-performance server chips, as Itanium machines were designed to run applications such as large databases and encryption programs much faster.

The Intel 64 fund extended Intel's age-old partnership strategy to the corporate market. Intel had years of experience using minority investments to help build consumer awareness and demand. Now it was deploying a similar strategy to stimulate a cadre of partners that supported its IA-64 architecture in the enterprise market. Intel refused to enter the corporate server market alone, but intended to assemble an armada to sail with it into these new waters.

# Rationale 9: Stimulating technology ecosystems to drive demand

As seen earlier in this chapter, demand for increasingly powerful Intel chips had been fueled traditionally by power-hungry software, often coming from Microsoft. While Intel's complementary relationship with Microsoft remained intact, over time Intel's portfolio of partners in areas such as digital content began to play a greater role in driving the demand for processors. In addition, investment funds from Intel's treasury moved beyond application software and digital content. Intel began to foster an ecosystem of enhancing and enabling technologies, pushing new developments in areas such as 3-D graphics, voice recognition, and Internet security. Some of these investments would drive demand for core microprocessors. Others would play a role in a new Intel, whose expanding core had been redefined to encompass Internet building blocks. A few of these companies would later be purchased by Intel and folded into this expanding core.

### 3-D GRAPHICS

Intel intended to seed the development of compelling 3-D graphics and actively invested in companies redefining how users would interact with PCs and other digital devices. Intel wanted to promote visual computing by improving 3-D capabilities. Unfortunately, a new generation of 3-D commerce and entertainment applications was slow in coming, testing Intel's resolve.

Intel invested in 3Dlabs, a supplier of semiconductors, boards, software, and related technologies for accelerating 3-D graphics on PCs and workstations. Intel next placed $24 million in Evans & Sutherland Computer (E&S). E&S developed systems for 3-D graphics and synthetic worlds used in desktop applications, simulation, digital studios, and digital theaters. Intel also invested in Think3, a developer of mechanical computer-aided design (MCAD) software used by designers to create 3-D models on a computer screen for objects from home appliances to specialty automobiles. Intel hoped these investments would drive demand for more processing cycles.

## VOICE RECOGNITION

Likewise, Intel made a number of minority investments in voice recognition—again driven by the potential of this technology to stimulate demand for higher-end processors. For example, Intel invested in a Belgian firm, Lernout and Hauspie (L&H), that developed speech recognition and language translation technology. L&H wanted to create voice recognition software that could control microwaves, televisions, and computers. It was also developing agentless call center services for ecommerce through iSail Solutions, an Intel-L&H joint venture that intended to support ebusinesses unable to afford human-intensive call centers. The L&H investment would prove troublesome, as the company was forced to file for bankruptcy protection, given bank pressure to repay loans after financial irregularities had been uncovered.

Intel invested in other telephony-based speech recognition software companies, such as SpeechWorks International and Nuance. Nuance, for example, worked to automate call centers in the financial services and travel industries. SpeechWorks technology could build voice portals for online services.

Speech recognition promised to have a greater impact than 3-D technology on hardware devices ranging from enterprise servers to consumer devices. Intel wanted to encourage its partners to tune their technologies to Intel's architecture. And a partner seemed to listen more carefully to an investor.

## INTERNET SECURITY

Reliable Internet security was essential for the growth of ecommerce and trusted web transactions. Intel created Common Data Security Architecture (CDSA) with IBM to promote applications for secure ecommerce. Intel also placed a large number of minority investments in security-related companies. Among other firms, Intel invested in eOriginal, which intended to make it possible to execute legally binding business transactions over the Internet through public key cryptography. It also invested in Veridicom, a developer of fingerprint identification technology, whose tagline was "Imagine a world where passwords, PINs, keys, and access cards are as obsolete as the vacuum tube."

Security was a vital element of Intel's Internet ecosystem because many applications and services would never succeed without appropriate assurance levels. Intel was building a portfolio of security investments that reflected its own enlightened self-interest.

# Rationale 10: Building multibillion-dollar divisions

Moore's law would not continue forever and was likely to become less relevant for the personal computer market. Intel needed to diversify its reliance on a PC microprocessor that had grown based on an increasing need for power. To broaden its product offerings, Intel decided to create new business units that could grow into billion-dollar-plus revenue centers. If Intel found a partner that was integral to one of its new business units, it would usually attempt to acquire the company outright. However, Intel structured some of its digital deals supporting this effort as staged acquisitions—a minority investment followed later by outright purchase. For example, consider three deals Intel made to support networking and communications, one of its target multibillion-dollar areas.

In 1998, Intel invested in NetBoost, a developer of software for increasing the performance of network applications by overcoming the limitations of firewalls and virtual private networks. Then a year later Intel bought NetBoost, stating that the company would complement Intel's communications chip products and enable companies to write software for Intel's networking chips.

Second, in 1999, Intel invested in Trillium Digital, which made communications software for high-speed data and telephone networks. The investment was the first for Intel's $200 million Communications Fund dedicated to support network-processing start-ups. The fund made equity investments of typically less than $10 million in companies doing work related to Intel's communications-chip business. Intel was now making a network processor, designed for use in equipment that routes data, voice, and video on computer networks. Then in 2000, Intel announced it would acquire Trillium for $300 million, and that Trillium would join Intel's Network Processing Group.

Finally, Intel also made a direct acquisition in networking and communications by acquiring Giga, a designer of high-speed communications chips used in optical networking and communications products. At a price of $1.25 billion in cash, the Giga deal was Intel's third largest acquisition to date. Intel continued to grow its networking communications division, focusing more on building a market presence than short-term profitability. Staged acquisitions and outright acquisitions both played a significant role in what the company hoped would become a major division.

## INTEL THE CONGLOMERATE?

Making hundreds of minority investments is an extremely complex endeavor. But Intel likes to portray itself as a simple and focused company. In a meeting with Les Vadasz, then Intel's Senior VP for Corporate Development, we once used the image of a conglomerate to describe his company's expanding business development efforts. Vadasz took offense at the reference, insisting that Intel was the most focused conglomerate he had ever seen.

In any case, Intel serves as a lighthouse example of how to place minority equity investments. It illuminates how companies can organize corporate ventures around a series of deal rationales driven by company strategy. Although expectations of blockbuster financial returns clearly played a significant role in both the scale and direction of its minority investments, Intel had also developed strategic rationales to guide its moves.

Over the next 10 years, Intel's focus will be challenged as it attempts to extend products, services, and brand to additional markets. Intel seeks to engage an ever-widening range of customers, geographies, and market value activities. The company's success or failure will be significantly influenced by its ability to select and execute smart venture deals that support strategic marketing initiatives.

## DIGITAL DEAL INSIGHTS

Whether a company is interested in taking money from a corporate venture capitalist like Intel or establishing its own investment division, there is much to learn from Intel's experiences.

# Taking corporate minority investment

As CEO of a growing company, should an executive take investment capital from a corporate backer? Certainly minority investment from an industry leader such as Intel can bring benefits that include new channels, R&D support, visibility, positioning for future financings, and endorsement. Here are some additional items to consider.

## VITALITY OF ECOSYSTEM

An organization may receive benefits from being part of an ecosystem or keiretsu-like network of companies within the corporate venture family. A corporate investor can provide introductions or even bring together executives from portfolio companies for formal meetings. (Cisco has been known to assume this role.)

In fact, a number of companies in Intel's investment portfolio have partnered with each other. For example, Styleclick.com, a 3-D ecommerce apparel site, joined with Intertainer, a program service company that provides entertainment over broadband networks. Styleclick and Intertainer would share revenues from the sale of the merchandise featured on Intertainer's services. Styleclick has also established an online partnership with iVillage (a women's Web portal and Intel investee) to integrate Styleclick's fashion content into iVillage's shopping infrastructure. However, it was unclear how much business would really flow through these partnerships. At the end of the day, the quality of partnerships matters more than the quantity.

Whether or not these intercompany partnerships are mutually beneficial depends on the vision and commitment of the corporate investor often at the center of the ecosystem. Will a corporate investor have the insight to identify meaningful partnerships between portfolio companies and the commitment to make something significant happen?

Furthermore, a number of new and traditional venture capital firms have also organized investment activities around developing an ecosystem of portfolio companies that provides complementary activities in a value web. For example, Blueprint Ventures, a San Francisco-based venture firm, has actively invested in next-generation communications infrastructure companies. A big part of Blueprint's strategy involves crafting value-added relationships through existing portfolio companies, institutional investors, and strategic affiliates. Similarly, Kleiner Perkins Caufield & Byers has long touted its ability to bring firms together in its "keiretsu" network.

Both corporate and private venture investors are using an ecosystem model. The core question is really whose ecosystem is more suited to a company's particular situation.

### THE HUMAN-INTERACTION QUESTION

How much ongoing quality attention will a company get from the corporate investor? Will a corporate business development manager be available for discussions on a regular basis? Will he or she be able to attend advisory meetings? Or will a traditional venture capital investor provide a more significant ongoing relationship? Will the business development manager who spearheaded the investment (and with whom an executive has developed good chemistry) be with the corporation in a year? Many corporate venture groups do not share gains from venture investments with venture teams. As a result some of the most talented people move on to traditional venture or other opportunities. In 1999, for example, managers from GE Equity's Internet investment team and Intel's Corporate Business Development group left to join traditional venture capital firms or establish their own funds. Of course, loss of key contact people can occur with any investment group—but the likelihood of loss may be higher with a corporate VC.

### THE TERMS QUESTION

Will special covenants be placed on the deal because an investor is bringing corporate money? For example, corporate investors may ask for an indemnification covenant in a deal agreement. Often taking the form of a side letter, the covenant may state, for example, that a company will not initiate litigation against the investor over intellectual property disputes. From the corporate VCs strategic perspective, this protection alone may be worth the investment.

### THE CACHET QUESTION

How shiny is the halo effect that comes with the corporate investment? For example, will customers, partners, and others see the investment as "Intel must feel that what you are doing is significant," or will the investment be viewed as "Intel gave *you* money too"? Will the cachet associated with an investment from a top-tier venture firm match or even exceed that provided from corporate money?

## THE CONFLICT QUESTION

Does a company want to do business with multiple competitors in the same industry? If so, taking money from one of them may put the company in conflict when working with the others. For example, one start-up developed a Web site where car owners could schedule oil changes and other auto services. In seeking seed funding, the CEO considered approaching Ford or GM's corporate investing groups, but realized that taking money from one manufacturer was likely to alienate the other. He decided to pursue traditional VC money instead.

Likewise, Chemdex, a company established to build B2B exchanges for chemical reagents, laboratory supplies, and other medical equipment, suffered from minority investment conflicts. Chemdex gave a 10 percent stake in the company (along with a seat on its board of directors) to a major distributor, VWR Scientific Products, which agreed to put its products on the exchange. However, following the deal, competitors of VWR refused to join the exchange. Chemdex's willingness to take this minority investment created conflicts with these suppliers, and Chemdex announced plans to shut down in March 2001.

## Making corporate minority investment

Although Intel was perhaps the king of corporate venture capital, many others coveted the throne. During 1999, venture investment by corporations comprised some 15 percent of all venture capital invested, according to the National Venture Capital Association. Compare that with 7 percent in 1998 and 2 percent in 1994. And this trend occurred during a time when the aggregate amount of venture capital was increasing.

From 1996 to 1999 the number of companies with venture programs more than tripled—from 49 to 163—according to Asset Alternatives. Even corporations known for caution when it came to venture activities, were swept up in the promise of staggering returns that had been associated with early-stage high-tech investments. Although caution returned after the Internet stock collapse of 2000, it seemed as though everyone had turned VC.

Here are key considerations for a corporation to consider in designing a digital deal strategy around minority investments.

## A RATIONALE FOR RATIONALES

Study the Intel method and follow it where appropriate. In particular, endeavor to connect investments to a set of deal rationales driven by organizational strategy. Doing so will strengthen the appeal of a company to target investees. To place too much emphasis on achieving opportunistic financial return will become problematic in the long run, even for sophisticated players such as Intel.

## WHERE NOT TO INVEST

Marketplace development investing, or funding areas that play a vital role in helping a company build its markets, has become increasingly common. This chapter mentioned the Intel 64 Fund, which has placed investments in partners that could help Intel develop and promote its emerging 64-bit architecture. However, an executive may choose not to invest in an area important in developing a marketplace if companies in that market are already getting adequate funding from other investors. For example, when the National Institute of Standards and Technology (NIST) in the United States analyzed where to invest to increase the export potential of the United States in a broadband world, a major consideration involved areas that would not get adequate funding from the private sector. Select investments that will make a difference in stimulating a company's markets.

## COUNTRY-SPECIFIC ECOSYSTEMS

If international and regional expansion is important to a company, an ecosystem perspective on a country-by-country basis can be extremely useful. For example, when Cisco wanted to understand what the company could do to drive broadband adoption in select countries around the world, it analyzed value activities and players in each region to see what was needed and what was missing. Cisco's partnerships or investments could then be targeted toward completing a vibrant ecosystem from its specific point of view.

## INVESTMENT FALLOUT

Be prepared to deal with fallout if investments are made in companies that are too close to each other. For example, when Intel invested in competitive local exchange carriers (CLECs) to stimulate broadband build out, it made minority investments in both Covad and NorthPoint. In doing so, Intel Capital ran the risk of alienating one or both of these players, which were going head-to-head for customers. A healthy ecosystem must avoid too much concentration in one value activity area.

## SMALL BETS AND DOUBLE-DOWNS

Consider making small initial bets and possibly following up with larger ones by participating in subsequent funding rounds or even via a staged acquisition. Intel continues to fund promising companies, often investing in multiple rounds. Chapter 6 demonstrated how Cisco has successfully followed a strategy of investing in a company, letting it develop without too much interference, and then acquiring the company at the right time. Cisco's role in providing attractive M&A liquidity events for emerging companies has endeared it to a number of venture capital firms, who view Cisco as less of a competitor and more of a partner.

# CHAPTER 9

# Advertising and Commerce Alliances

*"Pretty much anyone can be a content provider. . . . The challenge is to build an audience and that requires having great content under a great brand."* [1]
—Steve Case
Chairman, AOL Time Warner

On the seventh day of the new millennium, America Online (AOL) boasted the richest combination of content, commerce, and community on the Web. AOL's market capitalization hovered near $164 billion, making it the most valuable "media" company in the world. AOL was worth more than Time Warner and Disney combined! Looking at it another way, AOL was valued at some $8000 per subscriber, considerably higher than the $2000 to $3000 per subscriber valuation traditionally ascribed to cable companies. AOL enjoyed a valuation much higher than comparable companies. Why? Some thought an Internet bubble had inflated its stock. Others suggested that AOL's portfolio of brands, content, and business development partners justified the lofty valuation.

Then, three days later, AOL rocked the business world by announcing that it planned to acquire Time Warner. AOL would capture distinguished "old world" brands—including Time Magazine and Sports Illustrated—and gain the second largest cable network in the United States. *The Wall Street Journal* mused: "If an upstart online company can buy a traditional media company, merging the new economy with the old as never before, it raises the prospect that every industry could be reshaped as companies anxiously search for an edge in an increasingly competitive marketplace."[2]

This chapter focuses on AOL's business development deals, which had played a major role in driving up the company's valuation and thus allowing the unprecedented AOL-Time Warner deal. Immediately prior to announcing the Time Warner acquisition, AOL had built a $2 billion backlog (contracted, but not booked revenue) involving highly profitable advertising and commerce (adcom) deals.[3] Without this business development activity, the Time Warner acquisition would have been outside the reach of AOL.

This section also explores the deal rationales behind AOL's technology investments, especially ones that extended its possibilities for adcom revenue. In addition to analyzing AOL's adcom partnerships, the chapter also probes the extent to which other companies, both large and small, can replicate its success in this area. This case study demonstrates how partnerships are playing an increasing role in revenue generation, as successful companies sell to, through, and with partners.

# AOL BACKGROUNDER

Steve Case graduated from Williams College in 1980 and joined Procter & Gamble to market home perm kits. He then went to Pizza Hut, and after a short stint sourcing pizza toppings, he joined a video-game start-up named Control Video. Control Video later became Quantum Computer Services and repositioned itself in online content. In late 1989, Quantum Computer Services launched America Online, which later became the company's new name.

AOL went public in 1992. Case was named chairman and CEO in 1993, and that same year AOL unveiled a Windows version of its software. By the end of the year AOL enjoyed over 1 million subscribers, primarily in the United States. In 1995, it established a joint venture with

Bertelsmann, a German media firm, to form AOL Europe. (This JV was dissolved in 2000, after AOL announced its plans to acquire Time Warner, a Bertelsmann rival.) The next year, AOL started charging subscribers a flat rate for unlimited access, increasing the time users spent online and resulting in widely publicized service problems.

In 1997, MTV founder Bob Pittman became president of AOL Networks. Pittman focused on solving AOL's traffic problems and improving the company's sales efforts, which led to steady decreases over the next three years in marketing expenditures as a percentage of sales. In 1998, AOL traded its network services operations to MCI WorldCom (then WorldCom) in exchange for the CompuServe online services division and $147 million in cash.

By 2000, America Online stood tall as the largest provider of online services in the world. AOL offered subscribers email, conferencing, instant messaging, news, commerce, and entertainment, as well as general access to the Web. Revenues from Internet advertising and merchandising were rapidly increasing. AOL's brands included AOL, AOL.com, Digital Cities (local content), CompuServe (repositioned as low-end access), Instant Messenger, ICQ (communications portal), and MovieFone (telephone and online movie ticketing). AOL had also developed a stable of Internet music properties that included SHOUTcast, Spinner, and Winamp.

# CONTEXT FOR AOL DIGITAL DEALS

AOL's profitability depended on four primary metrics: subscriber growth and revenue, advertising and commerce revenue, network costs, and sales and marketing costs. AOL had over 23 million Internet service subscribers worldwide and about a 50 percent share of the ISP access market in the United States. AOL's network of Web properties (AOL.com being the most popular) was the most frequently visited destination on the Internet.

Just how profitable had AOL become? During the last quarter of 1999, Morgan Stanley pulled together a basket of 43 Internet companies with positive net income. AOL's net income alone accounted for 34 percent of the total profit pool![4]

As individuals spent more time online (in 2000, the average member lingered over one hour per day on AOL), the company started to generate a rapidly growing amount of advertising and commerce revenue. For example, during the year ending June 30, 1999, AOL earned $1 billion in advertising, commerce, and merchandising revenue, up from $543 million the previous year. By June 30, 2000, adcom-related revenue had grown to almost $2 billion. Although AOL did not disclose the cost of revenue by business segment, advertising revenue appeared to be yielding high gross margins, perhaps as high as 75 percent.

AOL also signed substantial advertising, marketing, and sponsorship deals. For example, in 1999 it signed a marketing agreement with First USA, valued at $500 million, to provide cobranded credit cards and financial services. AOL completed another deal with Travelocity.com (an online travel site) valued at $200 million. Aggressively building an experienced advertising sales force, AOL aimed to take a growing share of customers' network TV ad budgets. Some of these multiyear deals are examined later in this chapter.

In the late 1990s, AOL decided to outsource its highly capital intensive Internet access business to partners, such as MCI WorldCom. It also formed a broadband deal with SBC to offer DSL access in SBC's Pacific Bell, Southwestern Bell, and Nevada Bell regions. This announcement followed a similar deal with Bell Atlantic. Of course, the AOL-Time Warner merger signaled the reversal of this outsourcing trend, given the vast infrastructure owned by Time Warner Cable Systems.

AOL's costs continued to fall with scale, allowing the company to take more of its impressive revenues to the bottom line. For example, as AOL built its subscriber base, marketing expenses as a percent of revenues fell from 31 percent in 1997 to 20 percent in 1998, 17 percent in 1999, and 15 percent in 2000. This percentage was unlikely to drop significantly lower.

Even prior to the Time Warner deal, AOL had positioned itself through a series of partnerships and deals to deliver sustainable, quality earnings over the next several years from a massive subscriber base. With a growing cash cache of some $3 billion (end of fiscal 2000) and a respectable stock currency, AOL could also make additional acquisitions and minority investments to improve its positioning in technology, communications, and content.

# AOL DEAL RATIONALES

By 2000, AOL was extraordinarily active around the globe in a range of corporate development activities that included acquisitions, joint ventures, minority equity investments, and advertising-commerce deals. The company has used an array of deal structures in its adcom deals, including various combinations of up-front cash payments to AOL, direct investments by AOL, equity to AOL for placement on its sites, and revenue sharing.

Overall, AOL was driven by five primary deal rationales (see Figure 9-1):

1. Build a subscriber base.

2. Monetize its subscriber base.

3. Enhance content and service offerings.

4. Extend its reach through new technology.

5. Expand internationally.

| Deal Rationales | Sample Deals |
| --- | --- |
| 1. Build a subscriber base | |
|    a. By attracting partners' customers | Columbia House, Gateway |
|    b. Through brick-and-mortar partnerships | Wal-Mart, Blockbuster, United Artists |
| 2. Monetize subscriber base | Amazon, barnesandnoble, First USA, Drkoop.com, AmericanGreetings, Travelocity, Electronic Arts |
| 3. Enhance content and service offerings | Medscape, MarketWatch, PlanetRx, MovieFone |
| 4. Extend reach through technology | |
|    a. Mobile devices | Palm Computing, Tegic Communications, |
|    b. Through digital television | MapQuest, Hughes-DirecTV, OpenTV, TiVo, Liberate |
| 5. Expand internationally | Bertelsmann, Cisneros Group, Mitsui/Nikkei/DoCoMo, China.com |

**FIGURE 9-1**
*AOL's adcom-related deal rationales.*

This chapter especially emphasizes AOL's use of advertising and commerce deals to build and repeat a virtuous cycle of growing and then leveraging its subscriber base. This virtuous cycle is shown in Figure 9-2 and is described below.

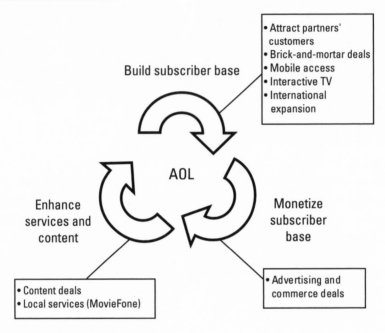

**FIGURE 9-2**
*AOL's virtuous cycle.*

## Rationale 1: Building a subscriber base

To attract lucrative advertising and commerce deals, AOL worked continually to grow its subscriber base. While it had taken the company 3371 days to reach its first million subscribers, by early 2000 AOL was adding a million subscribers approximately every 50 days.[5] To support subscriber buildup, AOL built a network of alliances.

### GAINING SUBSCRIBERS BY
### ATTRACTING PARTNERS' CUSTOMERS

AOL actively signed partnerships with other companies that commanded a large customer base that AOL could access. Some of these deals were exclusive; others were not. For example, Columbia House (a music club joint venture between Sony and Time Warner) had over 15 million members who purchased music and video products. In the years following the introduction of the CD, Columbia House thrived as consumers replaced vinyl collections with CDs. However by the late 1990s, Columbia House started to struggle and needed to find a new way to rekindle its business, perhaps as a more Internet-focused venue.

In 1999, AOL and Columbia House entered a three-year, multimillion-dollar alliance to cross-sell products through online and offline promotions. This was a nonexclusive deal, as Columbia House built similar business development alliances with Microsoft and Yahoo!. The marketing agreement included product bundling, direct mail initiatives, and comarketing campaigns. Columbia House guaranteed AOL a minimum number of new subscribers, provided cash payments to AOL, and developed cobranded promotions both online and offline. In exchange, AOL promoted Columbia House's video and music clubs on its Web properties, allowing Columbia to increase its membership base and identify opportunities to sell advertising.

The alliance enhanced AOL's plan to deploy a hybrid marketing strategy using both traditional and new media to grow its customer base. (In a sense, this deal foreshadowed the type of cross-promotion synergies that AOL hoped to gain from the Time Warner acquisition, which happened to be one of Columbia House's parents.) This deal allowed AOL to not only increase its membership base but also to monetize its current customer base with cash payments from Columbia House.

Some of AOL's other alliances secured access to a partner's customer base through complex deals where money and equity flowed in both directions. For example, in 1999 AOL invested $800 million ($180 million in AOL stock) over two years in Gateway, a popular PC manufacturer. AOL agreed to provide network operations, registration, billing, and customer service for Gateway.net, Gateway's Internet service (with over 600,000 subscribers). AOL would be promoted on the service. In exchange, Gateway would spend $85 million to market software and Gateway products on AOL's branded sites. The next year, the AOL-Gateway partnership continued to evolve as the companies worked together to introduce a line of Internet appliances.

## COMARKETING PARTNERSHIPS USING
## BRICK-AND-MORTAR VENUES

AOL has also partnered with brick-and-mortar retailers. These deals provide cross-selling opportunities for both partners, allowing them to promote their goods and services to new customer segments.

In 1999, AOL signed an agreement with Wal-Mart whereby AOL would promote Wal-Mart's Web site, and Wal-Mart would distribute AOL software in its stores. AOL gave Wal-Mart more than 20 million potential online customers, and Wal-Mart offered AOL access to 90 million brick-and-mortar customers each year. The following year, the partners extended their alliance to include international venues, such as the United Kingdom, where Wal-Mart's 240 Asda stores would distribute disks with AOL U.K.'s Internet service. Asda received preferred positioning in the AOL U.K. Shopping, Interests, and Lifestyle Channels as a food and drink retailer.

AOL also formed a three-year equity alliance with Blockbuster Video, the world's largest video chain. Both companies agreed to promote each other in stores, cyberspace, and traditional media. Blockbuster would give out AOL disks in their stores, play AOL's commercials on the in-store TV network, provide point-of-purchase promotional displays, and promote the service in direct mailings to its members. In exchange AOL would offer Blockbuster premier placement on AOL properties. The deal gave AOL access to Blockbuster's 40 million card-carrying customers in the United States. Like Wal-Mart, Blockbuster had a huge reach, having stores within a 10-minute drive of 60 percent of the U.S. population.

In late 1999, AOL cut yet another deal to capture customers in brick-and-mortar venues, this time with cinema chain United Artists (UA). Moviegoers would be able to get information and tickets for UA's network of theaters through AOL's online offerings. UA would get premier positioning on AOL MovieFone, the largest movie listing guide and ticketing service in the United States. (The UA theater chain alliance was the first one announced by AOL after it acquired MovieFone in 1999.) The success of online promotions for films like *Austin Powers—The Spy Who Shagged Me* and *The Blair Witch Project* had demonstrated that moviegoers were using the Web to get movie information and buy tickets. In fact, one in every five moviegoers used AOL MovieFone each week. UA was attracted to AOL for both its large cyberspace audience and its end-to-end logistical ability to provide tickets to the customer. AOL Movie-Fone became the exclusive provider of advance ticket sales for United Artists Theatres via the phone and Web. The companies would also offer the service over mobile Internet devices.

In line with AOL's push for presence in major brick-and-mortar venues, United Artists would distribute AOL disks at 300 theaters (with more than 2000 screens) in 24 U.S. states. These sites reached nearly 90 million customers annually. AOL sought exposure almost everywhere people went.

## Rationale 2: Monetizing a subscriber base

During the first quarter of fiscal 2000, AOL entered into more than 30 advertising-commerce agreements valued at over $1 million each. The company often structured the deals to participate in multiple, recurring revenue streams. Since the mid-1990s (when AOL started doing a significant number of adcom deals), its advertising and ecommerce revenue had been growing at an annual clip of 100 percent, and at the end of fiscal 2000 comprised almost 30 percent of the company's revenues.

Since AOL owned multiple Internet brands—including AOL (its private online service) and AOL.com (its Web site)—some of its deals carved off individual AOL brands, allowing it to sign deals with several competitors in a single market. Consider the following:

In December 1997, barnesandnoble.com and AOL expanded their online relationship. AOL would receive payments totaling $40 million over the four-year agreement to promote the bookseller's site exclusively on AOL's private online service. Earlier that same year, AOL had signed an exclusive deal with Amazon.com on AOL's Web site, AOL.com. Amazon and AOL established a three-year promotional agreement where AOL received $19 million with the possibility of additional payments if Amazon's revenues exceeded specified thresholds. Amazon would receive an "above-the-fold" front-screen button (visible without scrolling down) on the AOL.com homepage, linking users directly to Amazon's site. By separating its brands, AOL could sign lucrative deals with both rivals.

In February 1999, AOL announced an exclusive five-year deal with Bank One's First USA unit that was worth as much as a staggering $500 million. First USA would be the sole marketer of Visa and MasterCard credit cards on all of AOL's brands, including AOL, AOL.com, Digital Cities, and CompuServe. AOL would receive an initial up-front payment, in addition to performance payments based on customer acquisition benchmarks. Although AOL did not disclose the size of the up-front cash component, some analysts estimated the amount at $60 to $90 million. AOL would also receive a bounty per customer acquired and a percentage of the monthly credit balance. The credit balance payments represented a high-margin annuity revenue stream for AOL—the holy grail of corporate valuation. In addition to customer access, AOL had offered up its brand in the deal, as the credit cards would be cobranded AOL-First USA. First USA had been a partner of AOL's since 1996, but its contract was due to expire in May 1999. This new agreement suggested that AOL had overdelivered against the earlier contract.

AOL signed many other notable deals. For example, in 1999 Drkoop.com became the main healthcare-related content partner for five AOL brands in a four-year strategic alliance. Drkoop.com would pay $89 million to AOL, and in return it planned to work with AOL's 600+ sales-force to build advertising and ecommerce opportunities across all Drkoop.com properties.

However, by April 2000, Drkoop.com needed life support of its own and approached AOL for help. Not unlike other Internet companies, Drkoop was blazing through its cash and needed to renegotiate the terms of its AOL agreement. AOL agreed to bail out its partner, taking 3.5 million shares of Drkoop in lieu of cash payments, which gave AOL around 10 percent of the company and made it the third-largest shareholder.[6] Drkoop had only paid AOL about one-third of the original cash contract.

The Drkoop-AOL advertising commerce deal raised two general questions. How much softness existed in the advertising-commerce deal backlogs of companies such as AOL or Yahoo!? And how much was too much to pay for placement and promotion in Internet adcom deals? These questions are revisited at the end of this chapter.

Even though the specter of "backlog softness" continued to haunt AOL, the company moved to monetize its subscriber base across an even broader range of products and services involving many hundreds of companies. Some of the larger deals included the following:

◆ AmericanGreetings.com would provide greetings products on an exclusive basis across all AOL brands in a $100 million deal that would last five and a half years. AOL subscribers gained access to free online greetings products.

◆ AOL and Travelocity entered into a multiyear content and commerce alliance guaranteeing AOL up to $200 million over five years. Travelocity became the exclusive travel reservation engine integrated into all AOL properties.

◆ In late 1999, Electronic Arts (EA), a leading game software developer, forged an $81 million deal with AOL that would support AOL's game site. The partnership was likely to have significant repercussions on the online interactive entertainment industry.[7] In addition, Electronic Arts announced the spin-off of a newly created Internet division called EA.com, which would be partially owned by AOL.

### AN AOL ADCOM DEAL

Let's take a look at the AOL-EA deal in closer detail to demonstrate the subtlety and reach of AOL's adcom alliances.[8]

EA publishes and distributes games for PCs and console systems including the Sony PlayStation and Nintendo 64. The company's online gaming strategy was to generate 20 percent of its revenues from the Internet by 2003 or 2004. On November 19, 1999, EA and EA.com entered into a five-year interactive service agreement (beginning April 1, 2000) to be the exclusive game provider on all North American AOL properties, including AOL, CompuServe, ICQ, and NetCenter. EA.com was to launch the gaming site between June 1, 2000, and September 1, 2000. (In fact, the site went live on October 5, 2000.)

EA.com would offer games within three "channels": sports, family entertainment, and avid gaming. Not every online game would be available because some were too violent for AOL's content policy. In addition, EA.com agreed to produce four to eight titles per year exclusively for AOL Games. Games developed by EA.com for AOL would have budgets of under $50,000 for Shockwave games to over $5 million for high-end games. Development schedules ranged from several months to over three years.

*Select deal terms for Electronic Arts*

◆ Revenue goal is $175–$200 million by fiscal 2002.

◆ EA supplies all games and controls pricing for playing online games.

◆ EA obtains access to Time Warner's Road Runner broadband service.

◆ EA acquires WorldPlay, AOL's online parlor games development studio.

◆ EA sells games through AOL's online store.

◆ EA guarantees an $81 million payment to AOL. Specifically,

  • EA pays AOL a $50 million carriage fee, $25 million to be paid on the signing date of the agreement and $6.25 million for each of the next four years.

  • EA advances AOL $31 million, representing a minimum guaranteed revenue share for revenues generated by subscriptions and other commercial activities. Eleven million dollars of this amount would be paid on the signing date, followed by $5 million for each of the next four years.

◆ EA commits to spend $15 million in offline media advertising to promote its games on AOL.

◆ Deal is nonexclusive and allows EA to create similar agreement with other partners.

*Select deal terms for AOL*

◆ AOL receives 4.375 percent of gaming subscription revenue.

◆ AOL handles all advertising on AOL and receives 30 percent of all advertising revenue.

◆ AOL receives 5 percent of the gross profits EA derives from online sales through AOL.

◆ AOL will purchase 10 percent of the new EA.com tracking stock and warrants for another 5 percent.

◆ AOL has the right to extend the nonexclusive agreement for three successive two-year periods.

◆ Deal does not cover international AOL properties.

AOL was eager to work with EA. During the 1990s, Electronic Arts had built a reputation for strong brands (especially in the area of sports) and for skillfully managing ever-changing gaming platforms. It had also developed a proven online winner; EA enjoyed some 200,000 users paying $9.95 per month to play Ultima Online. AOL expected gaming subscriptions to become the deal's key revenue driver. EA was betting that online gaming was ready to be taken to another level.

The Electronic Arts deal illustrates how AOL could structure an advertising-commerce deal to participate in multiple revenue streams as well as the equity of a partner. Overall, AOL excelled at leveraging its subscriber base by cutting deals across an extraordinarily wide range of markets to generate substantial multiyear cash flows. These deals varied across several dimensions: (1) the number of participating AOL brands and channels; (2) how heavily content would be contextually integrated throughout the AOL properties; (3) the length of the agreement; and (4) the extent to which the deal involved up-front cash, performance features, recurring revenue streams, and equity participation. This vast portfolio of adcom deals allowed AOL to successfully monetize its extensive subscriber network.

## Rationale 3: Enhancing content and service offerings

In the late 1990s, as AOL established digital alliances to enhance its content and services, it became the rule, rather than the exception, that AOL got paid to host another company's offerings. Exposure and distribution—at least for a while—had become king. Which way money flowed boiled down to the classic "Who needs whom more" question. And everyone seemed to need AOL. AOL was in the enviable position of enhancing the reach and quality of its content while getting paid at the same time. (Although by late 2000, some analysts began to question the value of an AOL portal deal; some even called it an albatross around the neck—especially for an emerging company.)[9]

Consider AOL's deal with Medscape, a provider of authoritative health and medical information. In 1999, Medscape teamed up with AOL to launch "CBSHealthWatch by Medscape" consumer health sites on AOL, AOL.com, and Netscape Netcenter. Medscape had developed CBSHealthWatch through a strategic partnership with CBS, which took

32 percent of Medscape in exchange for $150 million worth of ads and promotions plus $7 million in licensing of the CBS brand.

The cobranded sites gave AOL direct access to Medscape's consumer-based health information. Medscape's offerings included an online medical journal edited by Dr. George Lundberg, former editor of the *Journal of the American Medical Association*. The prestigious content clearly benefited AOL subscribers. Yet, Medscape agreed to pay AOL $33 million over three years for the privilege of reaching the AOL audience. And Medscape's content would not even be the exclusive source of health information on AOL, which had struck a deal with Drkoop.com (and others). AOL was building a robust Health Channel through content partners.

In a similar deal, MarketWatch.com, a financial news organization with a presence on the Internet, television, and radio, joined with several AOL brands in a three-year alliance. MarketWatch.com became an "anchor tenant" on AOL's Business News Center, Investment Research, and Active Trader pages—all part of AOL's Personal Finance channel. Links across other AOL pages provided direct access to a CBS Market-Watch-AOL cobranded site. MarketWatch.com and AOL also started conducting scientific online polls, which were integrated into CBS MarketWatch.com radio and television programming. To consummate the deal, MarketWatch would pay $21 million in cash and promotional services to AOL.

AOL also signed commerce deals that would let subscribers buy almost anything they needed online. For example, in 1999 it formed an alliance to bring PlanetRx's online pharmaceutical and personal health-care products to AOL.com and AOL's Digital City sites. PlanetRx also became the premier online pharmacy partner in AOL's Health and Women's Channels and the only online pharmacy contextually integrated throughout the Health Channel. Among other services, shoppers could fill prescriptions online through PlanetRx and have medications mailed directly to their homes. Under the three-year agreement, AOL would receive payments from PlanetRx totaling $15 million.

As events unfolded, some of these AOL content and service deals came under pressure and were unlikely to continue in their initial form. In April 2000, for example, PlanetRx was pressed to renegotiate its marketing alliances. The company had spent nearly $100 million on marketing that fiscal year while generating revenues of only $26 million. AOL, however, didn't appear bothered by the trauma. If one content or service partner stumbled, a replacement company seemed to be waiting on its doorstep.

AOL's merger with Time Warner also raised questions about the future of these content-service deals. After all, AOL now owned an extensive portfolio of Time Warner content. What would happen to AOL's relationship with MarketWatch, for example, which was partly owned by CBS and thus a competitor to Time Warner's CNNfn? AOL's stock valuation resulted from its bevy of content and service deals. Would it de-emphasize these relationships going forward in order to more exclusively promote Time Warner content? Undoubtedly, each deal would be evaluated on an ad hoc basis at contract renewal time. AOL needed to carefully balance the opportunities arising from in-house content against those in its current portfolio of content and service deals with outside partners. Complicating matters, contract terms with a number of these partners prohibited AOL from heavily promoting other sites.

The acquisition of Time Warner would reflect yet another major transition in AOL's content and services strategy. Back in 1996, AOL had launched AOL Studios to move into content creation. The effort was short-lived, as the company's Entertainment Asylum site (and others) were not delivering adequate return on investment. The next year, AOL cut back on its entertainment efforts after an unsuccessful attempt at spinning off the division. In 1998, AOL ramped up its program to organize and distribute the online content of others. Content providers were treated as other retailers, paying for the privilege of exposure on AOL's brands. By 2000, another major content repositioning was afoot for AOL, as the company moved to acquire Time Warner and signaled its intent to aggressively create and own content.[10]

## LOCAL CONTENT AND SERVICES

AOL was also active in deals that enhanced local content on its Digital Cities site. Alliance partners provided ecommerce services in addition to local information, ranging from real estate to entertainment to auctioning. In some cases, AOL's Digital Cities brand was wrapped into content and service deals that also involved exposure on other AOL properties. Local content and services grew especially important as mobile digital devices providing Internet access became more popular.

In addition to these alliances, AOL wanted to own and control some local services itself. In February 1999, it acquired MovieFone in an all-stock transaction valued at $388 million. As noted earlier, Movie-Fone operated a telephone and Web-based movie ticketing business. This acquisition strengthened AOL's Digital Cities local content by offering an information and ticketing service that was used weekly by a growing number of moviegoers. MovieFone became a core AOL local service, attracting a substantial audience of entertainment enthusiasts.

## Rationale 4: Extending reach through technology

AOL had developed an impressive portfolio of digital deals that nurtured a self-feeding virtuous cycle: building a subscriber base, generating cash flows off of that base, and enhancing AOL's range of content and services. But to fuel this cycle, AOL needed to adroitly partner with and invest in companies creating novel technologies that could substantially extend its reach.

In particular, AOL began to make investments to aggressively position itself within two markets—mobile Internet devices and interactive TV. Under its "AOL Anywhere" strategy, the company wanted to extend beyond the PC to provide services for other devices and platforms. Although AOL did not make corporate minority investments on the scale of Intel (Chapter 8), AOL Investments, its corporate venture group, completed 30 deals in 1999 (up from 14 the year before). By April 2000, AOL had investments in over 70 public and private companies valued at $2 billion (not including a planned investment of $1.5 billion in Hughes Electronics and an $800 million investment in Gateway).[11]

MOBILE DEVICES

In late 1999, AOL decided to invest up to $80 million in Palm Computing, maker of the Palm Pilot electronic organizer and (at the time) a subsidiary of 3Com. AOL wanted to establish a presence on Palm's operating system, which had become a standard for mobile Internet devices by attracting an increasing number of licensees, including Motorola, Nokia, and Sony.

In another deal, AOL acquired Tegic Communications, a developer of text entry software used by mobile-phone makers. Tegic's software made it easier for users to type text on mobile phones. The rapid text entry could be used for instant messages, email, and other functions such as typing URLs into Web devices. At the time of the deal, Tegic was working with AOL to create a WAP-enabled AOL Instant Messenger application for digital devices.

AOL also acquired MapQuest, a developer of map, direction, and traffic information technology, in a $1.1 billion stock-swap deal. MapQuest's services were expected to become popular with mobile users looking for entertainment, restaurants, or other venues. MapQuest had already established partnerships with Nokia and Sprint to deliver travel directions to Internet-enabled phones. MapQuest was also developing a service to dictate driving instructions to users over the telephone.

## INTERACTIVE TELEVISION

AOL also began to structure partnerships to capture a leading position in entertainment-oriented interactive TV. In 1999, AOL announced a $1.5 billion investment in Hughes-DirecTV. The two companies would comarket a range of satellite services, including DirecTV and the AOL Plus high-speed service. However, by late 2000 a haze had settled over the AOL-Hughes partnership, as AOL's planned acquisition of Time Warner signaled an increased emphasis in cable delivery. Meanwhile, it looked likely that Hughes itself would go on the auction block with bidders such as News Corp. expressing interest. Hughes had also snuggled closer to Microsoft's interactive TV.

AOL made many other investments in technologies that supported its interactive digital television initiative. It invested in OpenTV, which enabled interactive services like email, chat, and instant messaging over digital broadcast video systems. AOL also invested in TiVo, a maker of personal digital video recorders. AOL would work with TiVo to combine AOLTV, an interactive television service, with TiVo technology. Furthermore, by the summer of 2000, AOL shipped its first AOLTV set-top box, which used Liberate software to support interactive television services. AOL had earlier invested in Liberate.

## Rationale 5: Expanding internationally

Like Microsoft (see Chapter 7), AOL pulled together a series of international joint ventures to build a global presence. Forming partnerships with local companies, AOL quickly became a player in Germany, Italy, Japan, France, Sweden, Hong Kong, China, and Mexico. By 1999, AOL's empire spanned 13 countries and 6 languages. The non-U.S. membership of AOL surpassed 3 million and was growing faster than the U.S. market. AOL structured most of these international deals as 50-50 joint ventures, with the partner providing cash or local presence and AOL providing brand and online expertise. AOL's international partners included several major players:

◆ Bertelsmann, a German media company joined AOL to form a 50-50 joint venture in 1995 involving AOL Europe and AOL Australia. Although the partnership looked promising, it was dissolved in 2000 following AOL's planned merger with Time Warner, a direct competitor to Bertelsmann. AOL purchased Bertlesmann's share of the venture for nearly $8 billion. Bertelsmann also entered into an adcom deal with AOL valued at approximately $250 million.

◆ The Cisneros Group of Companies (a 50-50 joint venture in AOL Latin America).

◆ Nihon Keizai Shimbun (Nikkei), Mitsui & Co, and NTT DoCoMo (a joint venture in Japan).

◆ China.com (AOL Hong Kong).

AOL wanted to replicate its virtuous cycle in each regional market. This time, however, it faced intense regional challenges, as local service providers and other global players learned from AOL's successful rise in the United States and fought back aggressively. AOL needed to continue building a distinctive portfolio of digital deals—tailored to each of its international regions—to emulate its U.S. success story.

## DIGITAL DEAL INSIGHTS

AOL's partnership strategy demonstrates the power of business commerce alliances to bring in subscribers, online content, and revenue. But was AOL just in the right place at the right time? What parts of AOL's strategy can other firms replicate? Here are six lessons that can be drawn from this case.

## New value of old eyeballs

The bits-versus-atoms value pendulum swung widely in 2000. Just a year earlier, value accumulated at digital companies like eToys, away from atomic counterparts such as Toys "R" Us. As 2000 wore on, value momentum reversed, moving in the direction of physical venues and traditional media. The new economy needed to attract a broader constituency of consumers, and firms raced to capture these new customers by building a presence where they "hung out."

This chapter demonstrated how AOL placed a heavy emphasis on deals with Wal-Mart, Blockbuster, and United Artists. Capturing customers in the physical world and converting them to Web customers became an important deal rationale. In addition to the aggressive cross-promotion of goods and services,[12] AOL's acquisition of Time Warner represented a fresh desire to combine old media with new to create third-generation media or "new" new media.

By late 2000, AOL boasted that its third-quarter advertising and commerce backlog consisted of deals with CitiGroup, Federated, Volvo, Pizza Hut, Target, and Office Depot. DrKoop, Travelocity, and others of the dot-com ilk got second billing.

Old-world media companies grew hip again for their enormous clout with potential Internet customers. Companies such as SportsLine (sports), ThirdAge (50ish adults), and Marketwatch.com (financial news) all swapped media exposure for equity positions in what was known as the CBS keiretsu. The benefits resulting from an Internet company being connected to traditional media were hardly automatic. Indeed, old media spin-offs such as NBC Internet, designed to capture a major slice of Internet adcom revenue, struggled.[13]

Nevertheless, old-world venues—from media to retail stores to movie theaters—enjoyed new appreciation (and value) in the digital economy. Knowing how to effectively combine physical with virtual would become even more important in an increasingly wireless world.

## Competing against a giant

In *Competing on Internet Time*, Michael Cusumano and David Yoffie discuss the challenges of competing head-to-head against a giant such as Microsoft.[14] The authors contend that smaller companies must use mobility, flexibility, and leverage to attack and defeat a larger opponent.

One David-Goliath contest in 2000 pitted Rob Glaser, CEO of Real-Networks, against his former employer, Microsoft. RealNetworks had developed a media player, RealPlayer, which let consumers listen to sound and view images over the Internet. RealPlayer had an early lead over Microsoft's Windows Media Player and enjoyed an installed base nearly four times as large.

The RealNetworks-Microsoft battle was reminiscent of Netscape's browser joust with Microsoft's Internet Explorer, and Microsoft employed similar tactics to overcome its sizeable installed base deficit. Microsoft integrated Media Player into Windows and established business development deals to promote its software with both content and technology companies.

Rob Glaser was unfazed. He predicted victory for his company, stressing that RealNetworks should not be compared to Netscape—which lost the browser battle—but to America Online, which had remained the dominant player in online services despite a Microsoft assault. RealNetworks enjoyed a huge lead in content partners, which, according to Glaser, would continue to attract more users. He stressed that music and other media companies would make more money by working with him—plain and simple AOL-style business development activity. While the outcome was far from certain, Glaser appeared to know where the battle would be fought.

## I wanna be like AOL

One of the more intriguing business development questions is the extent to which a company (large or small) can replicate AOL's adcom strategy. That is, how should a company go about reproducing a virtuous cycle consisting of: (1) building a user base, (2) monetizing the base, and (3) adding content and services that feed the cycle. Consider the following:

ThirdAge was founded in 1996 as a San Francisco-based company providing a Web destination site targeted at the 45 to 59 age group ("first-wave" boomers). ThirdAge's initial digital deals sought to drive traffic to its site. The company paid for exposure on AOL's Lifestyle channel and other highly trafficked sites. ThirdAge also leveraged its media exposure opportunities with CBS, an early investor in the company. By March 2000, ThirdAge registered its millionth user.

Simultaneously, ThirdAge moved to monetize its user base. While it brought in modest revenues from page-view advertising, ThirdAge was especially interested in more comprehensive sponsorship deals. The company had attracted a focused demographic—some 80 percent of its users were in the 45 to 59 age range (AOL, by comparison had less than 20 percent of its members in this age group). If a sponsor wanted to efficiently reach this sought after demographic, ThirdAge had become an attractive option. Companies including Procter & Gamble (Oil of Olay), Merrill Lynch, American Express Travel, and Merck (Zocor) all established sponsorship relationships that financially benefited ThirdAge, while simultaneously building the company's brand via association with quality content, products, and services.

ThirdAge attempted to emulate AOL's adcom strategy as an independent Internet company, but in November 2000 was acquired by MyFamily.com and consolidated into MyFamily's suite of Web sites. AOL's adcom model was replicable, but only if a company could achieve necessary scale at each step of the virtuous cycle.

## Portal deal—from jewel necklace to albatross?

The major Internet shakeout of 2000 challenged the business model of companies like AOL and Yahoo!. As the stock prices of their advertising and commerce partners plummeted—in some cases by as much as 95 percent—the cry for "profits now, not later" became an investor swan song. Analysts questioned whether AOL's adcom backlog of contracted payments from companies like Drkoop.com and 1-800-Flowers would really materialize.

Yahoo! was considered particularly vulnerable because some 60 percent of its revenues were based on advertising.[15] The company, like a venture capitalist analyzing "workouts," had to decide which companies to help through deal restructuring or strategic investments, and which partners to let die. For the fortunate ones, Yahoo! reduced ad placement fees by 90 percent and lead generation fees by 70 percent. How much had been too much to pay for an adcom portal deal? Boasting an adcom deal with AOL had once been like showing off a jewel necklace. Later, especially for some smaller companies, the portal deal turned into an albatross.

A digital deal needs to efficiently bolster marketing and other classic business functions. A smaller company must assess whether a large partner will really help build a commerce ecosystem that supports profitability. A more substantial company must occasionally help a struggling partner through tough times—even if it means reducing short-term cash flow.

## Which way does the money flow?

The story of AOL helps answer a recurring media question: Is content or distribution more important? Early on, AOL often paid for content as the company built its offerings and its brand. But by 2000, everyone lined up to pay AOL for exposure and distribution. Content, even great content, had been humbled. The answer to a classic deal question: "Who needs whom more?" was obvious—content needed distribution!

Yet, by the end of the year, forces were building that might push the pendulum in the other direction. AOL bought Time Warner, at least in part, for its exceptional content. And a major part of this content consisted of music, where MP3 digital file distribution through services like Napster made it easy to access content globally. Ironically, the widespread distribution of "free" music was likely to trigger a revaluation of content, as digital business models for music began to emerge. Content was once again reaching for the crown.

## Selling to, through, and with

America Online serves as a lighthouse example of how to leverage a media and distribution network through digital advertising and commerce partnerships. But a company need not be a media giant to build a lively ecosystem of commerce partners.

Consider Cisco. Although Chapter 6 featured Cisco's merger and acquisition activity, Cisco is no laggard in building commerce partnerships. In fact, Cisco has stated that in the 2000s, partnership ecosystems are likely to become more important than acquisitions. In 1999 Cisco announced its New World Ecosystem, composed of technology partners committed to working with Cisco to create solutions for service providers. Over 100 charter members would be involved in building integrated circuit-to-packet and packet-based solutions.

Internally, Cisco talks about selling to, through, and with a partner. For example, Cisco and SBC Communications formed a multibillion-dollar alliance where the two companies would jointly develop and sell data services. SBC also said it would buy more of Cisco equipment for its own telephone networks. As they sold products and services together, Cisco and SBC could promote their ability to offer a combined expertise in data communications and networking that would "give customers access to an ecosystem of infrastructure and service partners."

To . . . Through . . . With. Three words that permeated Cisco's culture as it built and managed a complex, but effective web of commerce partners that enabled the company to sell with market-by-market precision.

# CHAPTER 10

# Spin-offs and Tracking Stocks

*"This spin off will unleash both companies to realize their full growth potential."*
—Dwight Decker
Chairman and CEO, Conexant

Near the end of 2000, Conexant, a large maker of communications semiconductors located in Southern California, announced that it would spin off its high-growth Internet equipment business as an independent company. It was déjà vu for many of Conexant's employees; just two years earlier Conexant itself had been formed when Rockwell International spun off its semiconductor business. Although the earlier spin-off had initially proved an enormous success, Conexant's stock languished through 2000. The stock of competitors, such as Broadcom and Applied Micro Circuits, enjoyed much higher valuation multiples than Conexant.

According to one analyst, "Conexant's shareholders are not benefiting from that nugget of value [the Internet business] because it is a gem buried in a mediocre rock."[1] In spinning off its Internet equipment business, Conexant planned to mine its "gem" and increase the market visibility of this business. At the same time, Conexant's remaining divisions could focus on turning around their potentially valuable operations. The next day, Conexant's stock surged 45 percent, adding over $5 billion in market capitalization to the firm. Thirty days later, however, Conexant's share price had slumped back to the level prior to the announced spin-off. And in January 2001, Conexant postponed the spin-off citing adverse market conditions. Management expected to complete the separation once business and market conditions improved. The jury was out on the long-term value of this deal.

In the new economy, the number of corporate spin-offs has increased as many firms decide that size is not a virtue. Corporations are restructuring their businesses for a variety of reasons. Some firms, like Conexant, believe that public markets are not adequately valuing their assets and hope to catalyze stock gains. As dynamic markets trigger corporate change, what once looked like a pure play semiconductor company can evolve to resemble an unfocused conglomerate of networking products, modems, software, wireless, and Internet equipment. A spin-off can reorganize the company into market chunks that Wall Street can understand and value without a "conglomerate penalty."

Other companies spin off units for different reasons. Chapter 4 illustrated how Microsoft spun off its Internet travel business, in part to keep employees from leaving for smaller competitors. AT&T divested Lucent Technologies to eliminate conflicts of interest with potential customers (among other reasons). This chapter will examine a number of new economy rationales for spinning off a division.

But spin-offs are not a cure-all. In fact, a firm can sometimes awake from a restructuring only to suffer from a post-spin-off hangover. Having done the deal for questionable reasons, it becomes hamstrung by a poorly-performing cousin that drags down the brand or confuses customers. NBC, for example, bundled together a host of Internet assets (including Snap.com and Xoom.com) and spun off a new company, NBCi. The spin-off appeared to be driven by a desire to capitalize on a hot dot-com market. For a time the company enjoyed a $6 billion valuation, but it soon collapsed under an ever-changing strategy and questionable execution. NBCi's unique users and page views declined, its top executives quit, and its stock price crashed by 95 percent. NBC winced at its tarnished brand.[2] Firms need to execute spin-offs for the right reasons.

# HOW SPIN-OFFS AND TRACKING STOCKS WORK

A spin-off typically occurs when a firm carves out a new company from existing assets. After creating the new subsidiary, the parent company can proceed in a number of different directions. In a complete spin-off, the parent distributes all the entity's stock to its current shareholders—leaving the parent with no remaining interest. The shares of stock are normally registered with the SEC, so the spin-off's stock can trade freely on the public markets. As a result of this deal the subsidiary's shareholders are initially the same as those of the parent company. However, over time shareholders will buy or sell the subsidiary's stock separately from the parent's, and the shareholder mix of the two companies diverges. This was the process used by Rockwell to spin off Conexant in 1998.

In a partial spin-off (sometimes called an equity "carve out"), the subsidiary's stock is not distributed to the parent's shareholders at all. Instead, a minority stake is sold directly to the public markets through an IPO. The parent keeps the rest. Typically, a partial spin-off has its own management team and is essentially run as a separate company, although the parent may still exert substantial influence if it retains a large ownership percentage. For example, in 1999 Microsoft decided to spin off Expedia, its Internet travel business. It first separated out the relevant assets into a newly incorporated company, 100 percent owned by Microsoft. Next, Expedia filed an IPO to sell around 15 percent of its stock to the public, creating a liquid market for the shares. At the same time, the 150 Expedia employees had their Microsoft stock options canceled and replaced with new Expedia options with similar vesting schedules (significant secondary effects from this exchange will be examined later). Upon the completion of the IPO, Expedia became a separately managed company, but maintained a contractual relationship with Microsoft—which kept majority share ownership of Expedia.[3]

Sometimes firms combine both of these deals in a two-step spin-off. For example, the networking company 3Com decided to spin off its Palm unit, which would focus on handheld computing products. In March 2000, 3Com sold 5 percent of Palm's shares to the public in an IPO (it also sold shares to AOL, Motorola, and Nokia in a private placement). 3Com kept the remaining 95 percent of Palm's stock. Four months later, 3Com distributed the rest of Palm's stock to its shareholders, completely liquidating its ownership of the company. A two-step spin-off helps parents raise capital initially and also lets the market set the unit's value before the balance of shares are given over to the shareholders. AT&T spun off Lucent Technologies in the same manner.

Tracking stocks also allow a firm to separate out a business unit, but they work differently than spin-offs. The company creates a new class of stock that "tracks" the economic performance of a specific division. Unlike common stock, the tracking stock provides no ownership interest in the company. Instead, a stream of dividends is paid out based on the financial success of the tracked business unit. The share price of the tracking stock thus reflects the unit's performance. For example, in spring 2000 AT&T created a tracking stock for its wireless business through which each shareholder would be paid dividends that corresponded to the economic performance of AT&T's wireless assets. However, the owners of the tracking stock would have no control over the way that AT&T managed its wireless division. They could not elect directors, approve mergers, or exercise other major decision-making powers of typical shareholders. AT&T then filed an IPO for 20 percent of the tracking shares—at the time the largest IPO ever conducted—to create a public market for the stock. The pros and cons of tracking stocks will be explored shortly.

## WHY SPIN-OFFS?

For most companies, growth and size are fundamental goals. Why then might a firm take actions to shrink its business holdings? Occasionally, a firm may be forced to spin off a division to satisfy antitrust requirements (remember the greatest of all spin-offs—AT&T and the Baby Bells in 1984) or for other regulatory reasons. But most spin-offs occur today because companies believe that splitting out parts from the whole will create greater shareholder value, motivate human resources, or enable units to attack markets more effectively. In other words, there is some reason why the whole company is not functioning at an optimal level. Perhaps capital markets are having trouble valuing unrelated business units, or organizational issues are harming employee morale or skewing investment decisions. Let's look at three spin-off rationales that are especially relevant to the new economy.

## Rationale 1: Unlocking buried value

A major motivating factor for spin-offs is the belief that "reverse synergies" exist. In other words, two smaller firms will be worth more by themselves than in combination with each other. As seen in the Conexant example at the beginning of this chapter, spin-offs are almost always justified by their ability to accelerate growth and unlock buried value. This is called the *wealth effect* of spin-offs.

### MEASURING THE WEALTH EFFECT OF SPIN-OFFS

Unlike many other types of digital deals, spin-offs present a relatively clean opportunity to measure the results of the deal. Since both companies often continue to trade on public markets, researchers can study how the stock of the parent and spin-off performs after the deal is completed (adjusting for fluctuations that can be explained by market movements alone). Over the past 30 years, several of these research projects—commonly called *event studies*—have been conducted by academics and investment banks. Results tend to show a pattern of positive shareholder wealth effects from spin-offs.

Reviewing these event studies provides some clues regarding the types of spin-offs that are more likely to unleash buried value. Oppenheimer & Company studied 19 spin-offs that took place during the 1970s. In most cases, the combined value of the parent and spun-off subsidiary was greater than the market value of the parent alone before the deal. Fourteen of those spin-offs outperformed the S&P index for the six months following their deal.[4] In 1983, two academics, James Miles and James Rosenfeld, studied 59 spin-offs spanning nearly 20 years. They reported a positive stock price effect from these spin-offs, which was internalized in the parent's stock upon announcement (before the actual spin-off date). Interestingly, this uptick in stock value was sometimes accompanied by a decrease in the price of the parent's bonds. One way to interpret this bond price decrease is that the spin-off's assets and cash flow were no longer available to support the debtholder's interest payment.[5] Two more studies by JP Morgan in the late 1990s confirmed the prior work. Examining the stock prices of over 100 spin-offs, JP Morgan discovered a sharply positive stock price reaction around the announcement date of the spin-off. The study also analyzed the wealth effect by the size of the spin-off, and found that smaller spin-offs (under $200 million market capitalization) generally performed better than larger ones.[6]

On balance, there is evidence that spin-offs can create incremental shareholder value under the right circumstances. There are a number of reasons why this might be true. For example, it may be difficult for financial analysts to understand how well a particular business division is performing when it is buried inside a larger organization. Some argue that this leads to systematic stock market underpricing, especially for smaller divisions where detailed financial information is not provided. As the argument goes, spinning off the division leads to less market confusion because more information about the specific unit's activities and performance becomes available.

The exact reasons why a particular spin-off creates value can be hard to pinpoint. Certainly, spin-offs do not create wealth per se and at times have proved disastrous. Spin-offs are a tool for repackaging corporate assets. Sound underlying rationale for the spin-off and later execution, not the deal itself, creates the value.

## A SERIAL SPINNER

AT&T has probably conducted more high-profile spin-offs than any other U.S. company. However, these deals have met with mixed results. Some of AT&T's spin-offs have created enormous value, while others have floundered over time. Studying AT&T's spin-off strategy provides insight into when spin-offs unleash buried potential.

AT&T has undergone three major spin-off waves. In 1984, after 10 years of antitrust pressure from the U.S. Department of Justice, AT&T was forced to spin off its local telephone service into seven regional Baby Bells. The wealth effect from this deal was phenomenal, and the Baby Bells' growth into telecommunications giants (in some cases through recombination via merger) is well documented.[7] However, since involuntary spin-offs are not the focus of this chapter, let's move on to AT&T's later spin-offs (Figure 10-1).

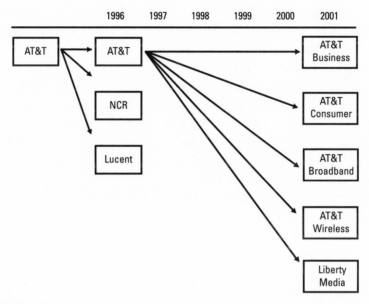

**FIGURE 10-1**
*AT&T's announced spin-offs (since 1996).*

The second wave of deals came in 1996. With the passing of the U.S. Telecommunications Act—which transformed the way that telecom firms could compete—AT&T decided to spin off two divisions and focus on its main business of providing telecommunications services. The first company that AT&T decided to spin off, computer maker NCR, had little relation to AT&T's core business. In fact, the deal was widely viewed as an admission that AT&T's earlier acquisition of the company had failed. In 1991, AT&T had purchased NCR to enter the personal computer business. But the merger flopped as AT&T struggled to find a "convergence" relationship between its telecommunications business and sales of computers. Conceding defeat, AT&T divested NCR in 1996. After the spin-off, NCR's stock "flatlined" at around $40 per share for the next four years. NCR was an unrelated, stagnant business, and while the spin-off may have provided focus for AT&T, it did not make much of a difference for NCR (although NCR's boring flatness had peculiar appeal in 2000).

AT&T's other 1996 spin-off, Lucent Technologies, proved more successful. AT&T gave Lucent its equipment manufacturing business along with Bell Labs, the world-famous research park. As Lucent took dozens of products to market, it even surpassed AT&T in market value during part of 2000. How did the spin-off unlock Lucent's buried value? Freedom from AT&T helped in a couple of ways. First, it uncoupled Lucent from conflicts that were arising between AT&T and the Baby Bells. Under the 1996 Telecommunications Act, AT&T began to wage fierce competitive battles with the Baby Bells as it pushed to reenter local phone markets. At the same time, the Baby Bells positioned themselves to offer long-distance telephone service in direct competition with AT&T. Because Lucent was no longer considered part of the "enemy," it was now able to sell more equipment to the Baby Bells. For example, in 1997 SBC Communications canceled a large agreement with Nortel to become the exclusive distributor of Lucent's office phone equipment in five states. That same year Lucent signed a $1 billion contract to upgrade the NYNEX network for Bell Atlantic. These contracts would have been impossible to win if Lucent had stayed with AT&T because Bell Atlantic and SBC were now viewing AT&T as a competitive threat. Over the next few years, Lucent continued to sell products to Sprint, Worldcom, and other fleet, well-financed start-ups that were building their networks from scratch.

The spin-off did more than remove Lucent's conflict of interest with potential customers. It also gave Lucent a flood of capital and its own stock currency. After filing a $3 billion IPO (at the time the largest public offering ever recorded in the United States), Lucent went on to conduct its own acquisitions, especially in the promising optical networking market (see Chapter 6). Freedom from AT&T had unleashed Lucent's potential to create value.

However, new economy markets are anything but static. By 2000, Lucent found itself under intense pressure from nimble start-ups and seasoned competitors such as Cisco. Lucent struggled to execute, missing earnings estimates again and again, forcing CEO Richard McGinn to resign. In October 2000, Lucent spun off another unit of its own, dubbed Avaya, which sold PBX systems used to control corporate phone lines and voice-mail systems. Lucent wanted to focus on faster-growing areas like fiber optic equipment and network systems. AT&T's descendant had inherited the spin-off gene.

Under the right circumstances spin-offs can unlock buried value. In particular, look for situations where latent conflicts of interest are preventing units from selling to potential customers. Likewise, keep an eye out for high potential units that have received limited investment due to internal conflicts.

## Rationale 2: Winning the war for talent

In the new economy, many firms describe their top challenge as attracting and retaining talented employees. In a war for talent, large companies have seen managers, engineers, and other personnel leave for more entrepreneurial organizations. A smaller firm can provide a more collegial atmosphere, more flexible working arrangements, and the perception of greater "headroom" in employee stock options. Spin-offs may offer larger firms a viable response. By allowing workers to join smaller, independent units, parent companies can give existing and new employees a start-up environment and stock options with more dramatic appreciation potential. This can help retain star employees that might otherwise have abandoned the firm.

Consider Microsoft's spin-off of Expedia, the Internet travel site. Expedia provides travel information and services—including airline, hotel, and rental car reservations—to business and vacation travelers. It was started in 1996, and for the first few years Expedia operated as a division within Microsoft. However, toward the end of the 1990s Expedia saw many of its employees leaving for smaller Internet start-ups, partly in search of more attractive stock options. Microsoft options were largely perceived as a stable, lower-growth currency, unlikely to enrich a new generation of programmers. In response, Microsoft decided to spin off Expedia to retain its employees and launch a blockbuster IPO. (Microsoft, not unlike many other organizations, was a bit jealous of the feverish dot-com market success during 1999 and early 2000.)

From a human resource perspective, the crucial question was how to structure the terms of the spin-off fairly. The big challenge was how to compensate Expedia employees with enough shares of stock to keep them excited about Expedia's future, without being unfair to Microsoft employees who stayed with the mother ship. Eventually the decision went to Bill Gates, who decided to allow Expedia employees to exchange each Microsoft option for six shares of Expedia, reflecting the difference in the two stock's share prices (Microsoft was trading around $84 a share, six times more than Expedia's expected IPO at $14 per share). But Expedia's shares quickly tripled once the IPO was launched, providing employees who went over to Expedia with a paper financial windfall. Steve Ballmer, Microsoft's then-President, was reportedly furious. The more attractive Internet spin-off threatened to drain Microsoft's most talented engineers and managers.

As with many softer human issues, there are no clearly right answers. Many employees who were affected stayed with Microsoft, and as time went on the grumbling subsided. Of course, the higher potential rewards of the spin-off also came with increased risk. The following year, Expedia's performance was mixed—its revenues and earnings continued to grow, but not fast enough to satisfy the changing expectations of investors. Expedia's stock fell back near the IPO price, rendering the original dispute largely irrelevant.

Regardless of its stock performance, the underlying rationale for Expedia's spin-off remains valid. In the new economy, talented employees, while harder to attract and retain than ever, are critical to a firm's success. As long as smaller companies continue to appeal to new economy workers, expect to see more spin-offs executed in an attempt to win the war for talent.

## Rationale 3: Freeing up a division for sale

A third rationale for spin-offs is straightforward—a parent company carves out a division to free it up for sale. This type of deal is cousin to the first rationale (unlocking buried value) in that the subsidiary will be worth more when severed from the parent. However, in this case, much of the value comes from combining the division with another owner that can put its assets to better use. Consider an example.

Near the end of 2000, General Motors explored spinning off its Hughes Electronics division in anticipation of a subsequent sale. GM had owned the division for roughly 15 years, purchasing Hughes Aircraft in 1985 and adding select electronics assets to create Hughes Electronics. At the time, Hughes was in fairly bad shape—it had lost a talented team of scientists and a number of government defense contracts. But over the next decade GM focused the company on satellites and commercial electronics. By 1995, as declining Cold War tensions reduced the need for defense satellite imaging, Hughes formed DirecTV to redeploy its satellite assets into a consumer business. This subsidiary, which broadcast digital movies and music to consumer subscribers, grew to become Hughes' prime asset with over 10 million customers.

However, it was unclear whether GM could put the assets of Hughes and DirecTV to their best use. GM had long insisted that DirecTV was a crucial part of its automotive business and would provide an Internet access platform for its cars and trucks. However, as GM explored ways that DirecTV could work with its automotive divisions, it realized that the businesses might not be as intertwined as originally thought. GM's CEO John Smith expressed continued frustration that he could not get a high enough valuation for Hughes while it was buried in General Motors. GM established a tracking stock for Hughes, but continued to explore ways to maximize the value of the division, especially as consolidation in the telecommunications and satellite industries picked up pace. In particular, GM wondered whether the satellite assets would be worth more in the hands of a global player like Rupert Murdoch's Sky Global or a broader-based media or technology firm like Walt Disney or Microsoft. A spin-off for sale would likely benefit GM's shareholders.

When should an organization consider such a spin-off? Fundamentally, the question is whether the company should sell a division. Can it use the assets to their highest potential? Are they mission critical to the other parts of the business? Would they be worth significantly more if combined with another company?

## USING TRACKING STOCKS

Let's revisit AT&T in 2000, as the company embarked on its third wave of spin-offs. Like the 1996 deals, these spin-offs sought to unlock buried value. Over the past few years, AT&T had assembled a vast collection of communications businesses. It spent over $100 billion purchasing cable companies—such as TCI and Media One—and updating their infrastructure to provide local telephony, high-speed Internet access, and digital television. However as the telecommunications services market splintered into more focused companies (such as Vodaphone, Nextel, or Global Crossing), AT&T's stock plunged, plagued by a conglomerate discount. At one point, its shares were estimated to trade at 35 percent below a conservative sum-of-the-parts valuation. Initially, AT&T decided to set up a wireless tracking stock to unlock shareholder value.

AT&T ran one of the largest wireless businesses in the United States, but while other wireless competitors enjoyed white-hot market capitalizations, AT&T's stock languished. Its prime wireless assets were buried in AT&T's cable and phone businesses. Furthermore, wireless infrastructure development required massive capital investment, and AT&T's competitors were using their high stock multiples to expand quickly. AT&T needed a new currency of its own to compete effectively.

In response, it decided to issue a tracking stock tied to the economic performance of the wireless business. Unlike common stock, the tracking stock provided no ownership interest in the company. Instead, a stream of dividends would be paid out based on the financial success of the wireless unit. AT&T would file an IPO for 20 percent of the tracking shares, and the rest of the shares would be distributed to common stock owners in the fall. AT&T expected the IPO to raise $10 billion, giving it cash to make additional wireless investments. It could also issue additional stock to pay for selected assets. Employees within AT&T's Wireless Group (as the unit would be called) were granted stock options for motivation. Unlike the previous deals, AT&T Wireless would remain a part of AT&T, under the leadership of long-time executive John Zeglis.

Tracking stocks offer an intriguing organizational compromise. Firms can create a stock that may receive better trading multiples by tracking the performance of a hot internal division. Employees can be awarded tracking stock options to provide clear financial incentives. At the same time, the deal can often be accomplished more quickly, with less regulatory scrutiny, and with better tax treatment than a complete spin-off. The parent also retains the ability to coordinate actions across the different business units.

But there are also some problems with tracking stocks. First, they are often considered shareholder unfriendly—the holders of tracking stock cannot exert ownership rights such as the power to elect directors and approve mergers. This can reduce the demand for a tracking stock as compared to a comparable spin-off. Second, tracking stocks often pose tricky conflicts of interest. Top management can face conflicts over which divisions, tracked or untracked, should pursue new opportunities. Finally, if the company fails, tracking stock shareholders will generally have no claim to the underlying assets (the stock is linked only to the performance of those assets). It also leaves the tracked assets on the books of the parent company, which may prove undesirable.

Tracking stocks are a "halfway house" to a spin-off. They offer a compromise between the status quo and complete separation, but the complications can outweigh the rewards. AT&T eventually turned to other methods.

## AT&T SPINS AGAIN

In October 2000, AT&T announced another major restructuring (see Figure 10-1). It would split itself into four distinct companies: wireless, broadband (cable), business services, and consumer services. The deal would be completed using a complicated constellation of spin-offs and tracking stocks. Under the plan, the business services company would retain core AT&T assets, including its brand, fixed line networks, and research labs. It would also remain the parent of the AT&T consumer business, which would operate the residential long-distance and Internet access businesses. A new tracking stock would be created for the consumer business, to be distributed in 2001. The AT&T wireless business would be completely spun off, with the existing tracking stock exchanged for normal shares. Likewise, AT&T would spin off the broadband business to shareholders.[8]

While this deal sounds convoluted (and it is!), it has the potential to create value over time. The high-growth businesses will be separated out with more focused strategic imperatives. These corporations will find it easier to attract new management and react adeptly to smaller attackers. AT&T business services may find it easier to receive management attention and investment, while the wireless unit will find it easier to pursue pure play acquisitions and partnerships. Facing a telecommunications market that was congealing around specialized subsectors, AT&T

reasoned that the only way to compete was through divestiture. Other telecom conglomerates may follow suit.

The rationale behind this third wave of AT&T restructuring is not confined to the communications market. Many companies, looking to execute a focused vertical market strategy, find themselves "conglomeratized" by nimbler players. In some cases size remains a powerful strategic advantage. However, as with AT&T, spin-offs are sometimes required to compete and to maximize shareholder value in dynamic competitive markets.

## And again!

In November 2000, AT&T announced yet another spin-off—this time it planned to "release" Liberty Media. Liberty owned interests in video programming, communications, technology, and Internet businesses. The company's investments included cable channels such as Discovery Channel and QVC. Liberty also owned 9 percent of Time Warner and 18 percent (nonvoting shares) of News Corp. Upon AT&T's acquisition of TCI, Liberty had become a subsidiary traded as a tracking stock.

The rationales for the spin-off were nothing new. The move enabled Liberty to raise capital on its own and forge partnerships with other companies, including competitors of AT&T. In particular, regulatory restrictions prohibiting one company from owning TV stations and cable in the same markets restricted Liberty's expansion. In addition, Liberty's desire to move closer to News Corp.'s Sky Global (an AT&T competitor) had become a significant conflict.

AT&T's nest was whirling. Liberty had been inside for less than two years, but it looked like centrifugal market forces could now propel it out.

# DIGITAL DEAL INSIGHTS

## Planning a spin-off

Once an organization has decided to conduct a spin-off, what planning steps are needed to get the deal done? Commonly, it takes about six months from the time that a spin-off is announced until the completion of the deal. Here's an overview of the essential issues.

The parent and subsidiary must first craft a restructuring plan, the agreement that governs the details of the spin-off. Executives from both groups will negotiate the plan to determine exactly how the spin-off will occur. Ultimately, the plan must be approved by directors of the parent and subsidiary, and often by the shareholders of the parent company as well.

The restructuring plan covers the exact relationship between the parent and subsidiary before and after the deal. Which assets and liabilities will go with the spin-off? How will intangible assets and liabilities (including pension liabilities) be treated? If the spin-off has historically operated as a separate subsidiary, much of this may have already been established. But if the deal involves a shuffling of assets, the restructuring plan may get extremely complicated. The agreement also covers the number of shares to be distributed, the record and payment dates for distribution, the exchange where the stock will be listed, and other details related to the issuance of new stock. The plan will contain any conditions necessary for the spin-off to be executed, such as favorable tax rulings or other regulatory approvals.

Finally, planning for a spin-off requires the parties to address personnel issues. Which employees will stay and which will transfer to the new company? Since many new economy spin-offs are driven by the need to retain talented employees, these details are extremely important. Stock option plans need to be rewritten, and the terms of these plans should be carefully crafted to ensure fairness to the parent, the subsidiary, and both sets of employees.

## Remembering those left behind

Spin-offs can create remarkable value. However, they are challenging and sometimes even painful deals to complete and should be executed only for the right reasons. This chapter described the organizational challenges faced by Microsoft as it spun off Expedia. In the digital economy, these human resource intricacies have become the rule rather than the exception. For example, a Conexant executive described to us his frustration the day his company's Internet spin-off was announced. He had suspected that a major corporate restructuring was afoot, but inquiries to the corporate planning group went unanswered. What's more, he seemed somewhat disappointed at being left behind with the "residual" division. He had no complaints about the jump in Conexant's stock but was even more interested in learning how the spin-off would affect him and his division. Some things don't change. In the new economy as well as the old, psychic income is as important as monetary income in maintaining employee commitment.

## When residual is regal

Sometimes the residual division after a spin-off is what's regal. In 2000 when Lucent spun off Avaya, its corporate network division, it gave the company a new economy name, but not necessarily the highest-growth assets. Lucent, itself, would retain the explosive (yet fiercely competitive) fiber optic equipment business.

A few months later, after severe earnings erosion, Lucent's board ousted CEO Richard McGinn and replaced him with Henry Schacht as interim head. Schacht had been Lucent's initial CEO after it was spun off from AT&T. Curiously, Schacht was now chairman of Avaya, a position that he resigned to reassume leadership of Lucent. As the personnel move indicated, Lucent (and not Avaya) was the main jewel to polish. The mother ship, clearly still regal, demanded the highest focus of attention.

## Avoiding wrong reasons

In 1999 the allure of sky-high Internet valuations was too tempting for many old economy firms to pass up. Company after company joined a parade of spin-offs where they cobbled together their Internet assets and presented a shiny new dot-com to public market investors. For a while, this allowed them to take advantage of hot public markets by developing a stock currency that allowed rapid expansion. But many of these firms went public long before they were ready. As investors relearned that high stock prices need to be supported by cash flow and earnings growth, they dumped many Internet spin-offs. NBCi, for example, dropped from $100 per share early in 2000 to trade at $5 only eight months later. NBC (and its parent GE) might have avoided painful brand bruises had it kept Internet operations internal. A spin-off should not be a knee-jerk reaction to new economy opportunistic fads.

Perhaps the worst reason for splitting up a company is to resolve a fight between company founders by providing each side with its own company. Breaking up the company may lead to a better managerial environment, but a spin-off is unlikely to be the best solution for this problem. In most cases, shareholders would be better off if another approach were used (such as encouraging one founder to resign). Under the right circumstances, spin-offs can create tremendous value. But a spin-off should not be a knee-jerk reaction to organizational pressures—it is a tool, not a tonic.

# PART 3

# Pulling It All Together

Crafting successful digital deals is challenging work. The same new economy forces that push partnerships to the center stage of corporate strategy obscure the competitive landscape. As markets endure a sandstorm of change, it becomes harder to see where to go and what combination of assets is required to thrive. Most firms know that strong partnerships are crucial but are not sure how to pick the right deals, the right partners, or the right structures. All-too-common responses—paralysis or promiscuity—don't cut it. Paralyzed firms pass on important deals and fall behind in changing markets. Promiscuous ones chase an endless array of partners but fail to invest in the deals that really matter. Winning deal strategies require both clear vision and considered approach.

Part 1 of this book provided a framework for developing a systematic deal strategy. It discussed how to map out market landscapes and select deal rationales that support strategic objectives. Those chapters argued that firms can earn a sustainable competitive advantage by planning and

*executing sound corporate partnering strategies—and by
developing the necessary information resources needed to
make them work. Part 2 of this book focused on five different
deal structures: mergers and acquisitions, joint ventures,
minority equity investments, advertising and commerce
alliances, and spin-offs and tracking stocks. In particular,
it explored the successes (and failures) of Cisco, Intel,
Microsoft, America Online, AT&T, and other industry giants
that have structured powerful partnerships.*

    *This final section is about fostering successful deals.
Chapter 11 explores the correlation between deal rationale
and deal structure. Do certain types of deals typically use the
same structure? Is a deal more likely to succeed when structured in a particular way? Why? Although firms will rarely
enjoy complete freedom to select the "perfect" deal structure
(politics, personalities, and other noncontrollables invariably
play too great a role), this chapter suggests how, all other
things being equal, a well-crafted structure plays a vital role
in building a business model. To illustrate, we will examine
how two firms, Amazon.com and VerticalNet, have structured
a wide variety of deals, not all of which have been successful.*

    *Chapter 12 offers specific guidance for building a sys-
tem that supports digital deal analysis and action. Its goal is
to highlight essential aspects to consider when designing
information resources that enable superior competitive positioning and partnership planning.*

# CHAPTER 11

# Linking Rationale and Structure

Choosing the right structure can substantially improve a deal's chance of success. Consider, for example, an established U.S. firm that wants to offer Internet security software to customers in India. It has no current Indian presence, but has identified an interested partner in Bangalore that appears to be a perfect fit. How should it structure the deal? According to one study, when firms in this situation—nonoverlapping geographies seeking foreign market entry—structure an alliance, it succeeds 60 percent of the time. By contrast, an acquisition only succeeds one out of every 10 times. However, if the deal involves overlapping geographies—say both companies have operations in India and the United States—then an acquisition in support of the rationale has a much higher rate of success than an alliance.[1]

This chapter explores the critical link between deal rationale and structure. Although firms rarely have the freedom to "clean sheet" a deal—there are invariably complex political and human factors that get in the way—it is essential to understand how deal structure might promote success or failure. The chapter starts by synthesizing insights from the previous five chapters around when to use a particular structure. It then illustrates these insights with additional case studies, exploring how two new economy companies, Amazon.com and VerticalNet, have selected different deal structures to support distinct deal rationales.

Selecting the right deal structure with appropriate terms can boost the odds of a successful partnership.

## CONTRASTS IN STRUCTURES AND RATIONALES

Part 2 of this book covered five common deal structures: mergers and acquisitions, joint ventures, minority equity investments, advertising and commerce alliances, and spin-offs and tracking stocks. These chapters highlighted types of deals that have been associated with different deal structures. Here's a high-level recap, comparing and contrasting the characteristics of these structures and why they lend themselves to particular deal rationales.

Not surprisingly, mergers and acquisitions are largely used for deals that demand the highest levels of control and commitment. For example, Cisco uses acquisitions to secure core technology, round out its product offerings, and feed a vibrant sales and marketing pipeline. Essentially outsourcing its R&D efforts, Cisco (and others following this strategy) monitors potential partners by tracking their development. As it becomes clearer that products work and markets are ripe, Cisco executes the acquisition. It believes that some technology is too important to leave in the control of others. Similarly, other acquisition rationales such as securing new business models, consolidating competitors, and blocking others from making an acquisition require high levels of control, commitment, and risk. The downside: Acquisitions typically require the buyer to pay a control premium and involve substantial execution risks.

Joint ventures are often created to go after new markets. For example, Chapter 7 illustrated how Microsoft has launched joint ventures to develop new products and services, expand into new geographies, and target new customer segments. JVs afford an excellent deal structure when resources and commitment are needed (and can be obtained) from two or more sides to capture the new market opportunity. But this deal structure may be the hardest to execute. No side enjoys absolute control, and a great degree of sustained coordination is required to make a joint venture succeed. This is especially true in ultradynamic new economy markets. Intel, for example, has largely avoided the JV structure and used minority investments wherever possible. Joint ventures can be very effective for pooling complementary skills inside a new entity, but this type of deal structure is a "dive with a high degree of difficulty."

The third deal structure, minority equity investments, is extremely common and flexible. As a consequence, firms use venture investments for a wide range of deal rationales and sometimes as a tool to achieve very subtle results. For example, when one company invests in two or more competitors at the same time, the goal can be to whip all players into more rapid action. Intel, for instance, invested in multiple broadband players (including Williams Communications, Covad, Northpoint, and @Home) to accelerate the broadband market and stimulate demand for its chips. It was far less interested in which specific horse would win the race. Intel has also made minority investments to mitigate its reliance on Microsoft by placing bets on firms developing the competing Linux operating system. However, firms placing a large number of minority investments need to monitor and manage the conflicts that may arise from their partnerships.

Minority investments typically require less effort and commitment than acquisitions or JVs, especially if the investment is largely financial and not strategic. An Intel senior executive chafed in one meeting when we called one deal a joint venture, insisting that it was only a minority investment. The deal had, in fact, been dubbed a JV in a press release, but inside Intel executives were, in general, clearly more comfortable with the level of commitment expected from a minority investor. The flip side is that minority investments offer less control than JVs or acquisitions. Microsoft found this out in 2000, for example, when it saw that its sizable investments in companies such as AT&T did not necessarily guarantee expanded use of its set-top box technology.

The fourth deal structure, advertising and commerce alliances, is probably the most frequently observed digital deal. AOL and others have built vast networks of alliances to grow their subscriber base, monetize distribution assets, and enhance online content and services. Although, as with AOL's advertising and commerce portfolio, some companies pay dearly for this type of deal, commerce alliances can be designed with less risk and commitment than other digital deal structures. This can be good if an executive wants to retain flexibility to work with others or monitor how the relationship evolves. But it may not be the best structure if the deal is central to a company's strategy. Some commerce partnerships (so-called fruit fly alliances) quickly diminish in importance or even die should one party find a more attractive partner. In fact, some deals are merely dead-on-arrival press releases—tossed out with the hope of securing a stock price kick, but signifying very little.

Many alliances do mature into important, and highly valuable, relationships. Undoubtedly, there is wisdom in getting to know one's partner before raising the ante—especially if speed is not a critical factor—but ultimately it is valence or strength of an alliance that matters. That means monitoring how much revenue flows from selling to, through, and with the partner. Key commerce alliances can be solidified by a minority investment or cross-ownership deal.

Finally, AT&T and others have spun off business divisions into new companies to unlock buried value, attract and retain employees, or free up a division for sale. Spin-offs sometimes create value by removing existing conflicts and allowing both old divisions and new entities to expand their web of relationships. For example, Lucent won a host of new customers and relationships by severing its ties to AT&T. Many accounting firms are spinning off their consulting divisions for the same reason. The liberated consultants often grow quickly by working with a range of new partners that had previously been unservable because they were competitors of audit clients. Essentially the inverse of an acquisition, a spin-off reduces control and coordination costs.

In summary, deal structures typically differ along the key dimensions of control, commitment, conflict, and risk. The rationale driving some deals shouts out for a prescribed structure. Complete command and control almost always mean acquisition. Other deal rationales can be supported through a number of different structures. For example, firms seeking geographic expansion have used all the deal structures mentioned above (and more!). Art, science, intuition, and system are all part of deal making. Let's look at two new economy cases to tease out some additional subtlety.

## AMAZON.COM'S DEAL EVOLUTION

Like many Internet pioneers, Amazon.com has changed dramatically over the past five years. Until 1997 it sold only books. Then Amazon expanded into music, movies, toys, electronics, software, tools, auctions, and more. Amazon has taken significant minority positions in online retailers of drugs, pet supplies, groceries, and sporting goods. It has established—and then shuttered—a joint venture with a venerable New York auction house, while launching alliances to promote wireless Internet shopping. In fact, much of Amazon's success—and some of its failures—can be traced to a rapid spate of alliances, acquisitions, minority investments, and joint ventures. The rationale and structure of these deals changed quickly as Amazon's needs moved from marketing exposure to brand extension to full utilization of its customer base.

Amazon provides a rich case study about a company pursuing a rapidly changing and diverse business development strategy. Since Amazon is a young company, most of its deals can be systematically examined. The variety of Amazon's deals—as well as the evolving rationales behind them—illustrates the relationship of structure to rationale. Why has Amazon made acquisitions in some cases, while using minority investments or alliances in others? What deals did Amazon reject, choosing to build internal capabilities instead? Why did some company partnerships not work? In analyzing Amazon's overall deal strategy, there is much to learn about designing structures to support the goals of digital deals.

## Starting out

In 1994 Jeff Bezos lived in New York, working as an analyst with investment bank D. E. Shaw. His job involved thinking up new business ideas, presenting them to his boss, and launching successful companies. As Bezos began researching the Internet, he grew certain that its rapid growth would lead to enormous shopping opportunities. He simply needed to pick the right product to sell—one that took advantage of the Internet's unlimited shelf space but could easily be shipped worldwide. Books seemed like a good choice; there were lots of them, and they were cheap to mail. But Bezos knew little about the book-selling industry. So he flew out West to attend a major booksellers conference in Los Angeles, spending the weekend lurking around publisher displays and chatting with distributors. It turned out that the largest book distributors had already developed electronic catalogs with information on millions of books. A massive online bookstore could be created quickly by putting these catalogs on a Web site. It seemed perfect.

D. E. Shaw disagreed. Although the investment bank accepted that the Internet would grow quickly, it was not excited about Bezos's book-selling scheme. But Bezos became obsessed with the idea. After a brief period of soul searching, he decided to risk it all, leaving his Wall Street job to start his own company.

New York was a lousy place to launch the venture, so Bezos moved to Seattle, where he would have a cheaper cost of living, more programming talent, and one of the largest book distributors. His brother gave him an old Chevy Blazer, and Bezos packed the car and headed across the country. While his wife drove, he pecked out a business plan on his laptop. When they finally arrived in Seattle, they rented a small house and converted the garage into an office. Extension cords snaked everywhere. Strapped for cash, Bezos drove over to the local Home Depot, bought a few doors, and hammered on some 2x4s to make desks. Eventually he raised a million dollars—mostly from friends and family—to buy computers and recruit a few programmers. Full of confidence, he interviewed new employees over coffee at a nearby Barnes & Noble. Amazon.com was off and running.

## Stages of deal strategy

Amazon's deals have evolved through three stages. Early on, it focused on marketing efforts that turned Amazon into a household name. It structured a series of alliances to build the brand and gain a critical mass of users. By 1998, Amazon had become prominent. It now turned to execute a style of deals that focused on growing the company, both geographically and via new product lines. To jump-start its growth initiatives, Amazon often relied on acquisitions or joint ventures. This pattern of corporate development continues, as Amazon selectively buys companies to extend its brand and sell new products. However, during 1999 Amazon also moved into a third stage of business development. As a more mature Internet company it began to pursue corporate venture capital, typically making minority investments in younger online retailers. Amazon could bring capital, customer access, and a stamp of approval to a start-up. In exchange, it sought huge financial returns and a relationship that could blossom into future product line extensions. These deals met with mixed results.

## STAGE 1: BUILDING THE AMAZON BRAND

Shortly after its Web site opened, Amazon started a program called Amazon Associates. Almost anyone who had a Web page could form a marketing alliance under this program. Here's how it worked. Associates would set up links to Amazon's retail pages, either to specific products or to Amazon's main page. In exchange for the promotion, the associate would be paid 5 to 15 percent of revenues earned from that customer on the click-through. Amazon also provided detailed reports of what was purchased, so associates could track the success of their links. This program was extremely flexible—since Amazon made variable cost payments to partners, it didn't need to take on a fixed cost risk (as it did, for example, when it paid AOL to promote Amazon's site). Associates could scale their efforts up or down as they saw fit. With a commission-based marketing alliance, everyone had incentives to increase sales. Amazon Associates proved immensely popular. Over the next two years, more than 350,000 partners signed up. The company had developed the largest indirect sales force on the Internet. Amazon also formed marketing alliances with the largest portals, including AOL, Yahoo!, the Microsoft Network, and Excite@Home.

In addition to its associates program, Amazon signed several cross-promotional agreements. It agreed to an alliance with Dell Computer in which both companies linked the checkout pages on their Web sites to new, cobranded Web pages offering Amazon and Dell products. Amazon also provided content to iVillage, a woman's Internet portal, in exchange for promotion on the site. It signed similar marketing agreements with Compaq Computers and with Intuit, a leading developer of personal finance software. These early alliances all focused on building the Amazon brand and winning a loyal base of customers.

## STAGE 2: ACCELERATING GROWTH

Amazon's early brand building worked well. Rewarded with a generous market capitalization, it moved into a second stage of corporate business development—rapid expansion. In this stage, Amazon often used its high-priced stock to acquire smaller companies, but also formed joint ventures and alliances if they would move the company forward. Amazon sought to grow in four ways: (1) via product line extensions, (2) via geographic expansion, (3) by acquiring new technology, and (4) by spurring demand for Amazon's core products and services. Let's examine each direction (see Figure 11-1).

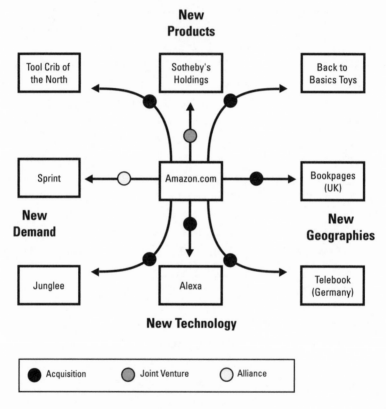

**FIGURE 11-1**
*Amazon's partnerships to expand the business.*

### Extending Amazon's product lines

On November 8, 1999, Amazon issued a terse press release: "Mr. Bezos will make a significant announcement regarding product line extensions that will impact the competitive landscape of online shopping." Throughout the year, Amazon had been extending its brand via new "tabs" for music, videos, and electronics. Now it would announce four new stores: home improvement, software, video games, and gifts. Bezos hammed it up at the press conference, wearing a cowboy-style hard hat and wielding a whirring power drill in each hand. He had a lot to be excited about; the Amazon machine was rolling on to offer more and more products that consumers wanted to buy online.

Behind the scenes, acquisitions paved the way for many of Amazon's new tabs. It bought Tool Crib of the North, which sold home improvement equipment and other tools. A few weeks later, Amazon announced it was buying Back to Basics Toys, a catalog and online retailer of classical toys, such as Slinkys and Raggedy Ann. These acquisitions served as the foundation for Amazon's product extensions. They combined the strong Amazon brand with knowledge and supplier relationships in the toy and home improvement markets. As Amazon raced to add stores, it could often move faster by purchasing an existing player that was familiar with a vertical space.

Yet Amazon did pass on some acquisition targets, electing to develop new markets on its own. For example, when the rumor leaked that Amazon was preparing to enter the computer software business, the stock of one leading online software store, Beyond.com, rose noticeably. Principals from the two companies were on close terms: Beyond.com's CEO had left Amazon to lead the software retailer. Shareholders expected Amazon to approach Beyond.com with an acquisition offer to jump-start a software tab. But Amazon chose another strategy, putting together an in-house team to frantically bang out product descriptions and learn everything they could about the online software business. Unlike product extensions in toys and home improvement, Amazon rejected the acquisition of Beyond.com and chose to go it alone.

How did Amazon decide whether to acquire capabilities through external deals or to grow them in-house? In this case, the cost of acquisition would not bring commensurate benefit. Beyond.com had spent millions building a brand, which would be virtually worthless to Amazon. In addition, Amazon's employees understood the software business and were able to secure key supplier and other relationships. In contrast, the home improvement business was something that Amazon did not understand well at all. It needed the instant know-how and supplier relationships that came from an acquisition such as Tool Crib.

Amazon also formed joint ventures to extend its product line. As mentioned in Chapter 3, Amazon put together a deal with Sotheby's Holdings to build an upscale online auction house. Amazon, seeing successful Internet auction companies like eBay and Yahoo! enjoy gross margins greater than 80 percent, was eager to expand its offerings in the auction business. A venerable company like Sotheby's seemed the perfect partner. Started back in 1744, Sotheby's rose to become the largest auction house in the world, authenticating, buying, and selling art internationally. Amazon craved Sotheby's established brand name and aristocratic image—its directors included Viscount Blakenham and the Marquess of Hartington—as well as its access to products and its imprimatur on authenticity. Sotheby's, on the other hand, enjoyed a well-known brand name, but recognized that the Internet economy would transform the auction business. It could benefit from Amazon's new-world brand and technological prowess. So 255 years after banging its first gavel, Sotheby's agreed to a joint venture with a company only four years old.

The boundaries of the deal were well defined. Each company continued to operate its own online auction in addition to the joint venture, which was named Sothebys.Amazon.com. Amazon's site focused on low-end products, competing head-to-head with eBay. Sotheby's stayed on the high end, offering pricier art masterpieces. The joint venture site, Sothebys.Amazon.com, offered products in the middle: rare coins, stamps, sports and Hollywood collectibles, and general art and antiques. Sealing the relationship, Amazon agreed to invest $45 million for a 1.7 percent stake in Sotheby's.

As noted earlier, this one failed to work as planned. Sixteen months later the partners disbanded their joint Web site, citing low traffic and customer confusion about the three different sites. Amazon also wanted to distance itself from Sotheby's, which was in the midst of an embarrassing U.S. Justice Department probe into antitrust violations. Sotheby's sterling brand had been tarnished. The partners scaled back their relationship, and Amazon learned about some of the unique digital deal challenges associated with a joint venture.

### Expanding into new countries

While the U.S. market had been a great place to launch an Internet business, Amazon had global ambitions. Europe—Germany and Britain in particular—seemed especially attractive. Amazon decided to use acquisitions to enter these two countries. In Britain, it bought a small online bookseller named Bookpages. According to Simon Murdoch, the managing director of Bookpages: "By combining Amazon.com's resources with Bookpages's in depth knowledge of the UK market, we could provide even better service and selection to our customers." It took time to implement the deal. Amazon spent over six months working with Bookpages before the site was rebranded with the Amazon name. In Germany Amazon followed a similar strategy, buying the largest online bookstore in the country, Telebook, and renaming the site Amazon.de.

Using acquisitions to fuel geographic expansion proved successful. Although a quarter of Amazon's sales was outside the United States, buying in Europe had traditionally meant expensive postage and long waits. Bookpages and Telebook gave Amazon access to European market knowledge, logistics, and management talent. As Amazon moved deeper into Europe and Asia, additional acquisitions were expected.

### Acquiring technology to spur sales

Amazon's growth required new technology. For example, as it kept adding product lines, Amazon needed more sophisticated search capabilities that could reach across the different product lines. If a customer typed in "the Jungle Book" Amazon wanted to offer the book, the movie, the soundtrack, and a stuffed King Louie animal. So it bought a company named Junglee, which had developed a software tool that could quickly search a range of Web-based databases to efficiently compare products.

Amazon made other technology acquisitions. One company, Alexa Internet, programmed software that latched on to users' browsers to track and send clickstream information (a chronological listing of where users go) back to a master database. Amazon bought Alexa in April 1999, hoping that the technology would help Amazon understand user patterns and how to get the right product in front of people precisely when they want to buy. Alexa's databases were 13 terabytes in size at the time of purchase, equivalent to 13 million books. Amazon felt that if it could mine this sea of information, it would have the Rosetta stone of marketing (although this deal came to haunt Amazon when consumers raised privacy concerns over the unauthorized gathering and use of this information). Amazon also launched a wireless shopping division (Amazon.com Anywhere) by acquiring Convergence Corp. for $20 million in stock. Convergence made Internet access software for cell phones, Palm Pilots, and other portable information devices. Amazon planned to use Convergence's wireless technology to serve mobile shoppers.

Why did Amazon acquire these firms instead of, say, licensing the technology? Fundamentally, it believed that the technology was directly related to its core commerce initiatives. By integrating the technology closely with its product databases and search capabilities, Amazon wanted to develop unique and insightful ways for consumers to shop online. The technology was so important to the firm that it wanted to control the applications exclusively and prevent competitors from using them.

### Generating derived demand

During this time period, Amazon also pursued a fourth major deal rationale: increasing the overall demand for ecommerce. Similar to Intel—which, as shown in Chapter 8, structured hundreds of deals to increase the need for high-powered computer processors—Amazon wanted to boost the overall volume of ecommerce. Bezos and his team knew that Amazon would receive a large share of the transactions. Unlike Intel, Amazon usually structured these deals as alliances—in part because it did not quite have the cash stockpile of an Intel. In December 1999, Amazon announced an alliance with Sprint to promote wireless shopping. Using an Internet-ready Sprint PCS phone, customers could now select Amazon.com from the phone's minibrowser and purchase any Amazon product directly from their phone. Expecting wireless shopping to be huge, Amazon also entered into alliances with Phone.com (which later changed its name to Openwave), Motorola, and AvantGo. Amazon expected these alliances to hasten the use of wireless Internet devices for ecommerce in general and its products in particular.

A few of Amazon's acquisitions had this same goal. For example, it bought the Internet Movie Database, a company that stores information on movies and television shows. Amazon wanted to use the company's content to increase derived demand for its products. Click for information on a movie, and an Amazon menu pops up next to the plot description where a customer can buy the movie on DVD, the soundtrack on a CD, or the book that inspired the movie.

## STAGE 3: REAPING THE BENEFITS OF SUCCESS?

After Amazon had built a prestigious brand and extended into new product lines and geographies, it began to craft new types of deals that attempted to capitalize on its early success. In some cases Amazon sought to leverage its vast user base. In other deals, it made a series of minority investments, acting as a corporate venture capitalist that could provide both money and endorsement (see Table 11-1). These new partnerships proved extremely risky, and while some investments paid off, many would cause Amazon headaches as the financial markets cooled.

**Table 11-1  Selected Amazon.com Minority Investments**

| Company | Estimated stake | Market | Status at the start of 2001 |
|---------|-----------------|--------|------------------------------|
| Drugstore.com | 20% | healthy and beauty | stock trading under $2/share |
| Pets.com | 30% | pet supplies | closed |
| HomeGrocer | 28% | groceries | merged with competitor Webvan |
| Gear.com | 49% | sporting goods | closed |
| Ashford.com | 17% | luxury goods | stock trading under $1/share |
| Kozmo.com | 32% | quick delivery | pulled IPO |
| Living.com | 18% | furniture | closed |
| Audible | 5% | music | stock trading under $1/share |

### Leveraging the customer base

As Amazon's customer base passed the 10 million mark, it began to aggressively pursue a new type of alliance. Mirroring AOL, which was earning significant sums from partners wanting to access millions of eyeballs, Amazon looked to monetize its vast user pool. In November 1999, Amazon signed an alliance with NextCard to launch a cobranded credit card; Amazon would promote NextCard's Visa in exchange for cash payments. If 1 to 2 percent of Amazon's shoppers signed up for the card, the deal would net Amazon $150 million. (It also obtained warrants to acquire up to 4.4 million shares of NextCard's stock, a stake representing almost 10 percent.) Jeff Bezos commented on this stage in his company's development: "As you achieve a critical mass of customers, you reach a tipping point. Suddenly, people are so eager to partner with you that you can negotiate the very best deal for your customers and also realize fantastic monetary value for Amazon."[2]

### Corporate venture capital

Amazon also made several high-profile minority investments. In these deals, one of Amazon's primary goals was to earn a large return on its investment by branding companies as "Amazon preferred" before their IPO. Amazon provided four resources to young partners: cash, ecommerce know-how, endorsement, and access to Amazon's customers. In return, Amazon sought extraordinary capital gains and relationships that might be used for future product expansions.

The company's minority investment in Drugstore.com is a typical example of VC Amazon. Amazon got involved early in Drugstore.com's history, coinvesting in the first round of funding (June 1998) with venture capitalist Kleiner Perkins. But while Kleiner put in $4 million in cash, Amazon didn't pony up a dime. Instead, it offered to share its Internet technology with Drugstore and sign a cooperative marketing agreement. Furthermore, Amazon provided intangible benefits according to Drugstore's registration statement: "Drugstore.com believes that the benefits of its relationship with Amazon.com include their promotion of our site and the beneficial aspects of our being associated with one of the premier ecommerce companies." Finally, Jeff Bezos teamed up with Kleiner's John Doerr to convince former Microsoft executive Peter Neupert to step in as CEO. In exchange for its backing, Amazon got 5 million shares of stock. Over the next few rounds of funding, Amazon continued to invest, this time paying cash to accumulate another 5.7 million shares. When Drugstore.com went public, Amazon snapped up another half million shares at the IPO price of $18. Over the next year, it continued to buy, and toward the end of 2000, Amazon owned nearly 13 million shares, slightly over 20 percent of the company.[3]

This minority investment made Amazon serious money (on paper) for a while. Drugstore's IPO opened at $50 and rose to a high of $70 over the next few weeks. At that point, Amazon enjoyed over $700 million in unrealized capital gains. Not a bad return on a $40 million investment—Amazon was starting to look like Intel. But the risk was enormous, and while Amazon kept buying shares, Drugstore.com's stock plummeted along with the rest of the e-tailing market. As its stock price dropped down below $2, the specter of failure hovered over Drugstore. An accounting of Amazon's position showed that it had now lost nearly $50 million and faced the possibility of losing the entire $75 million it had invested in the company.

Other minority investments proved equally sobering. In March 1999, Amazon coinvested with the venture capital firm Hummer Winblad in Pets.com, a provider of pet products, information, and services on the Internet. Amazon followed this $55 million investment with a second round of approximately $30 million in June. Scarcely a year later Pets.com shut down, dealing Amazon a painful loss.[4] Similarly, its stakes in Gear.com (a retailer of close-out sporting goods) and Living.com (an online furniture retailer) were wiped out when the firms went bankrupt. Early in 2000, Amazon invested $60 million to obtain an initial 23 percent stake in a company called Kozmo.com, which built up a fleet of vehicles and employees to make door-to-door deliveries of movies, snacks, and other whim purchases within the hour. Several months later Kozmo ended up pulling its IPO and laying off employees in the face of tough market conditions. All told, in the painful third quarter of 2000, Amazon took a $100 million charge for impaired investments and unrealized losses. In April 2001, Kozmo was shut down.

In hindsight, these minority investments look like bad decisions. But the lesson here is not that these deals were necessarily mistakes. Amazon found itself in what appeared to be the right place at the right time and could take equity partly in exchange for providing coveted customer access. It had a unique intangible asset, which it attempted to leverage by placing high-risk, high-return bets. Unfortunately, these investments failed to pay off as planned. Amazon experienced what many others were suffering in 2000: Venture returns required venture risk.

## Summing up Amazon's deal strategy

Amazon is a young company, but has already run the gamut of corporate business development. Early on, it structured thousands of small marketing alliances and struck business development deals with the major Internet portals to build brand, drive sales, and attract millions of customers. Its next wave of deals sought to grow the business via acquisition of new product lines and ventures with established players. Amazon then started placing minority investments, seeking positive financial returns, and possibly staged acquisitions.

Although Amazon had been burned by many of its high-risk venture investments, business development would no doubt play a major role supporting the company's future growth. In 2000, Amazon entered a fourth stage of digital deals, designed to accelerate its path to profitability. For example, Amazon struck a 10-year agreement with Toys "R" Us to tackle the online market for children's goods. Each side brought different strengths: Amazon offered a large customer base, strong brand, customer service centers, and warehousing skills. Toys "R" Us brought experience at purchasing and managing inventory risk associated with forecasting hot, seasonal items. Amazon would receive fixed and variable payments from Toys "R" Us, along with warrants to acquire 5 percent of Toysrus.com. In combining their strengths, both companies sought to reach profitability in this business more quickly than they otherwise would have. Amazon was likely to fashion similar deals in other product markets. At the same time, Amazon's business development team moved to structure additional deals that exploited commerce opportunities created by wireless and digital video technologies.

# VERTICALNET'S B2B DIGITAL DEALS

VerticalNet, a business-to-business ecommerce enabler, has actively used digital deals to position itself in a crowded field of competitors. Like Amazon, VerticalNet was founded in 1995 and rose to a prominent market position. VerticalNet is old enough to have a noteworthy track record of partnerships, yet young enough that its range of significant deals and deal structures can be studied comprehensively. VerticalNet had something else in common with Amazon, having snatched away its President, Joe Galli, to become CEO in 2000. (Galli's stint at VerticalNet was brief, however, as he left in early 2001 to become CEO at Newell Rubbermaid.) Over the past few years, VerticalNet structured dozens of acquisitions, joint ventures, minority investments, and alliances. In analyzing VerticalNet, pay special attention to how the rationale driving each deal relates to the company's choice of deal structure.

## VerticalNet's business

Headquartered in Horsham, Pennsylvania, VerticalNet ended the year 2000 with online communities for more than 50 markets, as diverse as solid waste, meat and poultry, dental supplies, and aerospace. The company was started by Michael Hagan and Michael McNulty, two college friends who quit their jobs and maxed out their credit cards to launch VerticalNet's first community, Water Online. Unlike many other B2B exchanges—which typically aggregate buyers to lower purchase prices—VerticalNet combined suppliers to create online communities of interest. Its Web sites offered a variety of features, including industry news, online catalogs, buyer's guides, job searches, and discussion forums. After receiving a $16 million investment from Internet Capital Group, Hagan and McNulty attracted Mark Walsh, a former senior vice president at America Online, to run the firm. VerticalNet continued to execute deals and build out vertical online markets. The company went public in 1999. Joe Galli came on as CEO the next year, departed in early 2001, and was replaced by Hagan.

VerticalNet was initially criticized for not being a "real" B2B exchange because the majority of its revenue came from advertising instead of commerce. In 1999, 82 percent of VerticalNet's sales came from online ads (slightly over $17 million). Skeptics scoffed that it was nothing more than a mishmash of online trade magazines. But having established an audience, VerticalNet quickly moved toward a much broader business model, including ecommerce revenue, exchange commissions, and maintenance and services revenue. In particular, it intended to increase sales of two commerce products, "storefronts" and "E-commerce centers." Storefronts—supplier-specific Web sites hosted by VerticalNet—allowed companies to display their products, generate sales leads, and sell a handful of items online. E-commerce centers were "souped-up" storefronts where vendors could sell many more products online. For example, a storefront might allow vendors to place 10 products online, while E-commerce centers would support more than 500 items. With these commerce products, VerticalNet earned a transaction fee on every sale. By the end of 2000, advertising still accounted for nearly $100 million in revenues, but this was now less than half of VerticalNet's total gross.[5]

Under Joe Galli, VerticalNet also restructured into three different business units. The first, VerticalNet Markets, consisted of the original 50-plus market communities. VerticalNet wanted to grow this division by expanding the portfolio of communities and by selling more storefronts and E-commerce centers at each site. The second division, VerticalNet Exchanges, focused on establishing direct, real-time open and spot markets for products. Revenues would come from exchange commissions. The final division, VerticalNet Solutions, would provide digital marketplace technology to a variety of industry alliances. This group would compete with Ariba, CommerceOne, and Oracle, as well as with other firms that offered technology solutions to online B2B exchanges.

## Deal structures

By 2000, VerticalNet had expanded beyond an advertising-driven revenue model, largely by forming digital deals. It was actively employing all five major deal structures—acquisitions, joint ventures, minority investments, alliances, and even a spin-off (see Figure 11-2).

### ACQUISITIONS AND SPIN-OFFS

VerticalNet completed over 20 acquisitions during its first five years for a variety of reasons. In particular, as was the case with Intel (Chapter 8), acquisitions gave VerticalNet the capabilities to build new divisions. In fact, two acquisitions initially formed the core of its Exchanges and Solutions business units.

Late in 1999 VerticalNet announced the acquisition of a 20-year-old Massachusetts company named NECX. Over the years NECX had built up the largest exchange for electronic components in the world. This deal not only provided an immediate presence in the important electronics market (an $80 billion industry) but it also provided VerticalNet with experience into how exchanges really work. NECX had warehouses, forklifts, and back-end processing capabilities that let VerticalNet get its hands dirty and learn how to operate real-time exchanges. This could help VerticalNet build similar exchanges for other market communities. In addition, with an established user base, NECX could also serve as a test market for a wide range of new offerings that VerticalNet was planning to roll out, such as auctions, reverse auctions, and real-time online markets.[6]

|  | Company | Primary Rationale |
|---|---|---|
| **Acquisitions** | NECX | Build VerticalNet Exchanges division |
|  | Tradeum | Build VerticalNet Solutions division |
| **Minority Investments** | Microsoft | Obtain 80,000 new storefronts and $100 million for acquisitions |
|  | ICG | Connect with B2B ecosystem |
|  | Sumitomo | Build overseas connections |
| **Alliances** | Excite | Increase customer base |
|  | EComm | Leverage customer base with cross promotion in foodservice |
|  | Environ | Cross promotion with environmental compliance site |
| **Joint Ventures** | Softbank | Launch VerticalNet Japan |
|  | British Telecom | Create VerticalNet Europe |
|  | Sumitomo | Build VerticalNet Exchanges in Japan |
| **Spin-Offs** | NECX | Refocus firm as software company |

**FIGURE 11-2**
*Selected VerticalNet deals.*

However in December 2000, VerticalNet announced it was spinning off NECX, selling the company to Converge, a B2B consortium created by 15 high-tech buyers and sellers including Compaq and Hewlett-Packard. VerticalNet would receive $60 million in cash and a 20 percent stake in Converge. Converge would buy $107.5 million in VerticalNet's software over three years. The move positioned Vertical-Net more solidly as a software solutions company, although it meant moving away from directly participating in the electronics components exchange space.

In March 2000, VerticalNet completed another major acquisition, buying Tradeum, a San Francisco-based provider of B2B transaction software. Tradeum sold a technology platform for building marketplaces that allowed multiple buyers, sellers, and transaction enablers to be matched in real time. Tradeum had also developed a number of scalable industry templates. This merger provided the bedrock for VerticalNet's new Solutions division, as Tradeum gave VerticalNet technology to compete with Ariba and CommerceOne. From Tradeum's point of view, the deal provided a strong brand, along with preferred access to a host of potential customers.

Why did VerticalNet structure these deals as acquisitions or spin-offs? As shown in Chapter 6, these deal structures are particularly well suited to support drastic business model shifts. VerticalNet needed to expand beyond an advertising-only revenue model. The company recognized that additional core capabilities were central to its new strategy and that it did not have time to build skills internally. Acquisitions allowed VerticalNet to get the capabilities and control necessary to aggressively morph its business model. The subsequent spin-off of NECX accentuated the future importance of the Solutions business unit.

MINORITY INVESTMENTS

VerticalNet enjoyed several well-heeled investors, including Internet Capital Group (ICG), Microsoft, and Sumitomo. Not surprisingly, these minority investors were investing to get more than financial returns out of the relationship.

Probably VerticalNet's most intriguing partnership involved a $100 million deal with Microsoft. In January 2000, Microsoft agreed to invest $100 million in VerticalNet to provide funding for strategic acquisitions. Microsoft would also give VerticalNet distribution and marketing support on its MSN network, the Microsoft bCentral small-business portal, and Microsoft.com. In exchange, VerticalNet agreed to accelerate its adoption of Microsoft technologies as underlying platforms for VerticalNet's community architecture. A few months later, VerticalNet and Microsoft expanded their relationship by signing a three-year strategic alliance to deliver business-to-business ecommerce services and content to small- and medium-size businesses. Microsoft agreed to purchase a minimum of 80,000 VerticalNet storefronts and E-Commerce centers and distribute them free to third-party businesses for one year. VerticalNet would build the storefronts, incorporate them with various Microsoft services (sales lead generation, for example) and place them in all of its B2B communities. From VerticalNet's point of view, the deal looked great—it would acquire money, customers, and a marquee partner.

Why was Microsoft supporting VerticalNet so strongly? Microsoft, crafting its B2B strategy, considered VerticalNet a perfect showcase for its next generation .NET technology and sought to demonstrate the scalability of its platforms. The deal also gave customers of bCentral the ability to participate in VerticalNet's 50+ industry information and trading communities and let Microsoft provide its instant-messaging technology to VerticalNet's customers.

## COMMERCE ALLIANCES AND JVS

In addition to these acquisition and equity investment deals, VerticalNet structured a broad range of commerce alliances involving many of its vertical markets. In a sense, VerticalNet was attempting to establish a "B2B mirror" of AOL's consumer-driven adcom channel alliance strategy (see Chapter 9). VerticalNet formed partnerships to broaden its business customer base through deals with Onsale (now Egghead), Excite, and Deja News. Next, VerticalNet began to leverage its traffic by establishing cross-promotional or preferred placement deals with companies such as Impresse (print procurement services), Ecomm Systems (food service equipment), and Environ (environmental compliance solutions).

VerticalNet also established joint ventures to support its aggressive international expansion goals. In early 2000, it teamed up with Softbank to launch VerticalNet Japan. A few months later, it struck a similar deal with British Telecom and ICG to create VerticalNet Europe. And, as mentioned earlier, Sumitomo, one of Japan's largest trading companies, invested $30 million in VerticalNet. The companies planned to cooperate on a number of joint initiatives, including the potential creation of VerticalNet Exchange Japan, which would follow on the heels of their NECX Asia joint venture in Singapore.

## Competing through deal strategy

Like many other Internet B2B firms in 2000, VerticalNet found itself in the middle of stormy financial markets. Although there was no guarantee that the company would thrive (or even survive), VerticalNet had clearly put together an array of partnerships to support its major goals. The company's deal portfolio included acquisitions and spin-offs, joint ventures, minority investments, and alliances to build new divisions, redefine its business model, enter new geographies, and expand and leverage its customer base. Going forward, digital deals were certain to play a significant role in determining the effectiveness of VerticalNet's strategy.

# RATIONALE/STRUCTURE MATRIX

This chapter explored the relationship between deal rationale and structure. In any given situation, a firm's appetite for risk, control, conflict, and commitment—combined with the unique context of the deal—will guide the choice of structure. Against the backdrop of Chapters 6 through 10, the deals of Amazon.com and VerticalNet tease out additional subtlety in the connection between rationale and structure.

There is no simple deal structure prescription for each strategic rationale. Commerce and deal making are too subtle, too political, too ego-driven to be completely subjugated to any rational system. Nevertheless, Table 11-2 lists the major digital deal rationales covered in this chapter and in Part 2, together with primary, secondary, and tertiary structures that tend to work well in supporting each rationale.

**Table 11-2 Summary of Connections between Deal Rationale and Structure**

| Rationale | Primary Structure | Secondary Structure | Tertiary Structure |
|---|---|---|---|
| Controlling technology | M&A* | Joint venture | Minority investment |
| Transforming a business model | M&A | | |
| Consolidating turbulent markets | M&A | | |
| Locking in synergies | M&A | Joint venture | |
| Building new divisions | M&A | Minority investment | |
| Penetrating vertical markets | Joint venture | M&A | |
| Expanding into new regions | Joint venture | Commerce alliance | M&A |
| Reaching new customer segments | Joint venture | | |
| Entering new value web activities | Joint venture | | |
| Building indirect demand for products | Minority investment | | |
| Obtaining home run financial returns | Minority investment | | |
| Whipping competitive horses | Minority investment | Commerce alliance | |
| Fueling an industry value web | Minority investment | | |
| Mitigating coopetive situations | Minority investment | Commerce alliance | |
| Extending brand | Minority investment | Commerce alliance | M&A |
| Stimulating an ecosystem | Minority investment | Commerce alliance | |
| Increasing customer base | Commerce alliance | Minority investment | |
| Monetizing a customer base | Commerce alliance | | |
| Enhancing offerings | Commerce alliance | Joint venture | |
| Extending technology reach | Commerce alliance | Minority investment | M&A |
| Selling to, through, and with | Commerce alliance | Minority investment | |
| Unlocking buried wealth | Spin-off | | |
| Retaining talented employees | Spin-off | | |
| Freeing up a division for sale | Spin-off | | |

*Merger and acquisition

This list is neither exhaustive nor exact; use it only as a starting point and then add additional context and subtlety. The right structure needs to be chosen on the basis of organizational practicalities along with a solid understanding of the deal's underlying strategic objectives.

Furthermore, as illustrated throughout this book, selecting an overall structure is only the beginning of deal configuration. Terms and conditions that motivate all parties, as well as mechanisms for ensuring deal execution, are essential interior build-outs of the structure.

Make no mistake, however: Deal structure is the central framework that can increase the chances of a successful partnership or investment. And deal rationale is the foundation of this framework.

# CHAPTER 12

# Conclusion:
# Analysis and Action

Superior business models increasingly require a network of deals, alliances, and other significant partnerships. The new economy has brought complexity, along with opportunity, to businesses throughout the globe. This means that executives need new information systems to help select and implement the right deals.

This book has presented a positioning and partnering framework for external market analysis and action. The building blocks for this market modeling system include players (companies), deals, and the submarkets to which players and deals are assigned. These submarkets, defined by combinations of products and/or services, geographies, customer segments, and value activities, comprise the new landscape where firms must compete. By assembling these building blocks in a meaningful way, companies can develop a comprehensive partnership strategy that supports top-level executive decisions.

Market modeling is emerging as an essential system for the new economy. It is a new genre of application, centering on information outside of an organization. As markets and competitive situations continue to grow in complexity, firms that dedicate the resources to effectively build these information systems will obtain a clear advantage over their peers. Forward-looking companies are already working to develop these types of systems. This final chapter concludes by offering some guiding principles on how to develop a market modeling system that structures analysis and inspires confidence in action.

# 1. DESIGN FOR DYNAMIC CONDITIONS

Above all else, a new economy market modeling system must be dynamic. Change is the hallmark of both opportunity and competition. New companies are born and existing ones die. Firms enter and leave markets. New deals are announced daily, as old ones are modified or terminated. New value activities in a market are established and existing ones become more or less important. Some international markets expand rapidly; others must be analyzed to understand "lighthouse" innovations.

As today's markets reel from the impact of digital disruption, external information systems must capture the turmoil. The decay curve showing the usefulness of market information over time is steep. Data has a short half-life. Static systems based on monthly inputs will fail. The unit of time for a market system update is often measured in days, sometimes hours.

# 2. DEDICATE RESOURCES

All vital organizational systems require resources, both technological and human, and a market modeling system is no exception. Dedicated analysts are needed to gather relevant company, relationship, and market research. This team must have the know-how, tools, and resources to obtain content that precisely supports executive decisions about competitive positioning and partnerships. Advances in knowledge management technology, including artificial intelligence-based classification engines, will make it easier for information to be automatically sorted in a meaningful way. But human intervention will always be required.

The effort must be systematic and ongoing. This is in sharp contrast with the processes of a typical news-driven publication, where the major effort goes from story to story, without adequate attention to building systematic resources. Targeted "chunk building" (as discussed in Chapter 2) should be the byword of market modeling.

There will inevitably be spikes of activity, driven by the current markets and related deals a company is considering, but even deal-specific research must be viewed as building an overall resource that supports an ongoing planning system. Research related to all relevant markets, companies, and relationships must undergo periodic review, and standards should establish the maximum time such information is allowed to stand without update.

A well-designed system supports the efficient and sensitive blend of publicly available market content on the Web with internal research and analysis. For example, company and deal database entries should automatically support hyperlinks to browse meaningful external content. Internal analysis relating to the company or deal entry should provide a context for the link.

# 3. INVOLVE FIELD AND BUSINESS DEVELOPMENT GROUPS

Robust market modeling contains more than publicly available information. Field sales personnel close to markets, companies, and relationships are critical sources of input. Corporate business development groups must view a market modeling system as their own and actively contribute meaningful content and analysis.

The goal is to get all vital organizational constituencies to use the system regularly in their everyday work—for information input, analysis, and action. The responsibility for the maintenance, updating, and consistency of knowledge should be in the hands of an analyst dedicated to the system. However, market modeling is both grounded and enriched from information in the field. This will happen if the sales and business development groups find that the system supports their core activities.

# 4. THINK GRANULARLY

This book has stressed the submarket as the unit of analysis for capturing company and relationship information. Recall that submarkets can be defined as the intersection of four dimensions: specific products or services, geographies, customer segments, and value activities. Digital deals are commonly made submarket by submarket. In fact, a partner in one submarket may be a competitor in another. Conversely, one arm of an organization can view another company as a competitor while a second arm considers the company its best friend. For example, in fall 2000, Sony Music bitterly opposed Napster's MP3 music service in court (represented by the RIAA). Yet, Sony Electronics belonged to the Consumer Electronics Association, which filed a friend-of-the-court brief supporting Napster. (Sony Electronics had introduced the Vaio music clip, a device that played MP3 files.)

The fact that market modeling must support competitive positioning and partnership analysis at the submarket level raises a challenging question: How granular should company and relationship information be? If content in the system is too broad, it will not support necessary subtlety in management thinking. On the other hand, if content is too detailed, information classification problems can become unwieldy.

The granularity of a market modeling system should be driven by executive need and subject to cost-benefit analysis. One needs to focus on building knowledge at an appropriate, yet manageable depth in any given submarket. In-depth knowledge of a submarket may be vital if an awareness of key competitor and potential partner movements in the market matters. On the other hand, to classify (and keep current) everything that thousands of companies are doing in dozens of markets throughout hundreds of countries will be overwhelming.

# 5. PREDESIGN ANALYSES

Market modeling should be tuned to support specific analyses such as:

◆ Deal structure classifications—highlighting mergers and acquisitions, minority investments, joint ventures, alliances, or other deal activity in a submarket

◆ Specific competitor profiles—summarizing partnership activities for a new or existing competitor

◆ Beachhead analysis—depicting a market segment or industry's evolution, including historical context, key statistics, tactical moves, and battles on the horizon

◆ Ecosystem analysis—selecting clusters of partners to support marketing and sales efforts for each submarket

◆ Conflict analysis—exploring what conflicts might result from partnerships or investments in a specific company

◆ What-if scenarios—simulating moves in a market to depict potential company and partner configurations

For example, Figure 12-1 depicts a simplified beachhead analysis developed in 2000, showing select Microsoft moves and challenges as the company positioned itself to enter the online gaming hardware market. The purpose here is merely to illustrate the type of analysis that market modeling might be designed to support.

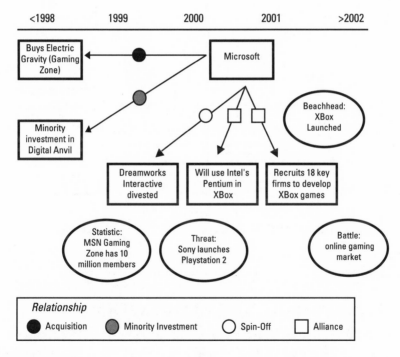

**FIGURE 12-1**
*Beachhead analysis: Microsoft moves into online gaming hardware.*

# 6. REDUCE COMPLEXITY

One could illustrate the complexity of markets, companies, and relationships by generating a graphic of Intel's minority equity portfolio, which, as discussed in Chapter 8, contains many hundreds of investments. But such an exercise would result in an illegible mess of lines and text. An effective market modeling system must be able to reduce market complexity into useful chunks of knowledge using appropriate search and filtering mechanisms. Once again, submarket filtering and search at appropriate granularity are keys to solving this problem. For example, showing Intel's minority investments in the submarket of Internet security presents a meaningful picture (see Figure 12-2).

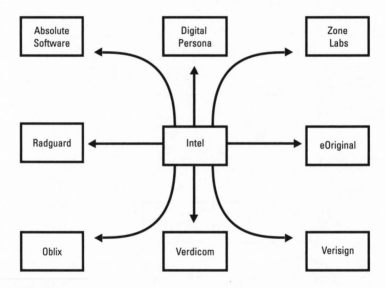

**FIGURE 12-2**
*Intel's investments in Internet security companies.*

# 7. SELECT PARTNERS SHREWDLY

Avoid extremes when selecting digital partners. The player universe of potential partners must not be limited to members of the country club. As this book has shown, successful business models now often depend on building ecosystems of partners with expertise not only in vertical product and service markets but also in technology and communications. A database of potential partners must be just that—a database—and not limited to a Rolodex or Palm Pilot address book.

On the other hand, a rule that experienced dealmakers have long used—do business with people you know—should not be ignored. Leveraging long-time relationships has been and remains one of the greatest risk-reducing mechanisms for selecting partners.

Semi-intelligent partner selection means expanding and refining the universe of deal partners through systematic market modeling. Intelligent partnership selection adds knowledge possessed by corporate insiders about outside organizations and people. In other words, market modeling coupled with personal Rolodexes yield the ultimate system for sourcing and selecting digital deals.

## 8. THINK STEWARDSHIP, STEWARDSHIP, STEWARDSHIP

Having partners is not enough. Partnerships must support coherent business models and deal rationales. They need to be grounded in underlying strategic objectives. Meaningful deal rationales can drive optimal structures, which, in turn, increase the odds of a successful outcome.

The essential role of deal stewardship has been illustrated throughout this book. Stewardship ranges from a merger and acquisition "cleanup crew" at Cisco, to marketing support for strategic corporate investments at Intel, to dedicated project managers at CNET who monitor alliance effectiveness after a deal is done.

A market modeling system, of necessity, embraces the key dimensions of implementation. This includes "follow-up" fields that monitor employee retention rates after an acquisition, product support resulting from a strategic minority investment, or new customer acquisition derived from a commerce alliance. Sustained follow-up closes the system loops of market modeling.

## 9. FASHION THE BUSINESS CASE

Digital deals must be linked to financial results. In 2000, AOL provided a clear example of how to do so through the use of long-term business commerce alliances. AOL built a multibillion-dollar backlog of adcom partnerships that showed at least some resistance to partner defaults. The next deal challenge: to develop a "new new media" business model and execute the Time Warner merger.

The call for "profit now, not later" trumpeted across the digital landscape. Hundreds of dot-coms died. Spin-offs that centered on financial engineering were abruptly halted. Market-share-grab strategies became tempered by classic economics. Speculation and speciation continued, but were subject to more intense financial scrutiny.

The need to integrate digital deals into traditional corporate functions—marketing, finance, operations, and organizational design—has been one of this book's main themes. Partnerships for revenue and profit—that help a company sell to, through, and with others—must be the ultimate goal of a vibrant market modeling system.

# Endnotes

CHAPTER 1: THE ERA OF DIGITAL DEALS

1. Thomas A. Edsall and Murray N. Charlton, "Nearshore Waters of the Great Lakes" (paper presented at the State of Lakes Ecosystem Conference, December 1997), 13-14, 29-30. Available: http://www.epa.gov/glnpo/solec/96/nearshore/nswmaste.pdf.

2. Bill Gurley, "The New Face of Internet Competition," *Above the Crowd*, February 22, 1999.

3. See, for example, "AT&T Lowers Earnings Expectations on Worries About Long-Distance Unit," *The Wall Street Journal*, May 2, 2000; "Cable-Telephone Target Poses Challenge for AT&T This Year," *The Wall Street Journal*, April 28, 2000. Ultimately these challenges led AT&T to announce a major breakup in October 2000.

4. Robert E. Spekman and Lynn A. Isabella, *Alliance Competence* (New York: John Wiley, 2000), 1.

5. For an analysis of AOL's backlog, see Scott Ehrens, Matthew Esh, and Matthew Adams, "America Online, Inc.: Baby's Got Backlog," Bear Stearns (January 4, 2000).

6. For a discussion of how strategic alliances can transform an industry's structure, see Benjamin Gomes-Casseres, *The Alliance Revolution: The New Shape of Business Rivalry* (Boston: Harvard University Press, 1996).

7. Nicholas Negroponte, *Being Digital* (New York: Knopf, 1995).

8. Lowell Bryan et al., *Race for the World* (Boston: Harvard Business School Press, 1999). See also Jeffrey F. Rayport and John Sviokla, "Exploiting the Virtual Value Chain," *Harvard Business Review*, November-December 1995: 75-85.

9. Bryan et al., *Race for the World*, 23-25. See also Frances Cairncross, *The Death of Distance: How the Communications Revolution will Change our Lives* (Boston: Harvard Business School Press, 1997).

10. Larry Downes and Chunka Mui, *Unleashing the Killer App* (Boston: Harvard Business School Press, 1998).

11.  For a good discussion of quantum technologies see Paul Taylor, "Race is on to Find Chips of the Future," *Financial Times: Survey on Information Technology*, January 2000.

12.  Carl Shapiro and Hal R. Varian, *Information Rules* (Boston: Harvard Business School Press, 1999).

13.  Bryan et al., *Race for the World*, 20.

14.  "Venture-Backed Companies Account for Half of All IPOs In 1999," The National Venture Capital Association, January 7, 2000.

15.  Gloria Tristani, UCLA panel discussion, January 2000.

16.  For an overview see Paul Krugman, "The Web Gets Ugly," *New York Times Magazine*, December 6, 1998. Two polar views are portrayed in Kevin Kelly, *New Rules for the New Economy* (New York: Viking, 1998), 55; and Shapiro and Varian, *Information Rules*, 18.

17.  R. H. Coase, *The Firm, the Market, and the Law* (Chicago: University of Chicago Press, 1988). For a classic discussion of transaction costs as they relate to alliance management, see Oliver E. Williamson, *Markets and Hierarchies* (New York: Free Press, 1975).

18.  Downes and Mui, *Unleashing the Killer App*, 37.

19.  The similarities between business competition and biological ecosystems have been explored in James F. Moore, *The Death of Competition: Leadership and Strategy in the Age of Business Ecosystems* (New York: HarperBusiness, 1997). See also Michael Rothschild, *Bionomics: Economy as Ecosystem* (New York: Henry Holt and Company, 1992).

20.  Joel Kotkin and David Friedman, "Why Every Business Will Be Like Show Business," *Inc. Magazine*, March 1, 1995. See also Kelly, *New Rules*, 111.

21.  John Seely Brown and Paul Duguid, *The Social Life of Information* (Boston: Harvard Business School Press, 2000). The authors continue to make the argument that a law of increasing firms is just as simplistic as a law of diminishing firms. Their point is that the world is more complex; technological gurus cannot just make linear predictions about the future of business but need to ground their thinking in the Byzantine interplay of technology and human social behavior.

22.  The effectiveness of vertical integration has been explored by Erin Anderson and Barton A. Weitz, "Make-or-Buy Decisions: Vertical Integration and Marketing Productivity," *Sloan Management Review* (spring 1986): 3-19. See also Kathryn Harrigan, "A Framework for Looking at Vertical Integration," *The Journal of Business Strategy* (February 1983): 30-37; R. D. Buzzell, "Is Vertical Integration Profitable?" *Harvard Business Review*, January-February 1983: 92-102.

23. Adam Brandenburger and Barry Nalebuff, *Co-opetition* (New York: Currency Doubleday, 1996).

24. Robert Porter Lynch, *The Practical Guide to Joint Ventures and Corporate Alliances* (New York: John Wiley, 1989). For an additional discussion of how to successfully implement geographic alliances see also Joel Bleeke and David Ernst, *Collaborating to Compete: Using Strategic Alliances and Acquisitions in the Global Marketplace* (New York: John Wiley, 1993); and Kathryn Harrigan and William Newman, *Managing for Joint Venture Success* (Lexington, Mass.: Lexington Books, 1986).

## CHAPTER 2: MARKET OVERVIEW AND PLAYER DATABASE

1. Herbert Simon, "What We Know about the Creative Process," *Frontiers in Creative and Innovative Management* (Cambridge, Mass.: Ballinger, 1985).

2. Peter F. Drucker, "The Next Information Revolution," *Forbes ASAP*, August 1998, 47-58.

3. National Research Council, *The Digital Dilemma: Intellectual Property in the Information Age* (Washington D.C.: National Academy Press, 2000).

4. Geoffrey P. Hull, *The Recording Industry* (Boston: Allyn and Bacon, 1998).

5. See National Research Council, *The Digital Dilemma*, Chapters 1 and 2, for more detail about the digitization of music and related policy issues.

6. MP3.com now enabled consumers to store digital copies of CDs they owned on MP3.com's Web site and offered consumers immediate digital copies of CDs they purchased from online retailers.

7. Our notion of traditional, hybrid, and digital value activities extends the classic value chain construct of Michael Porter, who posited a process view of the organization. Porter viewed a company as a system, made up of primary activities consisting of inbound logistics, operations, outbound logistics, marketing and sales, and service. See Michael E. Porter, *Competitive Advantage: Creating and Sustaining Superior Performance* (New York: The Free Press, 1985).

8. See A. Sasa Zorovic and John F. Powers, "The Online Music Report," Robertson Stephens (March 17, 2000) for a summary of activities along a digital music distribution chain.

9. See Sharon M. Oster, *Modern Competitive Analysis* (New York: Oxford University Press, 1994), 32-41, for a discussion of how intensity of competition in a market is determined by factors such as a large number of competitors, wide distribution in competitor size, and instability in demand.

10. For a primer on customer segmentation, see Art Weinstein, *Market segmentation: Using Demographics, Psychographics, and Other Niche Marketing Techniques to Predict and Model Customer Behavior* (Chicago: Probus Publishing Company, 1994).

## CHAPTER 3: DEAL DATABASE AND DEAL RATIONALE

1. This step could be viewed as part of Step 3. However, we view the determination of deal rationale as important enough to distinguish it as a separate step.

2. Kathleen Eisenhardt has written extensively about the connection between real-time information, speed, and quality of choice in strategic decision making. For example, see Kathleen M. Eisenhardt, "Speed and Strategic Choice: How Managers Accelerate Decision Making," *California Management Review* 32, no. 3 (1990).

3. For one analyst's estimates, see Jamie Kiggen, "AOL Posts Another Quality Quarter," Donaldson, Lufkin & Jenrette (February 12, 1999).

4. For perspective on First USA's problems, see "Bank One Names James Dimon Chairman and Chief Executive," *The Wall Street Journal*, March 27, 2000.

5. The notion of a deal constellation is explored in Benjamin Gomes-Casseres, *The Alliance Revolution: The New Shape of Business Rivalry* (Boston: Harvard University Press, 1998).

6. Infographics® is a term used by TriVergence (www.trivergence.com) in publishing constellations relating to technology, communications, media, and other markets. TriVergence was cofounded by George T. Geis.

7. This assumes, of course, that there is a rational or semirational pattern in the company's deals. In our judgment, some companies act irrationally or even neurotically in responding to market threats. Others act with impressive rationality.

8. It has become difficult to find a market day that does not generate at least one major news story about significant stock price movement in a company resulting from an alliance or partnership. This is especially true during volatile market periods. For example, during March 2000, the authors found at least one such story appearing in *The Wall Street Journal* or on the *Dow Jones Newswires* every business day of the month.

9. "Liquid Audio Adds New Releases from Atlantic, Arista, Bad Boy, Beyond, Capitol, Dreamworks, Elektra, Hollywood, MCA, Polydor, RCA, Reprise, Universal, Virgin, Wind-Up, Windham Hill and Warner Bros Records to Major Label Content it Distributes," *PR Newswire*, September 3, 1999.

## CHAPTER 4: SELECTING DEALS AND PARTNERS

1. For example, VA Linux Systems rose 698 percent and Akamai 458 percent during the first day that their stocks hit the public markets. There were many other short-term success stories.

2. Jonathan Rabinovitz, "The Internet Economy Gets a Reality Check," *The Industry Standard*, December 6, 1999, 85-88. This phenomenon became even more pronounced when alternative metrics such as hits-per-month, registered users, or connected desktops were used: Boris Feldman, "Metrics Fraud," *The Industry Standard*, March 6, 2000, 92.

3. "The Internet and Financial Services," Morgan Stanley Dean Witter (March 7, 2000).

4. Charles Gasparino and Rebecca Buckman, "Facing Internet Threat, Merrill Plans To Offer Trading Online for Low Fees," *The Wall Street Journal*, June 1, 1999.

5. In a Dutch auction, investors place bids over the Internet for the number of shares they want at the price they are willing to pay. When the bidding ends, the stock is offered to the bidders at the highest price at which all shares are spoken for.

6. "E-Commerce, Bonding on the Internet," *Euromoney*, February 10, 2000.

7. "Shifting Power to the Buy Side: Automating Fixed Income Markets," Meridian Research (1999).

8. "E-Commerce, Bonding on the Internet," *Euromoney*, February 10, 2000.

9. Don Tapscott, David Ticoll, and Alex Lowy, *Digital Capital: Harnessing the Power of Business Webs* (Boston: Harvard Business School Press, 2000).

10. See Judith E. Gallatin, *Adolescence and Individuality* (New York: Harper & Row, 1975).

11. Ed Christian, "Urban Hopes to Make a Major Out of Edel," *Billboard*, August 5, 2000.

## CHAPTER 5: STRUCTURING AND IMPLEMENTING DEALS

1. The event has been heralded as momentous, even though the connection cut off after only a few keystrokes.

2. Robert Porter Lynch, *The Practical Guide to Joint Ventures and Corporate Alliances* (New York: John Wiley, 1989).

3. While there are many other kinds of alliances, such as R&D partnerships, our focus will be on the advertising and commerce partnerships, where revenue generation has a direct role in the purpose of the deal.

4. See, for example, Kathryn Harrigan and William Newman, *Managing for Joint Venture Success* (Lexington, Mass.: Lexington Books, 1986).

5. Robert E. Spekman and Lynn A. Isabella, *Alliance Competence* (New York: John Wiley, 2000).

6. "The New M&A," *Fortune*, November 8, 1999.

## CHAPTER 6: MERGERS AND ACQUISITIONS

1. Laura M. Holson, "Whiz Kid: Young Deal Maker Is the Force Behind a Company's Growth," *The New York Times*, November 19, 1998.

2. J. Keith Butters, John Litner, and William L. Cary, *Effects of Taxation: Corporate Mergers* (Cambridge: Harvard University Press, 1951).

3. J. Fred Weston, *The Role of Mergers in the Growth of Large Firms* (Berkeley: University of California Press, 1961).

4. James Daley, "The Art of the Deal," *Business 2.0*, October 1999.

5. B. Alexander Henderson and Timothy Anderson, "Optical Networking Systems," SalomonSmithBarney (October 2, 2000).

6. Paul C. Judge, "The Savvy Behind Sycamore," *Business Week*, December 20, 1999.

7. See Andy Reinhardt, "Meet Cisco's Mr. Internet," *Business Week*, September 13, 1999; Daley, "The Art of the Deal."

8. Ibid.

## CHAPTER 7: JOINT VENTURES

1. Robert Porter Lynch, *The Practical Guide to Joint Ventures and Corporate Alliances* (New York: John Wiley & Sons, 1989).

2. John D. Carter, Robert F. Cushman, and C. Scott Hartz, *The Handbook of Joint Venturing* (Homewood, Ill: Dow Jones-Irwin, 1988).

3. See, for example, James Wallace and Jim Erickson, *Hard Drive: Bill Gates and the Making of the Microsoft Empire* (New York: Harperbusiness, 1993); Paul Andrews, *How the Web Was Won: How Bill Gates and His Internet Idealists Transformed the Microsoft Empire* (New York: Broadway Books, 2000).

4. "New Economy Stocks Join Industrials," *The Wall Street Journal*, October 27, 1999.

5. For additional discussion about each of these market-related fields, see George S. Day, "Assessing Competitive Arenas: Who Are Your Competitors?" in *Wharton on Dynamic Competitive Strategy* (New York: John Wiley & Sons, 1997).

6. Kevin Ferguson, "Laying it All Online," *The Las Vegas Review-Journal*, August 21, 2000.

7. Timothy M. Collins and Thomas L. Doorley, III, *Teaming Up for the 90s: A Guide to International Joint Ventures and Strategic Alliances* (Homewood, Ill.: Business One Irwin, 1991), 206.

8. "Ask Jeeves, Inc. to Establish Global Presence Through Ask Jeeves," *Business Wire*, December 6, 1999.

9. J. Michael Geringer, *Joint Venture Partner Selection* (New York: Quorum Books, 1988), 176.

10. Ibid., 176-187.

11. Kathryn Rudie Harrigan, *Strategies for Joint Ventures* (Lexington, Mass.: Lexington Books, 1985), 21.

12. Eric Young, "Why Pandesic Didn't Pan Out," *The Industry Standard*, August 21, 2000, 84.

13. Fara Warner, "Microsoft's CarPoint Plans Expansion in Canada, Europe," *The Wall Street Journal*, December 6, 1999.

## CHAPTER 8: MINORITY EQUITY INVESTMENTS

1. Michael E. Porter, *Competitive Advantage: Creating and Sustaining Superior Performance* (New York: The Free Press, 1985).

2. Andrew S. Grove, *Only the Paranoid Survive* (New York: Bantam Doubleday Dell Publishing Group, 1996).

3. Susan Moran, "Intel's Halo Effect," *San Francisco Chronicle*, November 13, 1997.

4. Ibid.

5. Julia Angwin, "Stealth Financiers," *San Francisco Chronicle*, November 13, 1997.

6. Dean Takahashi, "Intel Invests to Push Beyond the Usual Borders of PCs," *The Wall Street Journal*, April 14, 1997.

7. "Why Intel Is Involved in Health," www.intel.com/intel/e-health/internet.htm, December 24, 1999.

8. Adam Brandenburger and Barry Nalebuff, *Co-opetition* (New York: Currency Doubleday, 1996).

9. Andrew S. Grove, *Only the Paranoid Survive* (New York: Bantam Doubleday Dell Publishing Group, 1996).

## CHAPTER 9: ADVERTISING AND COMMERCE ALLIANCES

1. "Still a Cyber-Pioneer: AOL Chief Targeting the 75% of Households that Aren't Online," *Electronic Media*, November 9, 1998, 32.

2. Steven Lipin and Nikhil Deogun, "Other Industries May Become Fair Game in New Landscape," *The Wall Street Journal*, January 11, 2000.

3. See Scott Ehrens, Matthew Esh, and Matthew Adams, "America Online: Baby's Got Backlog." Bear Stearns (January 4, 2000).

4. Mary Meeker et al., "America Online/Time Warner: How Big is Big? Big!," Morgan Stanley Dean Witter, May 4, 2000, 19.

5. Ibid.

6. "Drkoop.com, Battling for Life, Restructures AOL, Go.com Links," *The Wall Street Journal*, April 26, 2000.

7. See Jon R. Estanislao under the supervision of George T. Geis, "The Game Is Just Starting: Interactive Entertainment," Anderson School at UCLA, 2000.

8. The deal specifics and economics are abstracted from EA proxy statements. See Electronic Arts Definite Proxy Statement filed February 28, 2000.

9. See, for example, Gary Rivlin, "AOL's Rough Riders," *The Industry Standard*, October 30, 2000.

10. For additional perspective on the AOL-Time Warner merger implications with respect to content, see Kara Swisher, "Playing Nice," *The Industry Standard/Grok*, September 2000, 109-119.

11. For a summary of AOL investments, see Nick Wingfield, "Fledgling Online Companies Flock to AOL as the Partner of Choice," *The Wall Street Journal*, April 3, 2000.

12. "The Failure of New Media," *The Economist*, August 19, 2000, 53.

13. "Some Peacock, Some Power," *Business Week*, September 4, 2000, 115.

14. Michael A. Cusumano and David B. Yoffie, *Competing on Internet Time: Lessons from Netscape and Its Battle with Microsoft* (New York: Free Press, 1998).

15. "Yahoo! To The Rescue," *Business Week*, September 11, 2000, 37.

## CHAPTER 10: SPIN-OFFS AND TRACKING STOCKS

1. Charles Boucher, Bear Stearns Securities Corp., as quoted in Karen Alexander, "Conexant Plans Internet-Chip Unit Spinoff," *Los Angeles Times*, September 14, 2000.

2. To some degree, NBCi's failure resulted from an ad hoc deal strategy. It acquired marginally related companies, such as Flyswat and AllBusiness.com, and then failed to make its assets work together. See, for example, Kenneth Li and Anjali Arora, "Well, It Seemed Like a Good Idea," *The Industry Standard*, September 4, 2000, 69-71; Dan Ackman, "At NBCi, the 'I' is for Inconsistent," *Forbes.com*, July 28, 2000.

3. Expedia Form 424B1, Prospectus filed in pursuant to Rule 424 (November 10, 1999). Available: http://investor.expedia.com/media_files/nsd/expe/Expedia_Final_Prospectus.pdf.

4. "The Sum of the Parts," Oppenheimer and Co. (January 14, 1981).

5. James Miles and James Rosenfeld, "An Empirical Analysis of the Effects of Spin-Off Announcements on Shareholder Wealth," *Journal of Finance* 30, no. 5 (December 1983): 1597-1606.

6. "J. P. Morgan's Spinoffs Study," June 6, 1995; "J. P. Morgan's Spinoffs Study," June 6, 1997. See also Ronald J. Kudula and Thomas H. McInish, *Corporate Spin-Offs: Strategy for the 1980s* (Westport, Conn.: Quorum Books, 1984); Leonard Vignola, *Strategic Divestment* (New York: Amacom, 1974); and Patrick A. Gaughan, *Mergers, Acquisitions, and Corporate Restructurings* (New York: John Wiley & Sons, 1999), 410-420.

7. See, for example, Barry G. Cole, *After the Breakup: Assessing the New Post-AT&T Divestiture Era* (New York: Columbia University Press, 1991); Richard S. Higgins and Paul H. Rubin, *Deregulating Telecommunications: The Baby Bells Case for Competition* (New York: John Wiley & Sons, 1996).

8. See, for example, Deborah Solomon and Nikhil Deogun, "AT&T Board Approves Breakup Proposal," *The Wall Street Journal*, October 25, 2000; "Ma Bell Does the Splits," *The Economist*, October 28, 2000, 57-58.

## CHAPTER 11: LINKING RATIONALE AND STRUCTURE

1. Joel Bleeke and David Ernst, *Collaborating to Compete: Using Strategic Alliances and Acquisitions in the Global Marketplace* (New York: John Wiley & Sons, 1993).

2. George Anders and Nick Wingfield, "Amazon.com, in Yet Another Expansion, Will Launch Credit Card with NextCard," *The Wall Street Journal*, November 10, 1999.

3. Amazon.com and Drugstore.com filings with the Securities and Exchange Commission.

4. For a discussion of Pets.com's collapse, see Pui-Wing Tam and Mylene Mangalindan, "Pets.com will Shut Down, Citing Insufficient Funding," *The Wall Street Journal*, November 8, 2000. For a more general discussion of Amazon's problems with its minority investments, see Lisa Meyer, "Are the Little Guys Dragging Amazon Down?" *Redherring.com*, August 21, 2000; John T. Mulqueen and Mike Cleary, "Amazon Partners Hitting the Skids," *Interactive Week*, October 2, 2000.

5. See Henry Blodget, "An Update on VERT," Merrill Lynch (October 10, 2000); Thomas Neuhaus, Jon Moody, and Mike Peasley, "Vert: Estimates Higher, Execution Concerns Remain in Near Term," *BB&T Capital Markets* (October 25, 2000).

6. See Mel Duvall, "NECX Unit to Expand VerticalNet's Community Reach," *Interactive Week*, May 8, 2000; Mark Gimein, "CEO in Motion," *Fortune*, September 4, 2000.

# Glossary

**Acquisition**
The combining of assets and operations of two firms to become one legal entity.

**Beachhead analysis**
Graphical depiction of the moves of a company or market segment over time. Shows not only key relationships, but also central events, including market statistics, tactical moves, beachheads, and emerging battles.

**Blocking move**
Competitor's deal initiative designed to blunt another company's strategy.

**Business development**
External partnership or deal activity engaged in to enhance company's revenue and profits. Can involve acquisition, joint venture, minority ownership, commerce alliance, spin-off, licensing, or other deal structure. *Corporate business development* is a term often used when equity investment is involved.

**Chunk building**
Developing a significant number of conceptual pieces of information relating to companies and relationships in a market. Implies systematic gathering of industry knowledge in a continual manner.

**Commerce alliance**
Occurs when firms work together to reap benefits that neither party could easily achieve alone, but do not create a separate business entity. Partners work within existing corporate structures and sell to, through, or with each other.

**Complementary value activity**
Supplementary market areas in which a company must partner or invest to buttress its strategy. Often involves efforts to support marketing, operations, finance, or organizational design.

**Conflict analysis**
Methodology used to evaluate potential clashes with other companies that could emerge from a deal under consideration.

**Co-opetition**
The act of cooperating and competing with one company at the same time. Cooperation occurs to grow the market, while competing involves slicing up the value created. Also used to describe when firms cooperate in one submarket, yet compete in another.

**Core value activity**
Central areas of strength possessed by an organization as it goes to market. These areas can highlight a company's attractiveness to prospective partners as well as identify the company's partnership needs.

**Corporate venture capital**
The minority equity investment one organization makes in another for financial or strategic reasons or both. The term implies an investment by an operating firm, as opposed to a traditional venture capitalist.

**Database granularity**
The degree to which company and deal information related to markets is categorized at an appropriate level of detail. Classifications that are too coarse inhibit meaningful partnership analysis, while classifications that are too fine lead to problems in data management.

**Deal constellation analysis**
The examination of clusters of partnerships or investments that a company or group of companies are undertaking to determine patterns that clarify deal rationale.

**Deal database**
A collection of information about relevant deals in a market. Often includes descriptive deal facts as well as structural and strategic information.

**Deal rationale**
Strategic motivation behind a company partnership. The "why" of the deal.

**Deal simulation**
A process used to anticipate deals or deal patterns that could happen in a market.

**Digital deal**
Deals in which partners team up to compete primarily using bits as opposed to atoms.

**Digital triangle**
Framework used to provide a high-level overview of a company's positioning in the digital economy. The triangle's corners consist of (1) product and service vertical markets, (2) technology, and (3) distribution and communications.

**Digital value activity**
Digital market segment where value capture occurs or where someone will pay more than it costs to provide the good or service. Example: ordering and receiving software online.

**Direct deal analysis**
The discerning of the rationale of a partnership or investment through assessment of the deal in relative isolation. Can be contrasted with deal constellation analysis.

**Ecosystem**
Synergistic collection of partnerships or investments. May or may not be centered around a central company.

**Event analysis**
Methodology for assessing the impact of a partnership or cluster of partners resulting from a significant company announcement. Alternatively used to describe the study of a company's stock price after a particular occurrence such as a stock split or spin-off.

**Gap analysis**
Graphical technique used to identify holes in a company's deal portfolio. Conducted on a market-by-market basis.

**Hybrid value activity**
Market area (part digital and part physical) where value capture occurs or where someone pays more than it costs to provide a good or service. Example: ordering books online, but taking physical delivery.

**Implementation**
The process of making the deal work as intended. The obtaining of desired marketing, financial, operational, or organizational results from a partnership through effective stewardship.

**Infographic**
Graphical depiction of a market consisting of companies and interconnecting relationships.

**Joint venture**
Cooperative business activity in which two or more companies create an independent business entity. The founding firms typically retain ownership and financial risks and rewards, while the new entity assumes operational responsibility.

**Market modeling**
An eight-step framework for analyzing a market and its players, and for selecting and structuring a firm's own partnerships.

**Market overview**
Step 1 of market modeling, a high-level overview consisting of the value activities of a marketspace.

**Massification**
The pursuit of a strategy of size or concentration.

**Metcalfe's law**

Value of a network increases exponentially with number of users. Has been a driver for digital deals.

**Minority equity investment**

The investment by one firm in another company in exchange for an equity interest, and possibly a management role, in the target firm. Investment may be driven by financial and/or strategic rationales.

**Moore's law**

For the same cost, computer processing power doubles every 18 months. Has been a driver for digital deals.

**New economy**

An economy where industry is being transformed largely through digital technology and communications.

**Player database**

A collection of information about companies actively involved in any given market or market value activity. Consists of both descriptive information and structural market information related to each company.

**Specialization**

The pursuit of a strategy of concentration of effort. Increasingly espoused within the context of reduced transaction costs in the digital economy.

**Spin-off**

The separation of a specific division or cluster of assets by a firm to form a new, independent business entity.

**Staged acquisition**

The process of purchasing a minority equity position in a company and then later buying the entire company.

**Structure**

The framework for a partnership or deal. Common deal structures include acquisition, joint venture or international joint venture, minority equity investment, commerce alliance, and spin-off.

**Tracking stock**

The creation of a class of stock by a company that is mapped to the economic performance of a specific set of assets within the company. Differs from traditional common stock in that no ownership interest is granted in the underlying assets.

**Transaction costs**

Efforts required to search out a buyer, advertise products, conduct negotiations, draw up a contract, and so on. The term is used within the context of the new economy to reflect the reality that digital technology is transforming such efforts.

**Value activity**
Market area where value capture occurs or where someone pays more than it costs to provide a good or service.

**Value web**
Both a linear depiction of market processes (production, marketing, distribution, retail, and so on), and an additional dimension consisting of traditional, digital, and hybrid value activities.

**Vertical integration**
The engagement in or control of a number of adjacent market activities by a company.

**Virtuous cycle**
A self-feeding business model. AOL's cycle of building a subscriber base, monetizing the base, and enhancing content and services is an example.

# Bibliography

Anderson, Erin, and Barton A. Weitz. "Make-or-Buy Decisions: Vertical Integration and Marketing Productivity." *Sloan Management Review* (spring 1986): 3-19.

Andrews, Paul. *How the Web Was Won: How Bill Gates and His Internet Idealists Transformed the Microsoft Empire*. New York: Broadway Books, 2000.

Bleeke, Joel, and David Ernst. *Collaborating to Compete: Using Strategic Alliances and Acquisitions in the Global Marketplace*. New York: John Wiley & Sons, 1993.

Blodget, Henry. "An Update on VERT." Merrill Lynch (October 10, 2000).

Brandenburger, Adam, and Barry Nalebuff. *Co-opetition*. New York: Currency Doubleday, 1996.

Bryan, Lowell, Jane Fraser, Jeremy Oppenheim, and Wilhelm Rall. *Race for the World*. Boston: Harvard Business School Press, 1999.

Buzzell, R. D., "Is Vertical Integration Profitable?" *Harvard Business Review* (January-February 1983): 92-102.

Cairncross, Frances. *The Death of Distance: How the Communications Revolution will Change our Lives*. Boston: Harvard Business School Press, 1997.

Carter, John D., Robert F. Cushman, and C. Scott Hartz. *The Handbook of Joint Venturing*. Homewood, Ill.: Dow Jones-Irwin, 1988.

Cartwright, Sue, and Gary L. Cooper. *Managing Mergers, Acquisitions and Strategic Alliances: Integrating People and Cultures*. Oxford: Butterworth Heinmann, 1992.

Christian, Ed. "Urban Hopes to Make a Major Out of Edel." *Billboard*, August 5, 2000.

Coase, R. H. *The Firm, the Market, and the Law*. Chicago: University of Chicago Press, 1988.

Cole, Barry G. *After the Breakup: Assessing the New Post-AT&T Divestiture Era*. New York: Columbia University Press, 1991.

Collins, Timothy M., and Thomas L. Doorley, III. *Teaming Up for the 90s: A Guide to International Joint Ventures and Strategic Alliances*. Homewood, Ill.: Business One Irwin, 1991.

Cusumano, Michael A., and David B. Yoffie. *Competing on Internet Time: Lessons from Netscape and Its Battle with Microsoft*. New York: Free Press, 1998.

Daley, James. "The Art of the Deal." *Business 2.0*, October 1999.

Day, George S. "Assessing Competitive Arenas: Who Are Your Competitors?" in *Wharton on Dynamic Competitive Strategy*. New York: John Wiley & Sons, 1997.

Downes, Larry, and Chunka Mui. *Unleashing the Killer App*. Boston: Harvard Business School Press, 1998.

Drucker, Peter F. "The Next Information Revolution." *Forbes ASAP*, August 1998, 47-58.

"E-Commerce, Bonding on the Internet." *Euromoney*, February 10, 2000.

Edsall, Thomas A., and Murray N. Charlton. "Nearshore Waters of the Great Lakes." (paper presented at the State of Lakes Ecosystem Conference, December 1997).

Ehrens, Scott, Matthew Esh, and Matthew Adams. "America Online, Inc.: Baby's Got Backlog." Bear Stearns (January 4, 2000).

Eisenhardt, Kathleen M. "Speed and Strategic Choice: How Managers Accelerate Decision Making." *California Management Review* 32, no. 3 (1990).

Feldman, Boris. "Metrics Fraud." *The Industry Standard*, March 6, 2000.

Ferguson, Kevin. "Laying It All Online." *The Las Vegas Review-Journal*, August 21, 2000.

Gallatin, Judith E. *Adolescence and Individuality*. New York: Harper & Row, 1975.

Gasparino, Charles, and Rebecca Buckman. "Facing Internet Threat, Merrill Plans To Offer Trading Online for Low Fees." *The Wall Street Journal*, June 1, 1999.

Gaughan, Patrick A. *Mergers, Acquisitions, and Corporate Restructurings*. New York: John Wiley & Sons, 1999.

Geringer, J. Michael. *Joint Venture Partner Selection*. New York: Quorum Books, 1988.

Gomes-Casseres, Benjamin. *The Alliance Revolution: The New Shape of Business Rivalry*. Boston: Harvard University Press, 1996.

Grove, Andrew S. *Only the Paranoid Survive*. New York: Bantam Doubleday Dell Publishing Group, 1996.

Gurley, Bill. "The New Face of Internet Competition." *Above the Crowd*, February 22, 1999.

Harrigan, Kathryn Rudie. "A Framework for Looking at Vertical Integration." *The Journal of Business Strategy* (February 1983): 30-37.

Harrigan, Kathyrn Rudie. *Strategies for Joint Ventures*. Lexington, Mass.: Lexington Books, 1985.

Harrigan, Kathryn Rudie, and William Herman Newman. *Managing for Joint Venture Success*. Lexington, Mass.: Lexington Books, 1986.

Henderson, B. Alexander, and Timothy Anderson. "Optical Networking Systems." SalomonSmithBarney (October 2, 2000).

Higgins, Richard S., and Paul H. Rubin. *Deregulating Telecommunications: The Baby Bells Case for Competition*. New York: John Wiley & Sons, 1996.

Holson, Laura M. "Whiz Kid: Young Deal Maker is the Force Behind a Company's Growth." *The New York Times*, November 19, 1998.

Hooke, Jeffrey C. *M&A: A Practical Guide to Doing the Deal.* New York: John Wiley & Sons, 1997.

Hull, Geoffrey P. *The Recording Industry.* Boston: Allyn and Bacon, 1998.

Hutchison, Scott G. *The Business of Acquisitions and Mergers.* New York: President's Publishing, 1968.

Inkpen, A. C., and P. W. Beamish. "Knowledge, Bargaining Power, and the Instability of International Joint Ventures." *Academy of Management Review* 22 (1997).

"J. P. Morgan's Spinoffs Study." (June 6, 1995).

"J. P. Morgan's Spinoffs Study." (June 6, 1997).

Kanter, Rosabeth Moss. "Collaborative Advantage: The Art of Alliances," *Harvard Business Review* (July-August 1994).

Kelly, Kevin. *New Rules for the New Economy.* New York: Viking, 1998.

Kiggen, Jamie. "AOL Posts Another Quality Quarter." Donaldson, Lufkin & Jenrette (February 12, 1999).

Kotkin, Joel, and David Friedman. "Why Every Business Will Be Like Show Business." *Inc.*, March 1, 1995.

Krugman, Paul. "The Web Gets Ugly." *New York Times Magazine*, December 6, 1998.

Kudula, Ronald J., and Thomas H. McInish. *Corporate Spin-Offs: Strategy for the 1980s.* Westport, Conn.: Quorum Books, 1984.

Lewis, Jordan D. *Partnerships for Profit: Structuring and Managing Strategic Alliances.* New York: Free Press, 1990.

Lynch, Robert Porter. *The Practical Guide to Joint Ventures and Corporate Alliances.* New York: John Wiley & Sons, 1989.

Meeker, Mary, Richard Bilotti, Mark Mahaney, and Celeste Mellet. "America Online/Time Warner: How Big is Big? Big!" Morgan Stanley Dean Witter (May 4, 2000).

Miles, James, and James Rosenfeld. "An Empirical Analysis of the Effects of Spin-Off Announcements on Shareholder Wealth." *Journal of Finance* 30, no. 5 (December 1983): 1597-1606.

Moore, James F. *The Death of Competition: Leadership and Strategy in the Age of Business Ecosystems.* New York: HarperBusiness, 1997.

Murray, Alan I., and Caren Siehl. *Joint Ventures and Other Alliances: Creating a Successful Cooperative Linkage.* Morristown, New Jersey: Financial Executives Research Foundation, 1989.

National Research Council. *The Digital Dilemma: Intellectual Property in the Information Age.* Washington, D.C.: National Academy Press, 2000.

Negroponte, Nicholas. *Being Digital.* New York: Knopf, 1995.

Oster, Sharon M. *Modern Competitive Analysis.* New York: Oxford University Press, 1994.

Porter, Michael E. *Competitive Advantage: Creating and Sustaining Superior Performance.* New York: The Free Press, 1985.

Rabinovitz, Jonathan. "The Internet Economy Gets a Reality Check." *The Industry Standard*, December 6, 1999.

Rayport, Jeffrey F., and John Sviokla. "Exploiting the Virtual Value Chain." *Harvard Business Review* (November-December 1995): 75-85.

Reinhardt, Andy. "Meet Cisco's Mr. Internet." *Business Week*, September 13, 1999.

Rivlin, Gary. "AOL's Rough Riders." *The Industry Standard*, October 30, 2000.

Rock, Milton L., Robert H. Rock, and Martin Sikora. *The Mergers & Acquisitions Handbook*. New York: McGraw-Hill, 1994.

Rothschild, Michael. *Bionomics: Economy as Ecosystem*. New York: Henry Holt and Company, 1992.

Seely Brown, John, and Paul Duguid. *The Social Life of Information*. Boston: Harvard Business School Press, 2000.

Shapiro, Carl, and Hal R. Varian. *Information Rules*. Boston: Harvard Business School Press, 1999.

"Shifting Power to the Buy Side: Automating Fixed Income Markets." Meridian Research (1999).

Simon, Herbert. "What We Know about the Creative Process." *Frontiers in Creative and Innovative Management*. Cambridge, Mass.: Ballinger, 1985.

Spekman, Robert E., and Lynn A. Isabella. *Alliance Competence*. New York: John Wiley, 2000.

Swisher, Kara. "Playing Nice." *The Industry Standard/Grok*, September 2000.

Tapscott, Don, David Ticoll, and Alex Lowy. *Digital Capital: Harnessing the Power of Business Webs*. Boston: Harvard Business School Press, 2000.

Taylor, Paul. "Race Is On to Find Chips of the Future." *Financial Times: Survey on Information Technology*, January 2000.

"The Internet and Financial Services." Morgan Stanley Dean Witter (March 7, 2000).

"The New M&A." *Fortune Magazine*, November 8, 1999.

"The Sum of the Parts." Oppenheimer and Co. (January 14, 1981).

"Venture-Backed Companies Account for Half of All IPOs In 1999." The National Venture Capital Association, January 7, 2000.

Vignola, Leonard. *Strategic Divestment*. New York: Amacom, 1974.

Wallace, James, and Jim Erickson. *Hard Drive: Bill Gates and the Making of the Microsoft Empire*. New York: Harperbusiness, 1993.

Weinstein, Art. *Market Segmentation: Using Demographics, Psychographics, and Other Niche Marketing Techniques to Predict and Model Customer Behavior*. Chicago: Probus Publishing Company, 1994.

Weston, J. Fred. *The Role of Mergers in the Growth of Large Firms*. Berkeley: University of California Press, 1961.

Williamson, Oliver E. *Markets and Hierarchies*. New York: Free Press, 1975.

Young, Eric. "Why Pandesic Didn't Pan Out." *The Industry Standard*, August 21, 2000.

Zorovic, A. Sasa, and John F. Powers. *The Online Music Report*. Robertson Stephens (March 17, 2000).

# Index

Note locators in **bold** indicate graphic material.

# ABOUT THE AUTHORS

**George T. Geis** is Adjunct Professor at the Anderson Graduate School of Management at UCLA, where he teaches in the areas of information technology (*Strategy in the Digital Economy*), accounting, finance, as well as statistical analysis. He has been voted Outstanding Teacher of the Year at the Anderson School four times (including in 1999 by the Executive MBA program) and has received a number of other teaching awards.

Geis is cofounder of TriVergence (www.trivergence.com), which provides software solutions, research, and consulting for business development and competitive intelligence. He is also Editor of *Alliance InfoGraphics*, a Web-based application (published by TriVergence) that tracks Intel and Microsoft investments and significant partnerships. Geis has extensive consulting experience and is a frequent lecturer on emerging trends in the computer, communications, and media markets.

**George S. Geis** is a management consultant in McKinsey & Company's Los Angeles office. He has served clients on alliances, strategy, corporate finance, marketing, and Internet issues. Geis is an active member of McKinsey's ecommerce, alliances, media and entertainment, and strategy practices. His recent engagements have all centered around structuring new economy partnerships and have involved planning deal strategies, supporting partner negotiations, managing the deal process, and driving the business development agenda. He has worked extensively with Internet start-ups, hardware manufacturers, new media firms, and a host of other technology companies.

Before joining McKinsey, Geis worked with the law firms of Wachtell Lipton Rosen & Katz in New York and Munger Tolles & Olson in Los Angeles and the accounting firm of Arthur Andersen & Co. He received a J.D. and an M.B.A. from the University of Chicago (both degrees with honors) and a B.S. in finance from the University of California at Berkeley.